Historia Discordia

HISTORIA DISCORDIA

THE ORIGINS OF THE DISCORDIAN SOCIETY

FEATURING ROBERT ANTON WILSON,
KERRY THORNLEY, AND GREGORY HILL
COMPILED BY ADAM GORIGHTLY

RVP Press
New York

RVP Publishers Inc.
95 Morton Street, Ground Floor
New York, NY 10014

RVP Press, New York

Illustration cover: Roldo
Cover design: Bruno Herfst

RVP Press™ is an imprint of RVP Publishers Inc., New York.
The RVP Publishers logo is a registered trademark of RVP Publishers Inc., New York.

Library of Congress Control Number: 2014939430

ISBN 978 1 61861 321 9

www.historiadiscordia.com
www.rvppress.com

Table of Discontents

Acknowledgements

MANY THANKS MUST be extended for such an ambitious endeavor as this. Eris certainly played a role, no doubt, and if I were remiss in mentioning our blessed Goddess, I'd soon find myself on the business end of her fiery wrath. (She'd probably clock me on the noggin with her golden apple, too!)

The principal party in making this party happen was Dr. Robert Newport (aka Rev. Hypoc Magoun). I can never thank him enough for sharing with me Greg Hill's Discordian archives, which will result eventually in a number of related projects in the years to follow, Goddess willing. (See, I'm still sucking up to Her!)

Robert Anton Wilson, as well, should be mentioned here, as his sage spirit hovers over most everything I do these days.

Christina Pearson for her support of this project, and for keeping her father's work alive.

Louise Lacey, another early Discordian Society member, remains a good and dear friend, and should not go unmentioned as a supporter of my many mad endeavors, particularly those infused with Erisian energies.

John F. Carr for his fond memories and photos of Camden Benares.

Jeff Stoner for maintaining the Discordian Archives East.

And, of course, Greg Hill and Kerry Thornley, without whom you would be holding nothing in your hands right now.

Lastly, I must give great thanks to the "new" artists involved in this project, whose contributions complement the many Discordian artifacts encountered herein:

Roldo Odlor for his Seal of Eris cover, in addition to a number of his rough sketches from the early 80s when he was collaborating with Thornley and Hill.

Michele Witchipoo for her Brunswick Shrine illustration.

Richelle Hawks for providing her wonderful Appendexia Discordia collage in homage to Greg Hill, the master collage maker of his generation.

Alan Moore for his chaotically crafted endorsement.

Oh, and let's not forget Brian Doherty, who came up with the title for this book. Hail Eris.

Let the good times (and apples) roll!

The Book of the Fnoreword

Ἵπποι ταί με φέρουσιν, ὅσον τ' ἐπὶ θυμὸς ἱκάνοι, πέμπον . . .

I   . . . and there is a Line, and it does not Start, either. (It's the same Line as before. Please pay attention, this gets complex.) Okay, let's try that again.

I   So it came to pass that the Wrong Reverend Houdini Kundalini, in the byways and whyways of his Meaderation around the Strange Fruits of Old, unknowingly unleashed the Seed from which grew the Plant that bore the Fruit that married the Rat which Jack built. But behold, Ἔρις did see what had occurred, and She did caress the Wyrd in dark erotic ways, so that it were Not the Strange Fruit, it were the Wildling Fruit—twisted-twin, far-fallen, fast-flowering, long-lost—which grew . . . and truly it were Truthy. And the Mad Ones gathered up this Fruit of the Fruit, and they Cast, and they Flung, and they Rejoiced, saying "This! This! This!" Except the ones that said "No! No! No!," for they were All Mad Here. And so the Wildling Fruit made a Bed of the World, and its Truthiness was Good, and Fair, and Nice, but it were Not the Strange Fruit, despite Popular Opinion. Citation Required.

II   And the Reverend Houdini saw through the Wilding Fruit's Shield of Truthy, and he saw that although there was a nice chunk of the Good, the Fair, and the Nice, Not All was entirely Good, or Fair, or Nice, with what he behelded, for verily it were Not the Strange Fruit. Although it had the Shape, it were lacking in the Heft. Although it had the Smell, it were lacking in the Taste. And although it had the Sunshine, the Moonlight and the Good Times, it were sadly Unboogical. And he swore then an Oath: that he, who had unknowingly unleashed this Thing upon the World, this Wildling Fruit, should take No Rest until he had quested and brought forth the Strange Fruit from the Prisons of the Past. And then, having sworn this thing, he had a Nice Lie Down. Citation Required.

III   Then in the morning, the Reverend Houdini did venture out, and he did drop by the Rev. Hypocrates Magoun's pad, to borrow a cup of sugar, for to sweeten his Bitter Tea. And having asked for the sugar, the Rev. Hypocrates did say unto him "Strange Fruit? I had some Strange Fruit here somewhere . . . lose my own head next," and the Reverend Houdini was about to correct him then, and say he wanted sugar not fruit, but verily did the Rev. Hypocrates bring forth Five Crates of the things. And the Reverend Houdini did Rejoice, and the Placid Dingo made thereof a Funky Video to tell everyone, and therein did the Reverend Houdini display for all to see the Beauty of the Strange Fruit. And all Rejoiced to see such a thing. Citation Required.

IV   Filled with the Joy of the Strange Fruit Revealed, the Wrong Reverend Houdini Kundalini swore then an Oath: that he, who had unleashed, from the Prisons of the Past, this Thing upon the World, this Strange Fruit, that he should take No Rest until he had shared the Bounty of the Strange Fruit with All The World, in a shiny new book, detailing the history, deeds, and best of all, the Words of the Strange Fruit, and likewise of the Gardeners and Propagators, the Growers and the Eaters. And then, having sworn this thing, he had a Nice Lie Down. And so it came to pass. And it were Good. Citation Required.

V   The Days of the Strange Fruit were without number, but it were less than Six. Surely it was the Ends of Days!

. . . κρῖναι δὲ λόγου . . .

Ex Catheter
His Holeyness the Slightly Rev.DrJon Swabey
Slutwyche, Oz, 2013
Still Still Not Dead, But Not For Want Of Trying

My Erisian Odyssey

THIS ENDEAVOR HAS BEEN a labor of Erisian love, an odyssey which began during research for *The Prankster and the Conspiracy: The Story of Kerry Thornley and How He Met Oswald and Inspired the Counterculture* (Paraview Press, 2003).

As previously revealed in *The Prankster and Conspiracy*, I received a cryptic e-mail from a certain Dr. Robert Newport in July of 2000 informing me of the solemn news of Discordian Society founder Greg Hill's passing. Although I had no clue as to who this Newport fellow was, I responded to his e-mail, informing him that I was considering a book project about Hill's cohort, Kerry Thornley, and asked Newport if he'd known Thornley, as well. To this, the mysterious Dr. Newport informed me that he'd been close friends with both Thornley and Hill, and had himself been a founding member of The Discordian Society!

How Newport knew to contact me at a private e-mail address (not the e-mail addy I display on my website and known only to a handful of friends and family members) remains a mystery. When I later brought this up, Newport himself was unclear as to how he came to contact me. One can only attribute this to the chaotic influence of Goddess Eris, I suppose. Whatever the case, this initial exchange with Newport was the prime catalyst that led me down the path (or rabbit hole, as the case may be) of researching and writing my Kerry Thornley bio.

Along the way I discovered that Newport was an old friend of author Robert Anton Wilson, an iconoclastic illuminary I'd much admired over the years, and it was through Newport that I had the good fortune of meeting Wilson at his apartment in Capitola, California, just a few months prior to 9/11. Wilson himself was a seminal Discordian, a major player back in its heyday during the evolution of *Principia Discordia*. Wilson used many *Principia Discordia* themes when he and Robert Shea (another card carrying Discordian) devised their legendary *Illuminatus! Trilogy* in the mid 1970s, the first book in the series dedicated to none other than Kerry Thornley and Greg Hill.

It was at Wilson's apartment that Dr. Newport first introduced me to the Discordian Archives (or a sampling thereof, as I later discovered.) A couple armloads of material, this modest booty was a veritable treasure trove of rare Discordian Society relics that Newport let me truck home and scan, a sampling of which later appeared in *The Prankster and the Conspiracy*.

Afterwards, I periodically checked in with Newport inquiring if, at some point, I could use these materials to produce a book on the history of Discordianism. Newport, bless his heart, always gave a thumbs up to this potential project, which sat on the Gorightly Productions backburner for the next several years. Every now and again I would touch base with Newport just to make sure he was still ok with my eventual use of the materials, and the answer was always positive and supportive. Then, in 2009, as I started getting a bit more serious about moving forward with the project, I yet again contacted Newport and as always he was totally down with whatever I wished to do. Additionally, Newport suggested that the next time I was down L.A. way I should drop by his place and he would give me the collection and "whatever else I wanted." Granted, I'm a little dense at times, so I wasn't quite sure what Newport meant, as I had assumed I'd seen the entire Discordian Archive contents back in 2001 at Wilson's apartment. Never one to let an opportunity pass, I took Newport up on his offer, and—at that time, by the grace of Goddess Eris—he passed on to me five boxes of the most wondrous and mind-blowing Discordian-related goodies, the results of which you now hold in your astounded hands, dear readers, taken directly from Greg Hill's Discordian Archives that were rescued from being tossed into a dumpster by my forever hero, the dutiful Dr. Newport.

Hail Eris! All Hail Discordia!

Adam Gorightly, K.S.C.
May 23, 2014

INTRODUCTION

All Hail the Goddess Eris

Robert Anton Wilson

SINCE MANY OF YOU out there are only unconscious Discordians so far, this first blast will be an introduction to Discordian atheology, to enable you to become conscious Discordians at once.

Nobody is excluded from the Discordian Society for reasons of race, religion, politics, sex, celibacy, being a cabbage, or anything like that. Every sentient being is an Honorary Discordian. We *accept* you, totally *whoever* or *whatever* you are.

This leads to an inevitable objection, which helpfully leads right into the center of Discordian metaphysics.

Some of you will distrust this universal good-vibe-ism and suspect an ulterior motive. Some will be so ornery as to refuse to be incorporated just because you are being offered it with no strings attached. Others will make a principle of recalcitrance and insist that we can't *accept* you without your consent.

It doesn't matter. You are still part of the Discordian Society. You are, to be precise, in the Accordian Society, a subsect reserved for those who reject Discordianism entirely.

Discordianism includes its own opposite, like all ideas above "the abyss" in Cabalistic language. (In Discordian language, there is no abyss. That region around Da'ath and those *unheimlich* places in general are called the Realm of Thud.)

Thus, we worship Eris, goddess of Discord and Chaos. (See Bulfinch for all the boring details.) Since Discord needs something to be discordant *with*, we also worship Her sister, Aneris, patroness of the Accordian Society.

The symbol of Eris is the Apple of Discord, which she threw into a party on Olympus (thereby indirectly causing Paris to get the hots for Helen, with results described by Lady Homer in the poems plagiarized by another Greek named Homer who later got all the credit.) The symbol of Aneris is the Pentagon, which represents Stability. Law 'n' Order. Nixonology, the Thule Society, and all sorts of dull, respectable, or patriotic forms of homicide.

Or in terms of over-simplification, Eris is the spirit of anarchy (Harpo), Aneris is the spirit of bureaucracy (Chico), and the Discordian Society is their synthesis in dynamic unbalance forever (Groucho).

Without Eris, no Aneris. Without Aneris, no Eris. Without unbalance, no progress: stagnation, death. Pasadena.

In the perpetual juggling of Eris and Aneris, Shem and Shaun, Discordian and Accordian. Hodge Podge. "Our social something bumps along bumpily" (as Joyce says in the Wake) in the form of "a human (pest) cycling (pist!) and re-cycling (past)."

There are five stages to each cycle, even though Joyce only knew about four, and poor old Marx only knew about three.

These stages are Chaos, or the thesis; Discord, or antithesis; Confusion, or the synthesis; Bureaucracy, or the parenthesis; and Aftermath, or the paralysis.

Eris, as spirit of Chaos (= 156 by Cabala and thereby equals Babalon in Crowley's less sophisticated system) broods over all ages of pure Chaos. This makes certain aneristic types uneasy, leading to:

Discord, or "How the West Was Lost"; the Marshall comes in looking like Clint Eastwood and the State is established, and things get more and more regimented, thereby creating or incarnating Aneris, spirit of Organization, creating Confusion, as everybody goes around asking, "Who's in charge here? What do I do next? Where can I hang my coat?" and things. Will has been divorced from body; each human is his brother's and sister's "Keeper"; conformity and slavery thrive (and the Freudian "unconscious" is created out of all the lost Wills, baffled Desires, surrendered Needs, etc.); whereby Aneris waxeth great, promoting Bureaucracy, which immediately begins to re-charge Eris according to the great Discordian equation

Imposition of order=

Escalation of chaos and the "papyraceous formation" of Proudhon is created: tons of decrees, laws, rules. Regulations etc. rain hard upon the increasingly frantic and disoriented population, leading to strikes, riots, insurrections, revolutions, anarchy and

Aftermath, in which things slowly evolve toward the original Chaos, and a new cycle starts.

So much for sociology. (Hah!) The same principles, Discordians claim (or are deluded into believing) hold throughout Existence (and Non-Existence) on all levels.

Protoplasm, for instance, is held together by the conflict of Erisian forces (electrical charge, driving each colloidal particle away from all others) and anerisian forces (surface tension, drawing all the particles together). As long as this dynamic unbalance remains, the protoplasm is "alive"; life is unbalance.

On the larger scale, the galaxies seem to be maintained, as Buckminster Fuller has shown, by opposing forces of tension (expansion) and compression (contraction).

Crafty readers will easily see how this Discordian/Accordian tendency appears in the amity-enmity of religious bodies: Christian, Moslem, pagan, or whatever.

Thus, if you only mildly oppose this Discordian atheology, you are only mildly Accordian, but still part of the Opposite which gives Discordianism a reason to exist; but if you violently oppose us (for reducing metaphysics to a clown-show, say), then you are a strong part of the Opposite and give us even more reason to exist.

Everybody is part of Discordianism; I repeat, because now you are ready to understand the profundity of the joke, somewhat.

Needless to say, this atheology is an expression in language of the great spiritual truth which the Master Therion expressed mathematically in the equation 0=2. Existence is the unreal resultant (0) of the imaginary conflict of two (2) non-existent forces.

The jewel is in the lotus: the Apple is in the Pentagon. We become what we love, but we also become what we hate. These are special cases of the general Sufi principle that *we become what we passionately imagine*. (Korzybski and Gurdjieff called this "passionate imagination" by the name *Identification*, if you are trying to translate this nonsense into one of the more familiar systems of philosophical or occult nonsense.)

Discordians do not enter into bliss like Buddhists or other low-level types like that. Entering into bliss is just another Accordian delusion, ignoring the Opposite again and thus remaining mired in Malkus on a higher level. Discordians are just as capable of entering into bliss as any other shamans, witches, magicians, yogis, dopers, artists and clowns, but Discordians are also capable of coming out of bliss and "re-incarnating." A fully, trained Discordian adept may re-incarnate as many as twenty times a day.

It has been objected in Certain Quarters that Discordianism is a "female chauvinist" plot, because both Eris and Aneris are ladies and there don't seem to be any male gods in this system.

The objection is easily met. Gods and goddesses, like space, time, mass, etc., are creations of the human nervous system, abstractions, symbols. (Nothing up either sleeve, you see; now watch what I do next.) Therefore, another symbolism containing the same truth is also true. Or, as Sri Syadasti said, "Truth is five but men only have one name for it."

In our alternative symbology, Eris remains female but Aneris is only a Veil before the mystery of the true God of law 'n' order, who is male. In fact, he is Eris inside-out, or *Sire*, the Father-spirit. Finally, in the New Aeon, Eris and Sire do a complicated 69 like Nuit and Hadit in the Stele of Revealing, and become *Risers* (Eris-Sire intertwined backwards), the twin spirits of Aquarian Consciousness also symbolized by Crowley's Horus twins.

Thus, Eris (moon-goddess) *is* Sire (sun-god) *is* Risers (star-gods), as in the 0 (Nuit), 1 (Hadit), 2 (Ra-Hoor-Khuit, Hoor-Par-Krat) symbolism of the *Book of the Law*. Neat? The full equation, which Crowley missed, is 0=1=2. This explains *all* the mysteries, East and West, North and South, everywhere.

(Cf. "The Star Ruby" with its formulae: "Father and Mother are One God. Father and Daughter are One God. Mother and Son are One God. Not six nor four nor two nor one nor none," etc.)

It will be understood by the Cabalistic reader that Discordianism is a system of transcendental Atheism, agnostic Gnosticism, skeptical Monotheism, and unified Dualism. In short, the Erisian revelation is not a complicated put-on disguised as a new religion, but a new religion disguised as a complicated put-on.

The Origins of the Discordian Society

IN THE LATE 1950s, two high school chums—Greg Hill and Kerry Thornley—witnessed a revelatory vision in a Southern California bowling alley which led to the founding of Discordianism, an apparent "spoof" religion based on the worship of Eris, the Greek goddess of chaos and discord. Subsequently, Hill and Thornley adopted the Discordian alter egos of Malaclypse the Younger and Omar Khayyam Ravenhurst and then set forth to enlighten the world—or at least tickle a few funny bones along the way. What evolved, in the years to follow, was the formation of the Discordian Society and the dictation of the holy writ, *Principia Discordia*.

Although Greg Hill was *Principia Discordia's* principal architect, Kerry Thornley would soon become the more famous of the two Discordian founders for reasons seemingly unrelated to Eris worship. Just the same, the Goddess works in mysterious ways . . .

In the spring of 1959, Thornley—then serving in the Marines—was stationed at El Toro Military Base, located near Santa Ana, California, and it was there that he became acquainted with the future alleged assassin of President John F. Kennedy, none other than Lee Harvey Oswald. This association later led some to suspect—such as New Orleans District Attorney Jim Garrison—that Thornley had been a participant in JFK's assassination. (Surely Eris had her five-fingered hand in all this!)

Thornley spent three months with Oswald at El Toro before he was transferred to Atsugi Air Base in June 1959. During his boat trip to Japan, Kerry started work on a novel called *The Idle Warriors*, the theme of which concerned the disillusionment of a young Marine as the result of overseas duty. The protagonist of Thornley's work-in-progress was a composite character based on several Marines he'd known during the period, including Oswald.

In October 1959, Thornley learned that Oswald had defected to the Soviet Union. This event immediately influenced a change of direction for the plot of *The Idle Warriors*, and from that point forward the protagonist would be re-shaped with Oswald as the main character (Johnny Shellburn) who defects due to his dissatisfaction serving with the Marines in the Far East. So, in essence, Thornley was writing a novel about Oswald more than three years before the Kennedy assassination!

Apocalypse: A Trade Journal
for Doom Prophets

IN 1960—FOLLOWING THORNLEY's Marine Corps discharge—he returned to Whittier, California and reunited with his friend and Discordian Society co-founder, Greg Hill. At this time, the two produced a humor magazine, *Apocalypse: A Trade Journal for Doom Prophets*, predating *Principia Discordia* by five years, which, of course, corresponds to the Discordian Law of Fives. (More on the Law of Fives later fnord.)

Hill and Thornley published only one issue of *Apocalypse*, mainly because no one else, besides them, found it the least bit humorous. As Thornley later noted: "Things we thought were funny, nobody else did."

ACKNOWLEDGEMENTS

We would like to thank Ernest Hemmingway, Dick Nixon, Ayn Rand and Mr. Jack Paar for their very helpful services in getting this issue to press.

Unfortunately, we cannot do so as they were of no help whatever.

This does not, however, prevent us from mention of Vance Packard.

We would also acknowledge the most needed technical advice of a Warren Shultz were it not for the fact that we have never heard of such a person.

We must, nonetheless, surely thank our good friend and intellectual genius Robert Doidge.

Without Bob's kind and open understanding, we could never have gotten permission to use his name in this section.

Thanks Bob,
THE PUBLISHER

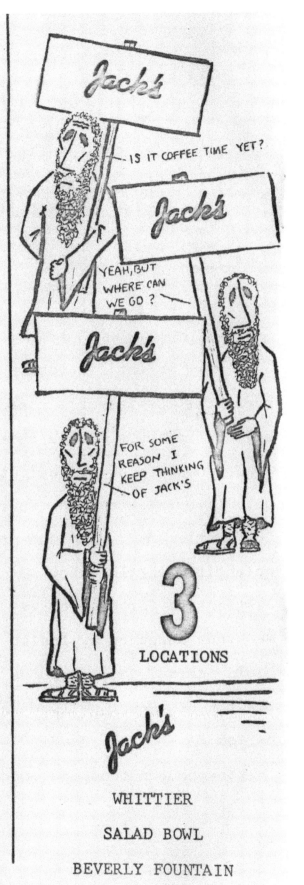

THE HAIRY MONSTER

science-fiction by
OMAR K. RAVENHURST

A very scientific looking nitrogen atom drifted over the professor's bald head as he spoke in scientific terms to his scientific audience.

The members of the scientific audience numbered but, like the elements, four.

"Gentlemen," said the professor, "in this very scientific little tube, I have one of the most destructive forces ever -- opps -- I dropped it -- that means an explosion which, if harnessed, could carry thirty pounds of wet toilet paper to the top of Mount Wilson every ten seconds for a period of --"

Vooooooooooooooooooooooooooooommmmmmmmmmm!!!!!!

OUR POET:

L. Q. vA. Kallisti made his first public appearance as an infant foundling, wrapped in old newspapers, at the pay-for-your-fines-here section of the local library. The child Kallisti (at that time 23 years of age) was dis-covered by an elderly woman, trying to sneak past the counter with a counterfeit library card, who had just lost her own son (while on a binge one day, she mistook him for a box of trash and sent him out with the family garbage.)

During his tender years of early childhood (from 31 to 47 years old) young Kallisti was very disturbed. Having heard rumors of his foster mother's son being lost as he was, Kallisti harbored a morbid fear of telephones (the connection is vague, but to him it made sense -- more evidence of how disturbed he was). This left him only one choice: become a writer for APOCALYPSE. More evidence of unbalance.

His young adult life (from 72 to 103) proved adventurous and he was seldom out of prison. During his most lengthy vaction on the "inside" he wrote his first book, an auto-biography titled Psycho. However, before he could copyright it, it was stolen, and even though it turned up years later, he never re-covered from the shock.

At present (age 218) he is very happy (though completely oblivious to reality) locked in a wine cellar of one of the old mansions around town.

KALLISTI AT HOME

He spends his time divided between writing profound poems, essays and stories and pondering on the highly philosophical problem of getting a cork from a bottle without the use of a cork-screw.

Every four days he sends his latest work to the landlady who forwards it to our office.

THE EDITOR

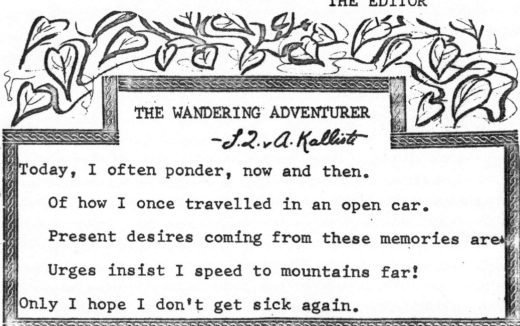

THE WANDERING ADVENTURER

-J.2.vA. Kallisti

Today, I often ponder, now and then.

Of how I once travelled in an open car.

Present desires coming from these memories are

Urges insist I speed to mountains far!

Only I hope I don't get sick again.

A NOTE BEFORE THE END

This paper, you will be glad to know, is at least one thousand years ahead of its time. Therefore, it would be excellent for you to stock up on several copies (one for each of your descendants in the thirtieth century) as they will doubtlessly be out of print within the week.

Before concluding, we wish to comment upon the fact that while there are over forty-nine thousand characters in the standard dictionary of China -- most of the characters on our staff are few indeed by over all comparison.

A study reveals, however, that indeed few Chinese ever compare overalls with standard dictionaries of any kind in the first place.

OUR STAFF   **editor**
GREGORY H. HILL

FOREIGN CORESPONDENT
       Omar K. Ravenhurst
CREATIVE GENIUS
       L. Q. vA. Kallisti
ARTIST
       Buzhil

THE STAFF MEMBER OF THE MONTH:
OMAR K. RAVENHURST

A year ago Castro nationalized the Ravenhurst
Manor in Cuba and left Omar penniless. Neverthe-
less, Omar -- an ardent liberal who is convinced
Castro's intentions are worthy -- let bygones be
bygones and joined Fidel's movement.
At present, Omar awaits execution in a Havana
prison from which THE HAIRY MONSTER, his most
critical piece on Castro to date, was smuggled.

APOCALYPSE - a trade journal for doom prophets -
is published monthly. It is distributed through
the advertisers.
© Kerry Thornley - 1960
Kerry Thornley * Box 349 * Whittier * California

APOCALYPSE ADVERTISING   OX 5-8863

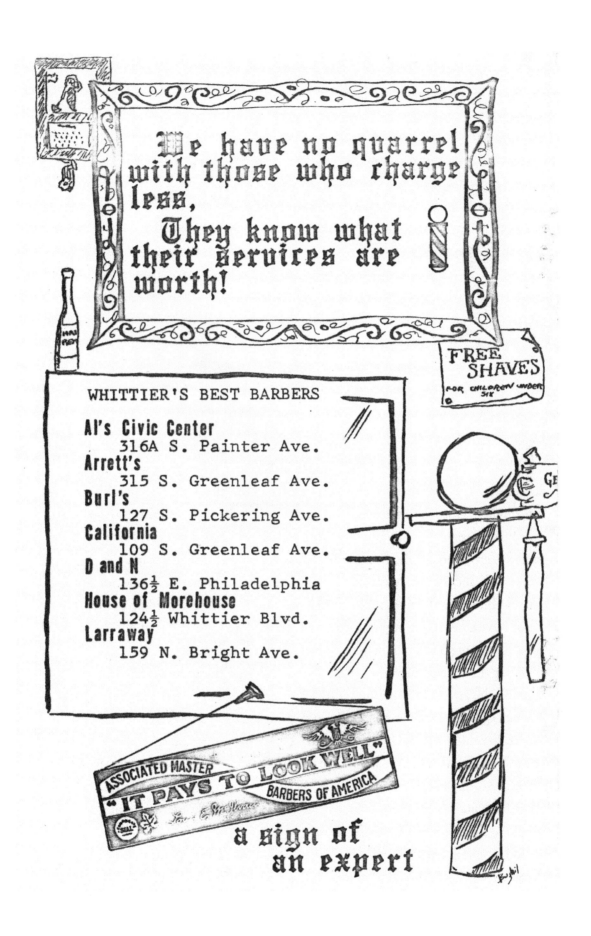

We have no quarrel with those who charge less,
They know what their services are worth!

FREE SHAVES FOR CHILDREN UNDER SIX

WHITTIER'S BEST BARBERS

Al's Civic Center
    316A S. Painter Ave.
Arrett's
    315 S. Greenleaf Ave.
Burl's
    127 S. Pickering Ave.
California
    109 S. Greenleaf Ave.
D and N
    136½ E. Philadelphia
House of Morehouse
    124½ Whittier Blvd.
Larraway
    159 N. Bright Ave.

ASSOCIATED MASTER "IT PAYS TO LOOK WELL" BARBERS OF AMERICA

a sign of an expert

The *Principia Discordia*
(Or How The West Was Lost)

L ATE ONE NIGHT, the founders of Discordianism were laughing and carrying on at the Thornley family house in Whittier when they woke up Kerry's parents. Having wreaked enough havoc on the Thornley household, the two went over to Greg's place and in due course woke up his family, too. So—as to not further perturb Hill's family—Greg and Kerry headed to downtown Whittier, where they figured nobody else could possibly be disturbed. Wrong!

As Hill and Thornley caroused along the main Whittier drag, the cops pulled up and informed them that they were in jeopardy of being picked up for vagrancy. "But I live here," Greg pointed out, to which the cops replied: "That doesn't matter: you're keeping odd hours with no general purpose in mind!"

After the officers drove off, Kerry said, "Let's go live someplace where it's not against the law to stay up all night!" To this, Greg suggested the New Orleans French Quarter, and so it was that he and Thornley moved there in early 1961, arriving the day after Mardi Gras. During this New Orleans period several new initiates were brought into the Discordian Society fold, among them Roger Lovin, Roderick "Slim" Brooks, and Barbara Reid. This period is chronicled in further detail in *The Prankster and the Conspiracy* and would later prove to be an important formative phase in the history of Discordianism.

In December 1963, following the JFK assassination, Thornley moved to Arlington, Virginia, which—it should be noted—is home to the second-most holy of Discordian Shrines, the Pentagon. It was during Thornley's Arlington period that the Law of Fives was revealed to him, which states that all things happen in fives, or are divisible by or are multiples of five, or are somehow directly or indirectly related to five.

This revelation was inspired no doubt by his veneration for the five-sided temple. At one point Thornley even attempted to secure a PO Box at the Pentagon to serve as the official Discordian Society Headquarters mailing address. As Discordian history instructs:

> The Pentagon refers to several things. For one, it specifically accords with the Law of Fives. It is also the shape of the United States Military headquarters, the Pentagon Building, a most pregnant manifestation of straightjacket order resting on a firm foundation of chaos, and constantly erupting into dazzling disorder; this building is one of our most cherished Erisian shrines. Also, it happens that, in times of medieval magic, the pentagon was the generic symbol for werewolves, but this reference is not especially intended; the Erisian movement does not discriminate against werewolves—our membership rosters are open to persons of all races, national origins, and hobbies.

The five-sided temple notwithstanding, Thornley's main motivation for his Arlington, Virginia move was to be within close proximity of Washington, D.C. where the Warren Commission hearings had just begun. Kerry figured that if he could arrange an appearance before the Commission it might help him land a deal for a non-fiction book he was then working on entitled *Oswald*. To this end, Thornley was indeed successful, testifying before the Warren Commission on May 18, 1964, at which time he recounted his interactions with Oswald during their service together in the Marines.

Meanwhile, back in New Orleans, Greg Hill was escalating his Discordian Society activities, as documented in a series of letters exchanged between Greg and Kerry during this period. Many of these Discordian discourses eventually evolved into the first edition of the *Principia Discordia (Or How The West Was Lost)*, published in 1965, consisting of a mere five copies. (There's that Law of Fives again. . .) Also in '65, Thornley's *Oswald* was published by New Classics House.

As synchronicity would have it, the *Principia Discordia (Or How The West Was Lost)*, was reproduced after hours on a copying machine in the office of New Orleans District Attorney Jim Garrison, who two years later would indict Thornley as part of a conspiratorial cabal that allegedly orchestrated JFK's assassination. This clandestine copying operation (which occurred two years before Garrison launched his JFK assassination probe) was allegedly perpetrated by Greg Hill's girlfriend, Lane Caplinger, who worked as a typist in Garrison's office. Later, Garrison theorized that the Discordian Society was a CIA front, an idea that Thornley—ever the surrealist prankster—heartily encouraged. Little did Garrison realize but that he was an unwitting dupe in this Discordian Society conspiracy by the covert use of his very own office copying machine!

Over the years, it has been speculated that all five copies of the first edition of the *Principia Discordia* had apparently disappeared. However, in 2009, Greg Hill's Discordian Archives were passed on to your humble author, and among these contents was discovered Hill's personal copy of the first edition the *Principia Discordia,* numbered 1 of 5. In the Greg Hill Wikipedia entry, it claims that the original edition of the *Principia Discordia (Or How The West Was Lost)* was discovered in 2006 in the "...President John F. Kennedy Assassination Records in the National Archives..." However, this is inaccurate, and only a portion of the first edition of *Principia Discordia* actually resides in this collection.

To follow, in its entirety, is a reproduction of the first edition of the *Principia Discordia (Or How The West Was Lost)*, seen here for the first time in nearly half a century.

===== <u>THE PRINCIPIA DISCORDIA</u> =====

or

HOW THE WEST WAS LOST

DISCORDIANISM ACCORDING TO

MALACLYPSE (THE YOUNGER), K.C.

beeing

the Officiale Handebooke of The

Difcordian Societye

ande

A Beginning Introdyctun

to

The Erisian Misterees

Which is Most Interesting

Written under inspiration by

MALACLYPSE (The Younger), K.C.

Omnibenevolent Polyfather of Virginity-in-gold
and High Priest of
The Heretic Fringe & Protestant Persuasion

ALL HAIL DISCORDIA!

TABLE of CONTENTS

continued on pg 1½

TABLE OF DISORGANIZATION: Official Discordian Document
#1-3.1-10:12:64.

===== THE DISCORDIAN SOCIETY =====

1. THE ERISIAN MOVEMENT

1. The House of The Apostles of Eris (The "Eristocracy")
    1. The Golden Apple Corps (Keepers of the Sacred Chao)
    2. Office of High Priesthood
        1. Erisian Orthodoxy
        2. Heretic Fringe & Protestant Persuasion
    3. Compilers of Truth--Esoteric
        1. Epistolary
        2. Holy Works
            (Inspirational, historical, philosophical, etc.)
    4. The Five Apostles, Saints, and Like Personages
    5. ~~Epistemoikos~~ *Council* of the Episkoposes
2. The Legion of Dynamic Discord
    1. Legionnaires
    2. Disciples of Eris
    (3. Second Degree Disciples)
    (4. Third Degree Disciples)
    (5. Fourth Degree, or "High" Disciples)
3. The Bureaucracy (alternately called The Administry)
    1. Bureau of Erisian Archives
    2. Bureau of Symbols, Emblems, Certificates, and Such
    3. Bureau of The Secretariat
    4. Bureau of Projects
    5. Bureau of The Miscellaneous

2. THE ERISTIC MOVEMENT

1. Eristic Avatars

2. Compilers of Truth--Lay

3. Eristianism at Large

3. THE ERISTESQUE MOVEMENT

1. Orders of Eris
    1. The Knights of the Five Sided Temple
        1½. The Communist Infiltrated Auxiliary of #1
    2. Ichabod College
    3. The Defamation League--Underground
    4. Apocalyptic Prophets Local #666
    5. The Bowel Movement

2. Eristesquianism at Large

NOTE: Together, the Erisian and the Eristic Movements
are called "Discordianism Proper"; and the Eristesque
Movement is called "Discordianism Improper".

ABOUT THE DISCORDIAN SOCIETY

The Discordian Society is a group (society) of people
with a common bound, that of DISCORD. It is quite true
that all men inherrently manifest discord (as all men
inherrently manifest order; the two principles being in
eternal conflict--which is itself discordant); but the
Discordian Society refers to an elite population, certainly
above and beyond the grasp of Mass Man.

There are three Discordian Movements about us (see
Note 1), and hence, three sorts of Discordians: The
Erisians, The Eristics, and the Eristesquians. It is
the first group, the Erisian Movement, that represents
the esoteric, religious fold that is dedicated to True
Wisdom, which they realize can be found only in The
Erisian Mysteries.

We of the Erisian Movement feel that the Greek
Goddess ERIS (or, under Her Roman name: DISCORDIA), the
Goddess of Strife, Discord, Chaos, and All Things Eristic...
Eris is the Divine Figure for our wisdom. It is Her after
whom we name ourselves, and She whom we worship (each
in our own little way). The word "Erisian" means: "of,
or about, Eris".

Consequently, it is The Erisian Movement about which
we are most concerned. Besides, nobody but the Erisians
even know about the others anyway; so you have to study
The Mysteries to find out much of anything in the first
place.

The Principia Discordia is the official handbooke
of the Erisian Movement; and together with the various
Holy Works and some of the Epistles and All That, it will
quietly, but exhaustively, explain everything that is worth
knowing. In the words of one of the Apostles of Eris,
Discordeaux (Jean the Eristentionalist): "Gorf stlikkter
heenoc queslipper flix." (see Note 2)

So we shall begin explaining the disorganization
of the Society--in all its glory detail--taking each part
and sub-part and sub-sub-part in its turn; and we guarantee
that any soul who finishes the work will have reached,
to some degree, the Divine State of Chaotic Understanding.

Hold the foregoing TABLE OF DISORGANIZATION in one
hand, the PRINCIPIA DISCORDIA in one hand (turn pages
with the other hand)...and welcome to the Erisian Mysteries.

THE DISCORDIAN SOCIETY SYMBOL

This magnificent emblem pictorally symbolizes The
Workings of the Forces of the Universe and What Those
Forces Are.
It is called THE SACRED CHAO.

Utilizing the symbolism of the Taoist "Ying & Yang",
we have The Sacred Chao divided into The Hodge and The Podge;
only instead of a Podge spot in the Hodge side there is
a PENTAGON, to represent The Eristesque Principle; and
instead of a Hodge spot in the Podge side, there is The
Golden Apple of Discord, to represent The Eristic Principle.
These two Principles--in eternal strife against each
other...bring forth most everything.

The Eristesque Principle: is, essentially, that everything that claims to be ordered is in fact only super-
ficially ordered, and imperfectly at that. In other words,
even the greatest orderers of all humanity, the scientists,
find that every time they get some kind of good scheme
going some damn thing or another doesn't fit and hence
every word of the 'knowledge' of science must be prefaced
with the understanding that it might all be scrapped if
the wrong evidence pops up tomorrow. Furthermore, every
scientist today is spending the bulk of his time trying
to figure out just what to do with all the bits of information that he already has that even now don't fit the
scheme. Anyway, it is all well and good because the order
is not really there in the first place--only primal chaos;
it is we that give birth to order, imposed on chaos, so
that we may utilize our environment and Lead A Good Life.
That is, ordering is essentially a Human Thing and is even,
in fact, essential to we mortals.
But what most people do not realize is that there
is another Principle at work also.

The Eristic Principle: is, essentially, pure bald
discord, the antithesis of order, in its unadulterated
state.
This Principle, too, is necessary for Life--for
without it, something or another would happen that must
be terrible--because we would be lacking something nec-
essary--but we poor humans lack the Understanding (so
far) to appreciate what that might be. But if you don't
believe that this Principle exists: LOOK ABOUT YOU!
Indeed, Discord is an inherrent Principle of The
Universe! Verily.

For a more complete dissertation on The Principles,
see "Metaphysics" in the incompleted Holy Work of Malaclypse
(The Younger), K.C., Summa Universalia ("A Summation of
the Universe"), which is probably not yet avaliable.
Also, for a more complete exposition of The Eristesque

Principle in particular, read his "Myth of Ichabod", included in the same Holy Work and also appended to this work.

The Pentagon and The Apple of Discord were chosen to represent these principles for the following reason:
We have found that one of the finest examples of Superficial Order resting on a solid foundation of Chaos is the United States Military Headquarters, The Pentagon Bldg. Furthermore, the Pentagon has five sides, which correlates with The Law Of Fives, which was discovered by the great Lord Omar Khayyam Ravenhurst, K.C., to be that everything happens in fives or is divisible into five parts (for a more complete explaination of this, read Book I "The Five Pillars of Rubbish" in his Holy Work The Honest Book of Truth). As one of the Five Apostles Of Eris put it: "The truth is Five, but we have only one name for it." (If you must know, that particular Apostle was Krishna Argumentium--I think.) *(see Note 3)*
On the other half, The Golden Apple of Discord was chosen to symbolize the Eristic Principle and refers to the only extant myth of the Greek Goddess of Strife and Discord, ERIS. That myth follows shortly.

The Official Colors of the Discordian Society are blue, red, green, chartruese, puse, heliotrope, tutti-fruitti, green, vermillion, navy black, and yellow; however, we usually render the emblem as silver bordered, with golden pentagon and apple, all on a black or darkened background, because that way it is sort of pretty.

NOTES CONCERNING THE PENTAGON:

1. About rendering the Pentagon: This symbol is included in many of the emblems of the various sub-divisions and in all cases (including the DS emblem it-self) it should be drawn in a particular position. You see, inherrent in every pentagon is a pentagram (made from drawing a line from each point to every other point) which is a very old Mystical Symbol. A strange thing aboutxxxxxx The Pentagram is that it could be used to mystifying Good or Evil; in white magic it was used with one point ascending and two points descending, and when used for black magic then it had two points up and one down. Well, we don't want to appear biased, so we always render one point to the left and two points to the right, which results in 1½ points up and 1½ points down--and everybody is happy, particularly Eris. *(see Note 4)*
2. The pentagon is also one of the basic geometrical figures; and geometry is one of the earliest applied logics. Geometry is also one of the earliest examples of the curious intermixing of logic and mysticism--read Pythagoras in the original, he was a nut. Hence, geometry is a Much Pregnant Symbol.

3. In times of Medieval Magic, the pentagon was the generic symbol for werewolves. The Discordian Society does not discriminate against werewolves: our membership roster is open to persons of all races and national origins.

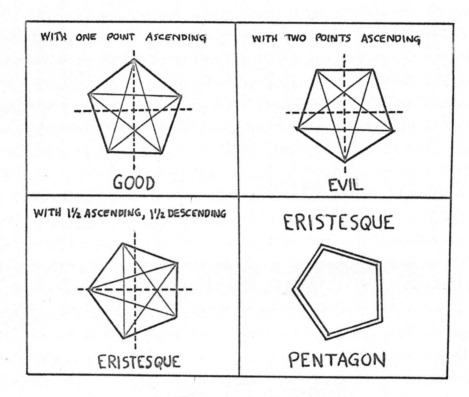

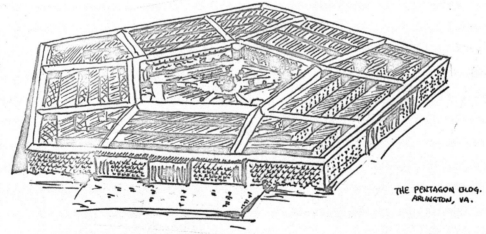

THE PENTAGON BLDG.
ARLINGTON, VA.

WHAT WE KNOW ABOUT ERIS

Disgustingly little.

However, we do know that She was worshipped by the ancient Greeks as the Goddess of Strife and Discord; and that the Romans appropriated Her and re-named Her Discordia.

The Romans seem to be the only ones who left a likeness of Her for posterity--She was presented as a grotesque woman with a pale and ghastly look, Her eyes afire, Her garment ripped and torn, and as having a concealed daggar hidden in Her bosom. Some Discordians of today question the validity of this picture, but that's what the Romans said.

Her geneology is amazingly confused (which is so appropriate to Eris, that it makes one shudder). She is the daughter of either a) Zeus and Hera (and the twin of Ares), or b) of Nyx. Now, Nyx was the daughter of Chaos and the Goddess of Night. She and her brother Erebus (how's this for a scandal?) begat Hypnos (sleep), Thanatos (death), Moros (doom), Cer (fate), Dreams (dreams), Momus (mockery, blame), Oizys (misery), Lachesis & Atropos & Clotho (The Three Fates), Nemesis, Deceit, Friendship, Old Age and Strife (ERIS). Zeus was scared to death of Nyx.

At least, it seems that she (Nyx) may by the daughter of Chaos. To quote from the New Century Classical Handbook: "In Greek mythology, chaos is the original formless state of the universe; or, the deity presiding over it. Perhaps no other myth exhibits quite so much confusion and variety as are found in the concepts of Chaos. The one thing common to all varieties was the idea of infinite space in which matter existed without form and in complete darkness; to some of the ancient poets, this was Chaos, and alone existed, but others said that Earth and Eros (not to be confused with ERIS--ed.) were coeval with Chaos. In some cosmogonies, the first of all things was Chronos (time), from whom proceeded Chaos and Aether (light, or upper air). But in another formulation, Chaos was the deity presiding over the formless mass with his wife Nyx (wife?--ed.). Their son Erebus (darkness) slew or dethroned Chaos (ho! another scandal!--ed.) and married his mother; from this union came Aether and Hemera (day), who with the aid of their son Eros (love) created Pontus (sea) and Gaea (earth). But in other accounts Gaea proceeded directly from Chaos and was the mother of Eros as well as of Tartarus (the nether world)."
And that is who Eris is related to.

But, all this aside, we have one nice little myth about Her.

The Myth of the Apple of Discord

It seems that Zeus was throwing a wedding banquet for Peleus and Thetis; and quite logically didn't want to invite Eris because he wanted it to go well. So everybody got invited byt poor Eris (we call this the Doctrine Of The Original Snub), and she got quite angry about it all.

Her cunning little mind clicking away madly, she took an apple of pure gold and inscribed upon it KALLISTI ("for the prettiest one") and rolled it into the banquet hall.

Needless to say, Her plan worked; three of the Goddesses immediately claimed the apple as theirs, exclaiming "It is obviously mine, it says so right accross the face of it!" and then their boy friends started defending them and soon began swinging at one another and an utter melee was in progress.

Now Zeus was taking all this in, and since he had previously decided that Earth was getting over populated and that something must be done, he too set his mind to work. So he announced that an arbitrater must be selected to decide whether Aphrodite, Hera, or Athena (the three Goddesses in question) should have the apple.

He sent the bunch of them to Paris, a shepherd of Troy, with the instruction to abide by his decision. But, (Oh, Eris knew these girls!) each went to Paris independently beforehand and offered him a bribe to answer in her favor; Athena offered Heroic War Victories, Hera offered something-or-another (I forget what), and Aphrodite offered The Most Beautiful Woman In The World. Now, being a healthy, red-blooded, young Trojan lad, he chose Sex; and Aphrodite manuvered it so that he could have Helen, then living with her husband Menelaus of Sparta (she couldn't always be found at home because she hopped from bed to bed throughout the Greek world). Anyway, unless you are some dumb clod, you should know that The Trojan War followed when Sparta demanded their queen back--and that the Trojan War was the proto-war for all the messes and problems of the world ever since.

A LITTLE NOTE:
The Greeks, not properly understanding that The Principle of Discord is not only necessary but GOOD and BEAUTIFUL and TRUE, thought that Eris was an evil Goddess and painted her as quite a bitch. But we modern Discordians know differently, and pass over their naieve and biased representation with a tolerant smile. (see Note Б)

THE FOUNDING OF THE DISCORDIAN SOCIETY

(Paraphrased from The Honest Book of Truth by
Lord Omar Khayyam Ravenhurst, K.C., Bull Goose of
Limbo and Protector of Switzerland; one of the founders
of the Erisian Movement)

Discordianism, as a disorganization, was founded
back in 1958 or 1959 or something when my colleague,
now Malaclypse (The Younger), K.C., and I were observing
the chaos spread out before us--the immediate vicinity,
the state, the nation, the world, verily: The Universe!;
when all of a sudden the air became still and no sound
arose from around us! And, for no apparent reason, the
place became black as the bowels of midnight! Then...
a piercing scream arose from my friend, hidden in the
dark, and the earth began to rumble--then light, of
brilliant intensity, from nowhere yet from everywhere;
and then nothing but stillness and I could stay concious
no longer. Presently, I came to, to find men in the
aisles weeping and women hysterically prostrate across
the lanes (we were in a bowling alley at the time); and
there before me: Malaclypse (The Younger) in a spasmatic
fit on the floor. Quite obviously, something profoundly
supernatural had occured. My friend was revived and
stammered out the following account of his vision:

"It is so obvious now! How blind we have been! All
of this chaos could not have just happened--it is no
coincidence that Pickering's Moon goes around in reverse
orbit, or that the Pentagon is riddled with--aye, founded
upon--confusion! Somebody had to put all this discord
here!"

"Yes, yes, yes," I shouted (for then it was clear,
now once stated).

Cried he: "And you, my friend, and I have a Holy
Appointment: together we shall found a new religion--
The True Religion--under the guidance of the Supernatural
Power you just witnessed: that of the Goddess of Discord."

And with that, he promptly swooned again, not to
awaken for five days and five nights.

Over the next five years, we, together, probed and
researched the philosophies of the world, discovering
that the Greeks and Romans had known Her (in an imperfect
form) and that She had lain all but dormant as a known
deity for two thousand years. As time passed, and the
work continued, and insight followed glorious insight,
the Erisian DISCORDIANSIM was born.

THE DISORGANIZATION OF THE DISCORDIAN SOCIETY

Following in reference to the Eristesque Principle, and in the footsteps of all Major Religions, the DS offers a complex structure and an Involved Hierarchy. For reference, see the Table of Disorganization to be found as page ii; that is, the page that you were instructed to be holding in one hand as you have been reading but hasn't been useful until now. (see Note 6)

Now it may appear that the Law of Fives is only partially operating in the Disorganization. Don't be fooled--that is not true. What happened is that all the various divisions and sub-divisions have not as yet been discovered. (see again Note 1)

We shall now explain the structure in detail.

THE ERISIAN MOVEMENT IN GENERAL

As has been mentioned (see Page 1), this is us-- the Enlightened Sages Seeking Wisdom Through ERIS. This movement has three divisions: The House of The Apostles of Eris, The Legion of Dynamic Discord, and the Bureaucracy.

The House of The Apostles of Eris

The House (as we lovingly call it) is the Eristocracy of the Erisian Movement. Any member of The House is called an Episkopos (which is a real honest-to-goodness Greek word that means 'over-seer', and from which we derive good words like 'epistle' and bad words like 'Episcopalian').and all of the Episkoposes are Eristocrats, which is the same thing. Now this is not to say that an Episkopos cannot be something else in The House also-- he can, if that something just happens to be a High Priest or a Compiler of Truth--Esoteric. In fact, it is quite likely that he will be a Compiler of Truth-- Esoteric; because that is probably how he became an Episkopos in the first place (but more on that later).

The fact that the sub-divisions of The House are numbered should not lead one to believe that this part is a heirarchy because that is not the case: with the grand exception of The Golden Apple Corps, which is in the attic. No Episkopos has any authority over any other Episkopos (with the same exception as mentioned)-- all are Eristocrats. But then, some Episkoposes do hold a higher place, but not because he is an Episkopos but because he is a something else too, and if that something else is the head of something. For instance, a High

Priest is the head of all those that follow his sect--
be they Legionnaires or Episkoposes--but he has no
authority over just any old body. Perhaps this will
become clearer as we go along (see Note 7).

The symbol for the House is the Golden Apple, with
KALLISTI written across the face of it (to represent
the Eristic Principle) surrounded by the pentagon (to
represent the Eristesque Principle). The apple is on
a darkened background. See Appendix for illustration.

The Golden Apple Corps:
This is the super-supreme-absolute-dictatorial-
tiptop of the Erisian Movement; it has the last word and
is answerable only to Eris Herself. It holds a position
somewhat similar to the (pardon the reference) Papacy
in heathen Christianity of the Catholic variety.

Now, don't get angry, it is not as bad as all that.

First, note that an Episkopos is pretty much his
own boss: he was ascended into The House because The
Keepers of The Sacred Chao felt that they could trust
his discretion. Hence, the only time that The Golden
Apple Corps would ever exert it's supreme authority would
be in case of disputes or in cases where a final authority is necessary.

Secondly, the fact that the Corps is closed to new
members (I guess I forgot to mention that), does not in
any way belittle other Episkoposes (see Note 8). The
Corps is for The Founders of Discordianism--and just
because you didn't happen to think of the idea first, it
doesn't necessarily imply that you are not as good a
Discordian as The Keepers of the Sacred Chao--even though
it is probably true.

A member of The Golden Apple Corps is called a
"Keeper of the Sacred Chao" and that is what that little
"K.C." after the founders' names means. Being two founders,
there are two Keepers of the Sacred Chao; namely;
Lord Omar Khayyam Ravenhurst, and Malaclypse (The Younger).
They, and only they, may authentically put "K.C." after
their names.

The emblem of the Golden Apple Corps is a single
golden apple (inscribed with KALLISTI) on a darkened
background--to represent the Founders affinity with ERIS.*

A NOTE ABOUT SYMBOLS:
The Golden Apple symbol is included in all Erisian
emblems, but not in its simple majesty--the Eristesque
Pentagon is also included in the others (symbolically
representing the two Principles together as the basic
Principle of Discord). The Apple is used as an Eristic
symbol for the Eristic Movement (to represent the Eristic
Principle alone) but does not include KALLISTI and, hence,
is not the Golden Apple of Discordia.

* See Appendix for illustration.

The Office of High Priesthood:
    Not long after the Discordian Society was founded,
there happened a schism (no great religion is without
schisms!). It seems that Malaclypse (The Younger)--
while under inspiration--realized that the Greeks did
not understand the Principle of Discord very well at all;
and that Eris should not be taken quite as literally as
had been done. And for about five days, Malaclypse
(The Younger) went through a Period of Rebellion, and
was heard making such comments as "Down with Eris" and
"Screw God" and other terrible things which made Lord
Omar very angry.
    Passing through his rebellious phase, Malaclypse
(The Younger) asked Lord Omar just what they should do;
for Lord Omar's inspirations told him that Eris was to
be taken literally--or nearly so, anyway. Well, they
went into conference at the Bowling Alley where ERIS
first presented Herself to them, and together they talked
things over with Eris.
    After much lengthy comtemplation, discussion, med-
itation, and consideration they concluded that it is
perfectly within the Discordian Philosophy to have Sex
(I mean Sects). And each appointed the other as the
High Priest of his particular interpretation.

    The Erisian Orthodoxy is the interpretation of Lord
Omar, and is more or less loyal to the ancient understanding
of Eris, and feels that she is a real live Goddess (sort
of). Any member of this sect should never, never take
Her name in vain, or so much as suggest that another
God or Goddess comes anywhere near Her. (see Note 9)

    The Heretic Fringe & Protestant Persuasion is the
interpretation of Malaclypse (The Younger). He feels
that She is not a real live Goddess but if there was one,
it would be She. Being a Symbolic Manifestation of The
Principle (which is what he calls Her), She does not,
he argues, always represent the appropriate specific.
Which means that sometimes a Fringe Heretic & Persuaded
Protestant can say "Hail Baccus" or "Hail St. Bokonon"
or "Hail Me" or something, if he feels that Eris is not
the appropriate symbol under the circumstances at the
moment. The liberal interpreters may take Her name in
vain on occassion; but do so sparingly, with kindness,
and not in the presence of an Orthodox Erisian (see Note 10).

    At the time that this is being written, these are
the only two sects and the only two High Priests. However, there is one way to become a High Priest yourself--
but that is a secret, and never let out of the Office.
The reason that it is secret is this: The High Priests
feel that being a High Priest and having followers is
quite a responsibility, and should not be avaliable to

just any one. So, if a person understands Discordianism
to the degree in which it is apparent to him, without
being told, how he can become a High Priest (if he wants
to), then he understands it well enough to qualify. So
don't ask a High Priest how he became one, because he
won't tell you. Incidentally, this is the only secret
that is to be found in the Erisian Mysteries--the reason
that we are "esoteric" is that nobody ever heard of us.

The emblem is a large pentagram (to represent the
mystically mysterious mysteries) with the inner pentagon--
that is inherrent in all pentagrams--outlined (to represent the Eristesque Principle) and a Golden Apple,
with KALLISTI, in the center (to represent the Eristic
Principle). See illustration in Appendix.

The Compilers of Truth--Esoteric
This is compiled truth. But this is not to be
confused with The Compilers of Truth--Lay, even though
both are Truth and both are Compiled. The difference
is that when an Episkopos compiles truth it is done in
specific regard to the Erisian Movement; which of course,
cannot be done by a layman who knows nothing about
Discordianism (though he may intuitively understand much
of Discordian Wisdom--which is why it is "truth" that
he compiled and not just any other old thing.)

This is a technical distinction and gives one no
authority or anything. If an Episkopos wishes, he may
call himself "Compiler of Truth--Esoteric" (if he has
compiled truth, that is), but usually this is not done.

The Epistolary is properly a part of the Erisian
Archives, but each Epistle itself is a compiled truth;
so it is properly part of this section too. More on
the Epistolary when we get to The Bureaucracy.

Holy Works are the best examples of compiled truths.
A Holy Work is a work done one, about, or in the name
of ERIS, and Discordianism. The Principia Discordia
(which you are now reading) is a Holy Work; as is The
Honest Book of Truth (the major work of Lord Omar) and
Summa Universalia (the major work of Malaclypse-The
Younger) and all of the trash that each Legionnaire
gets in his Initation Packet. Most of the Episkoposes
will have done some sort of a Holy Work by the time
they enter The House.

It has become a tradition of the Compilers of Truth--
Esoteric to dedicate their Holy Works to She For Whom
The Apple Of Discord Was Meant. Anything appropriate
to the following would do: "To The Pretty One," "For
The Fairest," "In Honor of The Prettiest," or simply
"KALLISTI".

The emblem is a large pentagon covered by crossed
quills (to represent authorship) covered by a small
golden apple. See illustration in Appendix.

The Five Apostles, Saints, and Like Personages

The Five Apostles of Eris are: Confusium, Krishna Argumentium, Discordeaux (Jean the Eristentialist), Eristotle, and Malaclypse (The Elder).

If you wish to know more about the Five Apostles, their history and importance: read Book II of The Honest Book of Truth, which is entitled THE GOSPEL ACCORDING TO OMAR. You will find it very enlightening (if you can find it at all).

Saints: At the time that this is being written, there are three Saints: St. Bokonon (sainted for his profound understanding of the function of religion), St. Quixote (sainted for his status in life as an Eristic Avatar), and St. Yossarian (sainted for his divinly inspired approach to life). It is interesting to note that our Saints are fictional, not factual-- but that is all right (St. Bokonon demonstrates that it certainly is all right). If you wish to know more about our Saints read (respectively): The Cat's Cradle, Kurt Vonnegut; Don Quixote, Cervantes; and Catch 22, Joseph Heller. As more Saints come to be recognized, all Discordians will be notified.

Like Personages: We just thought we would throw this in.

Council of The Episkoposes

An Episkopos is a member in general of The House. This is called a "council" just in case the Episkoposes get together someday. Everything else has pretty much been said, except:

How To Become An Episkopos: If a Legionnaire wishes ascendance into The House, he must first prove that he has a profound understanding of Discordianism. This is really necessary, for an Episkopos (unlike a Legionnaire) can do just about anything he wishes in the name of the DS. The only thing that he cannot do, is override The Golden Apple Corps. So, present yourself for examination before The Golden Apple Corps; and if it feels that your Erisian Judgement can be trusted almost unconditionally, then you will be ascended. The easiest way to present yourself for examination, is to write a Holy Work, such that you feel it demonstrates your ability to be an Episkopos, and present it to The Corps-- actually, this way is preferred, we like Holy Works. Ascendance into The House can be authorized only by The Corps.

One priviledge that an Episkopos has is that of giving himself titles, such as Bull Goose of Limbo and Protector of Switzerland (Lord Omar's Title) or like

Omnibenevolent Polyfather of Virginity-in-gold (Malaclypse-
The Younger's Title). Like your Sacred Name, your Sacred
Title is a very personal and individual thing and should
be chosen with care. Furthermore, he can also head
departments of The Bureaucracy and title himself ap-
propriatly; and he can officially usher in new Legionnaires
Converts; and ascend Legionnaires to Disciplehood; and
confer titles on Legionnaires and Disciples; and most
everything.
      As an Eristocrat in The House of the Apostles of Eris,
an Episkopos should carry his Honor with the appropriate
dignity.
      Episkoposes do not have a specific emblem because
it is they who use the other emblems of the House--and
they use whatever emblem is appropriate to what ever it
is that they are doing; or they may use the House symbol
by itself. See Appendix for lack of illustration.

                  The Legion of Dynamic Discord

      Of the rank and file of the Discordian Society,
The Legion is the file part (you are asked to politely
overlook the implication that The House is the rank part).
The bulk of our Fold, the following en masse, is The Legion.
      There are two sorts of Legionnaires: those who are
simply "Legionnaires" and those who are ascended to be
"Disciples of Eris". The latter is the more advanced,
and will be explained shortly.

LEGIONNAIRES:

      One may become a Discordian by simply stating to
any Episkopos his desire To Be Brought Into The Fold;
the Episkopos will then officially grant him membership
as a Legionnaire and notify the Bureaucracy (Bureau of
Erisian Archives) to add him to the books. When a
person expresses a desire to become a Discordian he is
saying, in effect: "I like Eris; I think She is the
True Goddess. I like the DS: I think it is the True
Religion. I wish to promote and understand ERIS by
becoming one with and working with the DS. I like
Chaos; and I need some help." The new Convert is now in
a position to gain Wisdom & Happiness & Goodness &
Meaning & Understanding & Insight & Beatitude & a DS
initation packet.
      The initation packet is liable to be most anything,
but it will surely include a handsome copy of The Sacred
Chao (see Frontpiece) and a certificate from The Legion
of Dynamic Discord acknowledging his entrance. It may
also include various pamphlets and miscellaneous information concerning the Discordian Society.

Every Legionnaire has the privelege of devising his
own personal Holy Name. He may choose his Name in any
way he wishes, and in reference to anything he wishes.
However, it is suggested that Holy Names be choosen
with the utmost care and with an eye towards originality--
for the Holy Name is the Outward Designation of your
Discordian Attitude; and it should be appropriate to
your own unique personality. When you have chosen a
Holy Name, notify the Bureaucracy (Bureau of Erisian
Archives) and it will be documented--after which you
will always be officially referred to by that name.
     The emblem for a Legionnaire is The Sacred Chao
with the words HAIL ERIS such that HAIL is inside the
border on top and ERIS is inside the border on the
bottom, which all around the outside of the border is
a sun burst (to represent a sun burst). See illustration
in Appendix.

DISCIPLES OF ERIS

     This is the advanced order of The Legion. A
Legionnaire becomes a Disciple when he demonstrates
that he is interested in actively promoting Discordianism, and so does.
     There are as many ways of becoming a Disciple as
there are ways of promoting Discordianism; and each way
has a Title which is conferred on the Disciple. To
cite a hypothetical example: Legionnaire John Anybody
adopts a Holy Name--say, Bacchus O. Bacchus--and is
tickled pink with Discordianism. He is so pleased that
he goes out and converts several friends, which he
introduces to an Episkopos (in person, or by mail) who
officially Ushers Them Into The Fold. Now when Bacchus
O. Bacchus converts five (5) people, it is felt that he
has made a significant contribution, and his effort is
rewarded. He notifies the Bureaucracy (Bureau of Erisian
Archives) that those converts should be credited to him
and he is ascended to Disciplehood--with the new title
"Evangelist". What used to be simply "Bacchus O. Bacchus,
Legionnaire" is now "Disciple Bacchus O. Bacchus,
Evangelist". How about that! And furthermore, every
time he does something particularly deserving he gets
another title to add on to those he already holds (and
becomes a Disciple of a Higher Degree). For instance,
say he writes, prints and sitributes 55 dopies of a
pamphlet to prospective people--he then becomes:
"Disciple Bacchus O. Bacchus, Evangelist, Public Pam-
phleteer. And so it goes; when he reaches Forth Degree,
he is called "High Disciple...etc." A few other examples
of Disciple-like activities are: a) making a pilgrimage
to a Holy Place, b) aiding an Episkopos in an administrative
duty, c) creating or helping with a Project, d) spreading

seeds of Discordianism, e) doing something that is
Divine in the Eyes Of Eris,...the list is endless.

A Disciple does not have any authority over a
plain Legionnaire but does have the significant distinction of being an _active_ Discordian, and does have
the priveledge to flaunt his well earned titles.

If a Disciple wishes to ascend to The House he
may do so via the approved route (see The House of The
Apostles of Eris; Council of The Episkoposes; How To
Become An Episkopos; page 12)

The emblem for Disciples is the Sacred Chao placed
on a shield-shaped banner supported by a staff. On
the banner, under the Sacred Chao, is the word DISCIPLE
and under that II or III or IV (depending on the
advancement of the individual). See Appendix for illustration.

THE LEGION AND THE SECTS

As previously mentioned (see The House of The Apostles of Eris; Office of High Priesthood; page 10) a
Discordian can be of the Orthodoxy or of the Heretic
Fringe & Protestant Persuasion--or can be non-sectarian.
Any Legionnaire, Disciple or not, may make his own
choice to follow under the auspices of High Priest Lord
Omar or of High Priest Malaclypse (The Younger) or
simply go independent. It is very confusing to go
independent because the two Keepers of The Sacred Chao
don't always agree on what Discordianism is and how it
should be handled (which is why the sects were formed
in the first place) and it is nice to have one dogma
you can always refer to while you just ignore the other.

Whichever Episkopos gets to you first will appear
to be attempting to influence you into thinking that
his own sect is the only sect that makes any sense--but
he is simply explaining Discordianism as he understands
it. He should inform you that you are free to join the
other (or neither) if you wish. Unless you otherwise
specify, then he will assume that you will follow his
sect because if he is the one who explains it to you then
it is likely that you understand Discordianism in the
same terms that he does.

The Bureaucracy (The Administry)

As its alternate name indicates, this handles the
Administrative Functions necessary for the propagation
of Discordianism. It is the responsibility of The House
and is headed by Episkoposes.

It has five sub-divisions ("Bureaus") each head of
which is called "The Keeper of...." ("of The Erisian

Archives", "of Symbols, Emblems, Certificates and Such",
etc.) except the Secretariat who is called "The Secretariat" but since we don't have one it doesn't make
any difference anyway. Each sub-division may have sub-
sub-divisions, and they can have their sub-sub-sub-
divisions, ad infinitum. Just keep track of what you
are doing.

This has an emblem, but The Keeper of Symbols,
Emblems, Certificates and Such (me) is keeping this
information classified at this time.

BUREAU OF THE ERISIAN ARCHIVES

Lord Omar, as Keeper of The Erisian Archives, has
in his possession: 1) the Epistolary and 2) all the
official Discordian Records--including copies of Holy
Works. The Epistolary is composed of copies of all the
Inspired Letters that have passed between the Keepers
of The Sacred Chao (or, if you like, passed between
the Chao's legs). Needless to say, these documents
will some day be Erisian Relics and should bring a
good price.

The rest of the Archives is everything else besides
the Epistolary.

The Polyfather also has much of this material in
his own Archives, which is officially called "The Erisian
Archives--Sub.Div."

Anyone who wishes may compile all of the Discordian
Material that they can get their hands on, and call it
"Unofficial Erisian Archives"--but it is not recomended
because it is a lot of trouble.

Anything that you wish to have officially recorded
in The Archives, please make duplicate copies and send
one to: United States Main Office; Lord Omar Khayyam
Ravenhurst, K.C.; c/o Kerry Thornley (his secular name);
~~4201 S. 31st St.~~ 4349: ~~Arlington, Va. 22206~~,* and send
the other to: Southern California Office; Malaclypse
(The Younger); c/o Gregory Hill (his secular name)--except
that you should put a little "K.C." after his Holy name
like I just forgot to do--; 1331 Ponderosa Ave.; Fullerton,
California 92631. Remember, two copies; carbon OK.

BUREAU OF SYMBOLS, EMBLEMS, CERTIFICATES AND SUCH

Malaclypse (The Younger), K.C., as Keeper of All
This, personally renders each hand drawn Certificate,
or Emblem or Such all by himself. He then has the master
duplicated (offset, Xerox, or something) and presents
it to whoever is going to get it.

Due to the expense involved in this operation, this
is one of the main areas in which The Treasury is emptied.

* Lord Omar's current address is to be found on the last page of this ms.

If you have any questions about the use of certificates, or what symbol is appropriate to what, or any
thing at all pertaining to this, just ask this Keeper
and if he doesn't have an answer ready he has the
authority to make up an answer to fit the question. All
the symbols and things so far, were for the most part
originally designed by him. All illustrations in this
manuscript can be blamed on him too.

BUREAU OF THE SECRETARIAT

This is the department that is in charge of typing
things, and mimeographing things and offsetting things,
and all that secretaries traditionally do.
It is here, also, that we have The Treasury.
And, too, any legalities that we must participate
in is done from here.
This is a pretty boring department.

BUREAU OF PROJECTS

Oh yes, we have Projects.
One of them is The University of Discordia, which
is still in the planning stage. When completed though,
it will have a whole catalog full of courses (with no
place to teach them) and will offer a Widower of Arts
degree to all Discordians interested. This should not
be confused with Ichabod College (see The Eristesque
Movement; Orders of Eris, Ichabod College)--The U of D
is avaliable only to upstanding Erisians.
The emblem for the U of D is a shield with the
words UNIVERSITY OF DISCORDIA across the top; with a
large sinking hand forming a "V" for victory in the
center; and a small pentagon enclosing an apple in the
lower point. On both sides of the shield is a large
burning torch, to represent knowledge or something; and
beneath the shield is the motto DIRUIT AEDIFICAT MUTAT
QUADRATA ROTUNDUS--HORACE. See appendix for illustration.

Another Project is Switzerland--it seems that Lord
Omar has discovered that there is a secret plot to overthrow Switzerland in which 11 small countries of Europe
will confiscate the gold in the Swiss banks. Being a
good natured fellow at heart, Lord Omar has offered the
Discordian Society Treasury for the purpose of Switzerland
to hide their gold in for safe keeping. The consulate
has not yet answered our offer (and our information about
The Plot), but we are sure that they will take us up on
it. For more information about this, read Book I of
The Honest Book of Truth, "The Fourth Pillar--Our Plan
to Liberate Switzerland". Those interested in this
Project may contact Lord Omar c/o Fair Play for Switzerland
Committee.

THE ERISTIC MOVEMENT IN GENERAL AND:
THE ERISTESQUE MOVEMENT IN GENERAL

Each of the two movements are not Erisian because they are not enlightened. They do not know of the DS, they are unfamiliar with ERIS, they (with possible exceptions in the Eristic Movement) do not recognize The Principle of Discord, they are ignorant of the Erisian Mysteries. However, they are obviously under the guidance of Eris Herself and must be acknowledged as citizens in our society of discord.

Each of the two movements represents one of the two Principles that together make up the Principle of Discord. That is, the Eristic Principle and the Eristesque Principle. These movements are living examples of these Principles at work in the universe. Their only problem is that they don't understand that a) they represent a principle, b) there is a counter principle, and c) these two principles in eternal conflict is the Basic Principle. And with the Eristesque Movement there is the further problem that they think that they are going just the opposite of what they are in fact doing.

THE ERISTIC MOVEMENT

As mentioned, this Movement is named after the Eristic Principle and the word "Eristic" is a real word to be found in any good dictionary. It's root (suprisingly enough) is "Eris" and it is defined as "Discordant or strife-ridden".

Those in the Eristic Movement, in one way or another, openly promote discord in a positive way.

The symbol is a silhouetted apple (no pentagon is included in any Eristic emblem).

Eristic Avatars

An Avatar is a physical manifestation, on this earth, of the Goddess Herself in the Other World. Such a person is 99 & 11/25ths percent Pure Chaos, and though he leads a frustrated life here on earth, his essence is of a Divine Status. Avatars (whole hearted Avatars, that is) are very few and very precious. To date, we have discovered only one: "The Prince of Dynamic Discord, Chaos Incarnate, Efficacious Paradox Con Carne, Our Eristic Avatar, Corporealeris, The Living One" (that is his title and Holy Name).

"Corporealeris" is his devine name and anyone who speaks it, hears it, reads it, or even thinks it is

necessarily endangering his place in the Eyes of Eris.
When referring to him "The Living One" is adequate,
providing one does not think of "Corporealeris" when one
is using that title in the shortened version. If one
says "The Living One" and does accidentally think of
"Corporealeris" then one must recite the entire title,
substituting the name Ichabod for Corporealeris (in
hopes of fooling Discordia into thinking that you actually
don't even know what his Divine Name is and that what
sounded like "Corporealeris" must have been a misunderstanding on Her part) while simultaneously not thinking
of the name Corporealeris, Five times foreward, and five
times backwards, with your head in a bucket of ice water
and your shoes on backwards.

The word "Avatar" is from the Hindus, and in Sanskrit
it means "down he goes".

Many Legionnaires, perhaps a little over exited with
their new found Discordianism, tend to ascribe the title
Avatar to everyone they can think of who is a little
chaotic in his actions--beware. An Avatar is very special
and very few exist. Now it is true that many people can
be discribed as "pretty unorganized" but remember that
all normal people exhibit both the Erisian and Eristesque
Principles--what you are confusing with Avatarism is
simply a small overbalance on the Eristic side of the
person. An Avatar is overwhelmingly Eristic. Those
individuals overwhelmingly Eristesque belong to the
Eristesque Movement; which we will be getting to any page
now.

The emblem for an Avatar is an Apple silouhette,
darkened, with the Holy Name printed accross the front.
See appendix for illustration.

Compilers of Truth--Lay

These are like Esoteric Compilers of Truth except
that they are not enlightened by Discordianism. But in
their writings they exhibit an intuitive understanding
of the fundamental importance of chaos. It is likely
that some would be active Discordians if they were aware
of our existance.

Two comtemporary examples of Lay Compilers of Truth
are Joseph Heller (author of Catch 22) and Kurt Vonnegut
(author of Cat's Cradle)--both of these books are Official
Discordian Textbooks and characters in these books have
been sainted (ie, St. Yossarian and St. Bokonon, respectively). Two classic example are Cervantes (Don
Quixote, also Sainted) and Lewis Carroll.

If you read something that you think may belong in
this catagory, pass it on to the House--we will be
interested in reading it. The emblem for Compilers of
Truth--Lay is a darkened apple silouhette with crossed
quills accross the front. See appendix for illustration.

THE ERISTESQUE MOVEMENT

The Eristesque Principle, if you recall (and I'm not about to let you forget), is the principle of superficial order resting on a firm foundation of chaos. It is false order, a sham. But this fascade is strong enough to compete with its counter Principle, the Eristic, which is honest chaos.

The Erisian and Eristic Movements, together, are called Discordianism Proper; and the Eristesque Movement is called Discordianism Improper. All Eristesquians have the following in common: they are convinced that they are fighting for order and against disorder, but they in fact are born of disorder and promote chaos in spite of (or because of) themselves.

Eristesquians are negative and are all bad guys-- but we don't fight them because they are really helping our cause--which actually doesn't need any help because the Principle of Discord is a Basic Truth and operates whether we like it or not.

The symbol for the Eristesque Movement is a pentagon, but with no apple.

The Orders of Eris

These are basic catagories the membership of which may or may not be very organized. They will be explained one at a time.

1. THE KNIGHTS OF THE FIVE SIDED TEMPLE
This is the counterpart to the Eristic Avatar. Such people are almost invariably found to be either bureaucrats or militarists (frequently both). The Five Sided Temple referred to is The Pentagon Bldg. itself where there is an incredible concentration of Knights. In your own experiences with military service and bureaucracies, you will have noticed many people with a heavy tendency towards the Eristesque Principle, but every so once in a while you will find a person who is absolutely wound up in all sorts of fantastic technical and formal order which due to its own weight ends up only in a comical-absurd cross-referenced maze of nothing; and such a person who lives, thinks and breaths in such terms--he is a Knight.

1½. THE COMMUNIST INFILTRATED AUXILIARY OF THE KNIGHTS OF THE FIVE SIDED TEMPLE
This is just what it says it is, and refers to a counter comical-absurd cross-referenced maze of nothing with a different set of fantastic technical and formal order built especially for the destruction of the first comical-absurd cross-referenced maze of nothing and the promotion of its own comical-etc. Each is convinced that

It Knows What It Is Doing and that the other is a Malevolent
Enemy.

If there is ever a Russian branch of the DS, its
Eristesque Movement will have a Capitalist Infiltrated
Auxiliary of the Knights of the Five Sided Temple.

The emblem for the Knights is a jousting shield,
crested with a jousting helm; with battle axes crossed
behind. Draped from one battle ax to the other is Red
Tape. The shild carries a Bar Sinister and two abatements
a) a darkened wavy border, and b) a point rising from
the lower center of the border (see Note 12). In the
center of the shield is a dimensionally drawn pentagon,
with sunburst. See appendix for illustration.

The emblem for the Communist Infiltrated A of T K
o t 5 S T is exactly the same but rendered in red ink.

2. ICHABOD COLLEGE
This, not to be confused with The University of Discordia,
is especially designed for those who have been exposed
to Discordianism and don't understand it.

Since lack of understanding is a pre-requisite for
entrance, then everybody flunks and no classes need be
held.

The emblem is an open book with the motto IGNOTUM
PER IGNOTIUS accross the pages; with a burning lamp of
wisdom on the page and a pentagon on the other; the book
is surrounded by a sunburst. This is enclosed by a
circular border with ICHABOD COLLEGE accross the top and
OF MISSAPPLIED ARTS AND SCIENCES accross the bottom.
Within the border on the left and right are five (5)
"plus signs" (+) such that the center plus is 90° from
the center of the emblem and the first and fifth are
45° from the center. The pluses should be positioned
such that the first and fifth pluses are tilted to
form an "x" (x) rather than a "plus" (+) while the second
and the fourth areinbetween. All this represents (from
the center plus) the ascention and descention from
positive (+) to unknown (x). Very clever. See appendix
for illustration.

3. THE DEFAMATION LEAGUE--UNDERGROUND
Not much is known about the Defamation League because it
is underground. However, it is easy to identify members:
they are people like assassins, bomb-throwers, anarchists,
rabble-rousers, anyone who makes it a practice to mal-
iciously throwm monkeywrenches into the works.

The Othodoxy feels that the Defamation League is an
enemy of the DS (because they frequently are referred to
as sowers of discord and throw bad light on the DS) and
does not even belong in the Eristesque Movement. The HF&PP
however, suggest that though others call them sowers of
discord, they themselves are convinced that they are solving
the worlds problems and, hence, promoting order. This,

we argue, is the common attitude of all Eristesquians.
Both sects agree that, regardless of the classification,
such actions cannot be officially condoned.

Their emblem is a black splotch with a pentagon in
the center. See appendix for illustration.

4. THE APOCALYPTIC PROPHETS LOCAL #666
Malaclypse (The Elder) was the first Doom Prophet and he
carried a sign that said "Doom". The sign had a novelty
appeal and ever since that day there have been Doom
Prophets walking around with signs displaying such encouraging messages as "The End Of The World Is Coming"
or "Repent, Your Time Is Had" and such nonsense.

None of these persons since the time of Malaclypse
(The Elder) knows what he is doing! All have misinterpreted
his message; all have corrupted his wisdom; all have
misrepresented his Divine Understanding.

All are honorary members of Local #666.

Just what the True Message Of Malaclypse The Elder
Is will soon be revealed by his only true follower the
Younger Malaclypse, K.C., in a portion of his Holy Work
Summa Universalia (which is not yet available).

The emblem is a "Doom" sign covering a pentagram
superimposed on a thick pentagon. Between each point
of the pentagram, and inscribed on the pentagon, are the
words WAR, FAMINE, PLAGUE, DEATH, CHAOS; all on a
darkened background and surrounded by a circular banner.
Accross the top, the banner reads BROTHERHOOD OF APOCALYPTIC
PROPHETS and on the bottom center it reads LOCAL #666,
which is the Sign of The Beast. Perched on top of the
banner is a raven. See appendix for illustration.

5. THE BOWEL MOVEMENT
This is a movement that is specifically Anti-Discordian.
It's members are those who have been exposed to the DS
and violently oppose it and those who were once members
but have fallen into disrepute. Needless to say, all
these people are forced into Ichabod College.

We do not fight these people but quietly condone
their noisey vulgarisms for we think that opposition is
a good thing (see The Books of Bokonon).

Their emblem is a black area in the form of a
pentagon with a large gapping hole repped from the center.
See appendix for illustration.

+ + + + +

And that, dear reader, is the structure of the DS.
                              All Hail Discordia

THE OFFICIAL DISCORDIAN DOCUMENT NUMBERING SYSTEM

The Keeper of Symbols, Emblems, Certificates and Such feels that no organization should be without a system for numbering it's official releases. This is ours:

It is composed of three sets of numbers, each seperated by a dash. The first represents the Movement appropriate to the document; the second to the sub-div(s); and the third is the date. Example: #1-2-4:11:64 would mean that it is Erisian, what it pertains to The Legion of Dynamic Discord, and that it was documentd on April 11th, 1964 (or 1864).

What to do with sub-sub-divisions: In the above example, there would be no way to diferentiate between a Legionnaire's document and a Disciple's document; so a Disciple's document would be two point one (2.1) whereas the Legionnaire's would be two point two (2.2), and when there are several more sub-catagories, just add a period and another number.

To find the appropriate numbers for the catagories, check your Table of Disorganization (Official Discordian Document #1-3.1-10:12:64) which whould have everything numbered for you.

About dates: Any given thing is liable to be revised without notice at any given time; so, if you have conflicting information, check to see which is the latest-- and follow it. Anything that is duplicated from this office will have an Official Document Number with the date. The reason that the date has colons and not slashes between the numbers is to make it not look like a date, which we thought would be nice.

Oh yes, the Orthodoxy uses a different system entirely.

1. Actually there are five movements, but two of them are remaining hidden and we cannot find them.

2. It seems that Discordeaux frequently succombed to spells wherein he could only speak a Divine Tongue of some sort that no one could understand but himself. We are sorry that we have no translation of this most apt comment.

3. See last paragraph of Note #4.

4. "The pentagon is said to be the star which lead the Magi to the manger where the infant Christ was laid." (Encyclopedia of Occultism, Spence; University Books)
    One of the ancient Egyptian symbols for the underworld was an irregualr 5 pointed star within a circle.
    These are just two more examples of the interrelationship between The Law of Fives, The Pentagon, and the intervention of Eris in the history of mankind.
    From DS Memo 14, Feb 1964 from OKR to Mal 2, on record in the DS Epistolary: "I am glad to discover that he was not also a virgin. I refer, of course, to your quotation from Spence: '...the manger where Christ was laid.' Naturally the five-sided pentagram enabled the Magi to discover this. I find the Law of Fives to be more and more manifest the harder I look."

5. This is a plug for the Heretic Fringe & Protestant Persuasion.

6. If you really took the page out and held it all this time when it wasn't needed...then you're too dumb to be a Discordian.

7. And perhaps not.

8. ...very much.

9. Lord Omar, after reading this explaination of The Orthodoxy states that no Protestant should ever be relied on to explain The Orthodoxy.

10. He might hit you.

11. There is no Note #11.

12. An abatement, in heraldric terms, is a mark of dishonor. A bar sinister is a sign of bastardy.

APPENDIX

ADDENDAE

MISCELLANEOUS

&

ET CETERA

THE MYTH OF ICHABOD

There once was a huge boulder, perched precariously, on the
edge of a cliff. For hundreds of years this boulder was there,
rocking and swaying, but always keeping its balance just perfectly.
But one year, there happened to be a severe windstorm; severe enough
um it was, to topple the boulder from its majectic height and
dash it to the bottom of the cliff, far far below. Needless to say,
the boulder was smashed into many pieces. Where it hit, the ground
was covered with a carpet of pbbles--some small and some large--
but pebbles and pebbles and more pebbles for as far as you could
walk in an hour.

One day, after all this, a young man by the name of Ichabod
happened on the area. Being a fellow of keen mind and observational
powers, naturally he was quite astounded to see so many stones
scattered so closely on the ground. Now, Ichabod was very much
interested in the nature of things, and he spent the whole afternoon
looking at pabbles, and measuring the size of pebbles, and feeling
the wieght of pebbles, and just pondering about pebbles in general.

He spent the night there, not wanting to lose this miraculous
find, and awoke the next morning full of enthusiasm. He spent many
days on his carpet of stones.

Eventually he noticed a very strange things There were
three rather large stones on the carpet and they formed a triangle--
almost (but not quite) equilateral. He was amazed. Looking further
he found four very white stones that were aranged in a lopsided
square. Then he saw that by disregarding one white stone and thinking of that grey stone a foot over instead, it was a perfect square!
And if you chose this stone, and that stone, and that one, and that
one and that one you have a pentagon as large as the triangle. And
here a small hexagon. And there a square partially inside of the
hexagon. And a decagon. And two triangles interlocked. And a
circle. And a smaller circles within the circle. And a triangle
within that which has a red stone, a grey stone and a white stone.

Ichabod spent many hours finding many designs that became
more and more complicated as his power of observation grew with
practice. Then he began to log his designs in a large leather
book; and as he counted designs and described them, the pages
began to fill as the sun continued to return.

He had begun his second ledger when a friend came by. His
friend was a poet and also interested in the nature of things.

"My friend," cried when Ichabod, "come quickly! I have
discovered the most wonderous thing in the universe." The peet
hurried over to him, quite anxious to see what it was.

Ichabod showed him the carpet of stones...but the poet only
laughed and siad "It's nothing but scattered rocks!"

"But look," said Ichabod, "see this triangle and that square
and that and that." And he proceeded to show his friend the harvest

of his many days study. When the poet saw the designs he turned to
the ledgers and by the time he was finished with these, he too was
overwhelmed.

He began to write poetry about the marvelous designs. And
as he wrote and contemplated he became sure that the designs must
mean something. Such order and beauty is too monumental to be
senseless. And the designs _were_ there, Ichabod had showed him that.

The poet went back to the village and read his new poetry.
And all who heard him went to the cliff to see first hand the carpet
of designs. And all returned to the village to spread the word.
Then as the enthusiasm grew there developed a group of those
who love beauty and nature, all of whom went to live right at the
Designs themselves. Together they wanted to see every design
that was there.

Some wrote ledgers about just triangles. Others discribed
the circles. Others concentrated on red colored stones--and they
happened to be the first to see disigns springing from outside the
carpet. They, and some others, saw designs everywhere they went.

"how blind we have been," they said.

The movement grew and grew and grew. And all who could see
designs knew that they had to have been put there by a Great Force.
"Nothing but a Great Force," said the philosophers, "could create
this immense Beauty!"

"Yes," said the world, "nothing but a god could create such
magnificent order. Nothing but a God."

And that was the day that God was born. And ever since then,
all men have known Him for his infinite power and all men have
loved Him for his infinite wisdom.

Excerpted from a treatise concerning The Nature of Gods and The
Eristesque Movement, to be found in the SUMMA UNIVERSALIA, the
Holy Work of Malaclypse (The Younger), K.C., Omniscient Polyfather
of Virginity-in-gold, and High Priest of The Heretic Fringe and
Protestant Persuasion of the ERISIAN MOVEMENT of the Discordian
Society--Hail Eris.

Official Discordian Document #1-1.2.2-4:11:64

ALL HAIL DISCORDIA!

(The House of the Apostles of Eris)

THE GOLDEN APPLE CORPS

(The House of the Apostles of Eris)
COMPILERS OF TRUTH--ESOTERIC

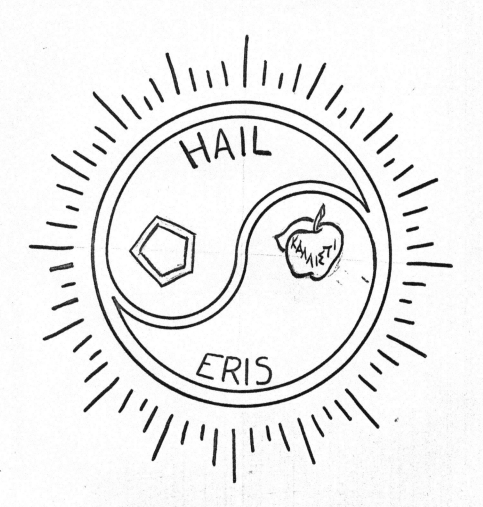

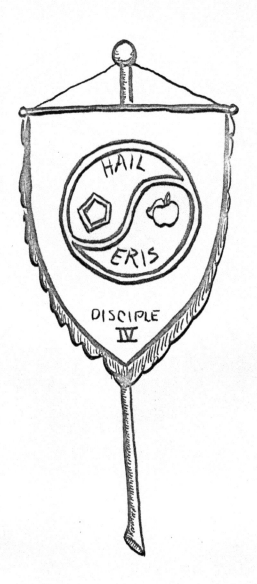

PROJECT CONCERNING THE UNIVERSITY OF DISCORDIA

"He pulls down, he builds up, he changes
square things into round."   --Horace

(Orders of Eris) THE KNIGHTS OF THE FIVE SIDED TEMPLE

(Orders of Eris)   THE DEFAMATION LEAGUE--UNDERGROUND

(Orders of Eris) ICHABOD COLLEGE

"The unknown explained by the still more
unknown."

(Orders of Eris)   THE BOWEL MOVEMENT

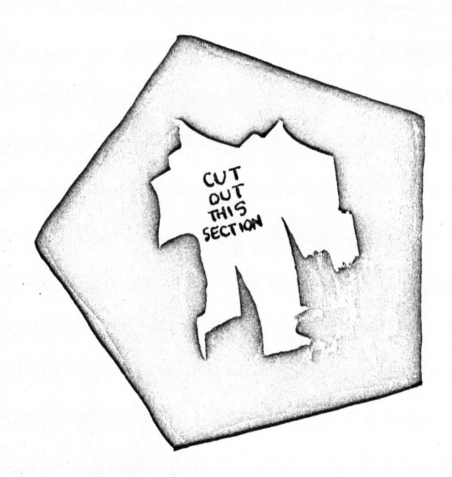

Official Discordian Document #1-1.3.2.3-4:1:64

5 more spaces ⟶

<u>WHY</u> <u>WE</u> <u>THINK</u> <u>THE</u> <u>DS</u> <u>IS</u> <u>A</u> <u>HOT</u> <u>ITEM</u>

We think the DS (Discordian Society) is the hottest item to
hit the holy market since Islam; here are a few of the reasons:

1) Organized Religion can no longer serve the inspirational
needs of the modern consumer; it cannot keep up with the swift
pace of scientific discoveries, which now all the really good nothing
religious ideas must do at least long enoughto to become accepted
as traditions too sacred to examine. The DS offers an alternative
to Organized Religion, thus evading such problems entirely: Disorganized Religion.

2) Disorganized Religion hits the spot. What else, in the
name of <u>one</u> God and <u>one</u> collection box, can take five different
stands on, say, birth control--all at the same time?

3) DR (Disorganized Religion) offers, to those who have
courage enough to maintain it, what the Eristentionalist philosopher, F.J. Discordeaux, aptly calls "a disintegrated view."

D) DR, and only DR, recognizes the basic principle of everything: The Law Of Fives, whthm which was so recently rediscovered for
science by the Eristitivist philosopher and mathematician, Lord
Ravenhurst; that is, as Krishna Argumentum put it: Truth is five,
but men only have one name for it.

E) Our competitors offer nothing but outworn stories about
men who died long ago, but DR, and only DR, has an Eristic Avatar
here on earth now! When we say, "He lives," we mean it! Further,
He works for the Post Office!!!!! How's that for being down to
earth?

5) The DS was founded some years ago by two people. Today
its growth has more than tripled. Further, it is already infiltrated by a <u>genuine</u> Communist, has lost one book form its Bible,
THE HONEST BOOK OF TRUTH, and has suffered several major ideological
controversies!

We hope you are impressed. Nothing but DR offers <u>everything</u>
for so little. Get yours today.

Lord Omar Khayyam Ravenhurst, Bull Goose Of Limbo & Protector Of
Switzerland. House of the Apostles of Eris; United States Main
Temple of the Eristic Orthodox Branch of the Discordian Society;
Box 55555, Pentagon Bldg., Washington, D.C. 22206. Hail Eris.

ON THE LAW OF FIVES

~~WHO SAYS?~~

From a treatise concerning NATURAL LAW, found in the (as yet unavailable)
SUMMA UNIVERSALIA, incompleated holy work of Malaclypse (The Younger), K.C.

It has frequently been brought to my attention that the name ERIS has
only four letters, and it has been claimed that this disproves the Law of
Fives. Nonsense! Observe the following proofs that, as always, the Law of
Fives necessarily holds true even here:

#1 The name ERIS begins with the letter 'E'. As was first observed
by Lord Omar, the eminent discoverer of the Law of Fives, the position of
'E' in the alphabet is that of FIFTH.

#2 The name DISCORDIA has nine letters; the name ERIS has four.
Not only is the fourth letter 'D', the first letter of 'DISCORDIA', but
9-4=5 (FIVE).

#3 The letters E,R,I,S correspond as the 5th letter, the 18th,
9th and 19th. Now, 5+18+9+19=51. Fifty-one starts with FIVE.

#4 The first two letters of ERIS (E,R) correspond to five and
eighteen (18-5=13). The first two letters of DISCORDIA (D,I) correspond to
four and nine (4+9=13). The total number of letters in ERIS (4) plus the
total number of letters in DISCORDIA (9) sum to thirteen (9+4=13). Obviously,
the number 13 is important.
The letters of DISCORDIA correspond to 4,9,19,3,15,8,4,9,1 which add up
to 118. Add that to the all important thirteen (established above) and
118+13=131, which is six more than 125 (five squared five times). Six is
important because:
a) it is what five and one equal (remember proof #3 which ended in
five and one).
b) when you add 51 (referred to in 4-a) to 118 you get 169, which when
subtracted by the all important thirteen equals 156, which is 6(!) more
than 125 (five squared times five) plus 25 (five squared); that is,
156=6+125+25 and twenty-five is FIVE FIVES.

#5 Five to the fifth power is 3125. If you observe closely, you
will note that there is but one number missing from the series to form a
1 to 5 progression, the number 4--which is how many letters there are in
the name ERIS.

#6 As in the case of Lord Omar's five proofs of the truth of the
Law of Fives, there are five proofs here--FIVE. If it appears to you that
there are now six, then simply recall proof #3 which has 1 left over (five
and one). Subtract that from 6 and 6-1= FIVE.

This should dispel any doubts about the reliability of the immutable
Law of Fives.

O.D.D. #1-1.2 -3.5.65

This fifth day of March, 1965
In the name of Our Lady of Discord

Malaclypse (The Younger), K.C.
Omniscient Polyfather of VIG

* 1+3+1 = 5

UNDERSTANDING DISCORDIANISM

You are not expected to understand Discordianism; the question is, rather, "Do you just don't understand it?" or "Is it that you don't understand it in the same sense that even Discordians don't understand it?"

If the former: then pass on to exoteric oblivion; if the latter: welcome to our esoteric ranks.

Under the Divine Guidance of Eris, there is no sure way of deciding whether your lack of understanding is ~~crass or~~ vulgar or sophisticated; but if this preposterous essay makes any degree of sense to you — then to that degree you are probably Discordian material.

Mal 2 9-24-64

ADDENDUM

Official Discordian Document #1-1.3,2.2-4:11:64

ON BEHALF OF ERIS

THE DISCORDIAN SOCIETY PRESENTS AN OUTLINE-GUIDE-OF-THE-HIERARCHY-
OF-ARGUMENTS-TO-USE-ON-POTENTIAL-CONVERTS FOR THE BENEFIT OF OUR
DISORGANIZATION MEN IN THE FIELD (OR, IF YOU PREFER: PASTURE).

The Socratic Approach should always be used to open the con-
versation with the victim. That is what asking questions to start
an argument is called. You approach the victim and simply ask:
"Did you know that God is a female? And that her name is Eris,
Goddess of Discord?" If the victim says "yes", then he's either
lying or you've picked a fellow Discordian, idiot. If he doesn't,
then proceed to

THE BLIND ASSERTION. This is where you say, "Well, She is a
woman and her name is Eris." Now see if the victim appears to be
convinced. If not, proceed to

THE FAITH BIT. "But you must have faith! Faith is wonderful,
etc.! I feel sorry for you if you don' have faith!" And then add

THE ARGUMENT BY FEAR. "Do you know what happens to those who
don't believe in Goddess?" If the victim says "no", don't tell
him whatever it is you think happens to unbelievers, just shake
your head sadly and go to

THE FIRST CAUSE PLOY wherein you point to all the chaos around
you and ask, "Well who do you think made all this then, wise guy?"
If he says "nobody, just impersonal forces", then go on to

THE ARGUMENT BY SEMANTICAL SYMNASTICS wherein you say that
he is right and that those impersonal forces are a female and that
her name is Eris. If he still objects to your objectionable presence,
then go to the

FIGURATIVE SYMBOLISM DODGE wherein you explain that all
sophisticated people know that Eris is just a figurative symbol
for discord, but that the Discordian Religion is a magnificent
work of art--portrait of chaos, so to speak. If nix....

Quietly draft him into Ichabod College where he may flunk
to his heart's stupid content.

Written by LORD OMAR KHAYYAM RAVENHURST, K.C.; Bull Goose of Limbo
and (same personage) Protector of Switzerland; Keeper of The
Erisian Archives

A PERSONAL NOTE FROM LORD OMAR

WHAT THE
PHILOSOPHICAL FUNCTION OF THE DISCORDIAN SOCIETY IS:

For centuries, men have probed the secrets of nature to discover and explain the laws of the universe, to find out the shape and source of order. Today, that search is ending. It used to be the function of religion to provide explainations for the order of things which science discovered but was unable to explain. Today, that function is vistigal.

So interested have men been with order, throughout history, that they left another field entirely neglected: DISORDER.

Science is unable to explain, for example, why today's world goes right on ignoring science--paying more tribute to superstition, totalitarianism, and war.

Why are the secrets of the atom used to promote chaos among men? Why are the most generous motives of men played upon to produce slavery? Why do otherwise sane people attend church on Sunday?

The purpose of the Discordian Society is to provide false, comforting answers to questions of this sort; to give mystical reasons for the disorder around us; to promote unworkable principles of discord--in short, to provide the world with a workshop for the insane, thus keeping them out of mischief as Presidents, Ambassadors, Priests, Ministers, and other Dictators.

Lord Omar Khayyam Ravenhurst, K.C.
April 11, 1964
Arlington, Va.

A PERSONAL NOTE FROM MAL 2

_____

ARE DISCORDIANS "SERIOUS"?

As one of the founders and authors of the Discordian
Society, I am frequently met with the following comment:
"You don't really believe all this stuff, it's too silly
to be serious. Sure, some of the satire is serious,
and parts of the underlying philosophy are sound, and
you've done a great deal of work on it; but you can't
believe what you say you do--do you?"

This question cannot be answered "yes" or "no"--only
that the question itself is inappropriate.

You see, in authoring Discordian material, some things
I write I mean to be taken seriously, literally, as you
would if you were reading any philosopher; other things
I mean to be taken seriously, but analogously, as if you
were reading any poet; other things I mean to be taken
fasceously, as if you were reading any critic-satarist;
still other things I mean to be taken humorously, as if
you were reading any humorist; and a few things I don't
expect to be taken at all, for they were put there for
my own private amusement and their references are too
obscure to be expected to be understood.

But all this is really secondary, for if you can
understand what it is that the philosopher is stating,
and what it is that the poet is expressing, and what it
is that the satarist is criticising, and why it is that
the humorist is humorizing, and how it could be that
such an author might then have the audacity to include
private references that can only confuse his readers--
in short, if you can understand Discordianism--then you
can see that Discordianism absolutely destroys the
distinction between "being serious" and "not being serious".

Ask me if I believe in "Eris", ask me if I believe
in "truth", or in "reality", or in "myself" or...hell,
ask me if I believe at all. If you were to recieve any
answer whatsoever; it would be the same answer to each.

                    Malaclypse (The Younger), K.C.
                    September 24, 1964
                    Fullerton, Calif.

APPLICATION FOR MEMBERSHIP IN THE ERISIAN MOVEMENT OF
+++++   THE DISCORDIAN SOCIETY   +++++

1. Today's date:_____ ___, 19___   Yesterday's date:_____ ___, 19___

2. PURPOSE FOR WHICH THIS APPLICATION IS SUBMITTED:

    a. () Legionnaire in The Legion of Dynamic Discord
    b. () Disciple of Eris in The Legion of Dynamic Discord
    c. () Episkopos in The House of Apostles of Eris
    d. () Secretary for Cultural Affairs for the Legation of the People's
       Republic of Bulgaria in Washington D.C.

If you have checked 2-a, you will be immediately accepted as a Legionnaire.
If you have checked 2-b or 2-c, please enclose a statement of the reasons
you have to believe that you should be ascended; it will be considered.

3. NAME_____

   HOLY NAME_____

   ADDRESS_____
If you have reason to believe that this addres will be temporary, please,
add here a "permanent address" from which mail can always be forewarded
(parents, friend, etc.)_____

4. DESCRIPTION:

a. Born: ()yes ()no   b. Eyes: ()two ()other   c. Height:____fluid ounces
d. Last time you had a haircut:_____, 19___; reason:_____
e. Race: ()horse ()human   f. IQ: ()150-200 ()200-250 ()250-300 ()over 300
g. Marital status: ()single   ()married   ()separated   ()shacking up
h. Identification print: on the lower left hand corner place one of the
following ()fingerprint of middle finger of right hand ()toeprints of
entire left foot ()noseprint ()name print ()please print

5. HISTORY:

a. Education: circle highest grade completed 1 2 3 4 5 6 ()over 6th
b. Professional: on another ream of paper list every job since 1937 from
which you have been fired   c. Medical: on a seperate sheet of paper,
labeled "confidential", list all major psychotic episodes experienced within the last twenty-four hours.

6. SNEAKY QUESTIONS TO ESTABLISH PERSONALITY TRAITS:

a. I would rather ()live in an outhouse ()play in a rock & roll band ()eat
caterpillers   b. I wear obscene tatoos because_____
c. I have ceased raping little children ()yes ()no; reason_____
d. "None of your goddam business." (Write a question to fit this answer.)

7. IN CASE OF ACCIDENT please notify ()mother ()father ()God

==IDENTIFICATION PRINT:==   FOR   OFFICE   USE   ONLY:
                                     ()accepted ()rejected ()burned
                                     Official Discordian Document (ODD)
                                                #1-3.3-3:5:65.

LEGION OF DYNAMIC DISCORD

Hark! Recognize that the
DISCORDIAN SOCIETY
Doth hereby certify

As a LEGIONNAIRE
GLORY TO THE CHILDREN OF ERIS!

PRESENTED UNDER THE AUSPICES OF OUR LADY
OF DISCORD; ERIS; BY AN EPISKOPOS OF
THE HOUSE OF THE APOSTLES OF ERIS

signed: _____

(title) _____ date:

OFFICIAL DISCORDIAN DOCUMENT # 1-2,2.3-4:11:44

 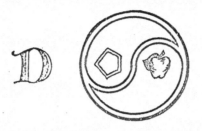

forsooth

The Discordian Society

announces that

has been

and that (check one) *he, she, it deserves all due honors appropriate and will not go to hell*

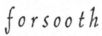

DECLARED AND DOCUMENTED ON THIS ____ DAY OF _____,
IN THE HOUSE OF THE APOSTLES OF ERIS, IN THE NAME OF
OUR LADY OF DISCORD—ERIS, BY THE HAND OF:

(Name) _____

(Title) _____

(Authority) _____

special all-purpose DS document

Official Discordian Document #1-1.2.2(1.3.2)-11:6:64
Chicago, Ill.

<u>NOTICE</u>

1. This manuscript is the property of the Discordian
Society (Administry: Bureau of Erisian Archives, Discordian
Library) and whoever has possession of it is kindly
requested to personally <u>guarantee</u> its return to an
Episkopos or to Malaclypse (The Younger), K.C. If mailed,
please write "Principia Discordia" on back of mailing
envelope. If another Discordian or a sincere prospective
Discordian wishes to take it, then pass it on to him--
provinding he personally <u>guarantees</u> its return.

2. Permission is hearby granted to quote from or
to reproduce this manuscript on the following conditions:
a) that credit is given to the DS and the author; b) that
any money made from the direct result of using this ms
be forewarded to the DS treasury to be used by the DS
at large (c/o Gregory Hill). Any deviation from the
above conditions requires written permission by Malaclypse
(The Younger), K.C. Note that "The Myth of Ichabod" is
legally copyrighted.

MALACLYPSE (THE YOUNGER), K.C.
c/o GREGORY HILL
1331 PONDEROSA AVE.
FULLERTON, CALIF. 92631

THIS IS COPY _1_ OF FIVE (5) COPIES

Operation Mindfuck
and the Bavarian Illuminati

IN 1968, KERRY THORNLEY was indicted by New Orleans's District Attorney Jim Garrison as part of an alleged JFK assassination conspiracy directed by elements of the CIA [Figure 4.1]. (Hail Eris!)

During the course of the Garrison investigation, Thornley discovered that one of Garrison's aides, Allan Chapman, was of the belief that JFK's assassination had been orchestrated by the Bavarian Illuminati, a secret society much ballyhooed by right-wing conspiracy theorists as being behind communism and damn near every other conspiracy then corrupting the world and "poisoning our precious bodily fluids."

In response, Thornley devised a covert campaign dubbed Operation Mindfuck, which included a series of announcements Kerry sent out claiming that he (aka Lord Omar) was an agent of the Bavarian Illuminati, just to further confound Garrison and his staff.

Operation Mindfuck went into full swing in late '68, when fellow Discordian and *Playboy* editor Robert Anton Wilson — in cahoots with Thornley—composed a letter & answer in the *Playboy Forum*, which Wilson was then editing. This spurious correspondence (appearing in the April '69 issue) put forth the theory that the wave of political assassinations then besieging America had been orchestrated by (you guessed it!) those Bavarian Illuminati bad boys. In addition, this *Playboy Forum* letter & answer mentioned a Cal Berkeley campus group which also identified itself as "The Illuminati" and issued press releases on all sorts of weird subjects, the intent of which was to give people who wanted to believe in conspiracies something to point to, and thus become more paranoid about.

Tampan Subpoenaed by Garrison

By THOM WILKERSON
Tribune Staff Writer

A Tampa free lance writer yesterday was subpoenaed by Dist. Atty. James Garrison of New Orleans in connection with Garrison's probe of the assassination of President Kennedy.

Kerry Wendell Thornley, 29, of 726 51st St. S., said at his home here that he has nothing new to tell Garrison but said he would appear in New Orleans Feb. 8-9 "if I'm legally required to do so."

Garrison, in announcing the subpoena, said Thornley hadn't told the Warren Commission everything about his association with Lee Harvey Oswald, described by Garrison and the Commission as a Marine Corps buddy of Thornley's.

"I've been half expecting this," said Thornley, who has lived at the 51st Street address with his wife, Clara, since last October.

"I'm very, very skeptical that Oswald killed Kennedy or had anything to do with it. The last time I saw him was

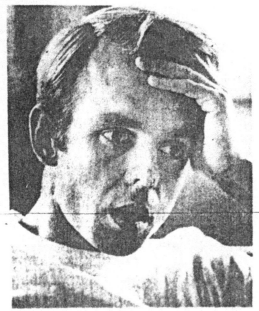

—Staff Photo by Mark Foley

Thornley Expresses Mild Surprise
... says he has nothing new to tell Garrison

in June 1959. I never saw him in New Orleans. I told the Warren Commission in April, 1964 in Washington all I knew."

Thornley said Garrison's action was prompted by information supplied by Barbara Reid, a New Orleans practitioner of witchcraft. He said he knew Oswald at El Toro, Calif., in 1959.

The Tampan is the author of, "Oswald," a book on the accused assassin published in 1965 by New Classics House, Chicago.

"I don't think Oswald had any best buddies," said Thornley. "I was a close acquaintance. One time, I remember, we had an argument about waiting on a parade and I told him, 'Well, comrade, comes the revolution and you'll change all that.' Everybody in the outfit (Marine Air Control Squadron 9) put him down as an atheist and communist."

He said Oswald didn't appear to be insane but was "a little bit of an oddball."

Thornley said his and Os-
(Continued on Page 11, Col. 1)

Figure 4.1 *Tampa Tribune* interview with Kerry Thornley following his February 1968 subpoena by Jim Garrison

---

Formed in 1967, the Cal Berkeley Illuminati branch eventually merged with the Discordian Society's Operation Mindfuck, and among its members was Louise Lacey, who—synchronistically enough—had edited Thornley's 1965 book, *Oswald*, for New Classic Books in Chicago. In the mid-60s, Lacey relocated to the Bay Area where she worked as research director for *Ramparts*, the cutting-edge political/activist magazine of its day. One of her main projects during this time was a series of exposés on the Kennedy assassination.

In an August 1968 letter to Louise Lacey, Kerry addressed the forthcoming *Playboy Forum* mindfuck, and further outlined a plan of clandestine action with the creation of Hassan-i-Sabbah X, a modern-myth-in-the-making [Figures 4.2–4.4].

Similar to the *Playboy Forum* prank, Wilson and *Illuminatus!* co-author Robert Shea penned a series of articles advancing this Bavarian Illuminati conspiracy, one for the March 1969 issue of *Teenset*, a popular music magazine, and another for *The Roger Spark*, a Chicago neighborhood anarchist newspaper [Figure 4.6].

The *Teenset* article, entitled "The Most Sinister, Evil, Subversive Conspiracy in the World"—written under the pseudonym of Sandra Glass—documented an in-

7Aug68

Dear Louise -

The name your black writer writes under is Hassan-i-Sabbah X --
this name he chose as a somewhat whimsical put-on, as Hassan i
Sabbah was the Moslem heretic who founded the Assassins, after
which was patterned the Roshaniya (or Illuminated Ones), after
which were patterned the Alumbrados of Spain and the Illuminati
of Bavaria.

Formerly, he was a student at Berkeley, where he joined the
Berkeley psychedelic anarchist group, the Bavarian Illuminati,
and then dropped out to become a full-time revolutionist, for
the Illuminati. Previous to all of which he was a rank-and-file
brother in Black Islam.

On a self-assigned mission for the Illuminati Conspiracy, he
was jailed for "revolutionary activities." It is from prison that
his manuscripts are smuggled via an "underground railway" to you,
Lady L., whom he has asked to act as his literary agent.

Naturally you cannot reveal the country in which Hassan-i-
Sabbah languishes at present nor his real name, for to do so would
be to imperil those unsung heroes who transmit his work to the
world, not to mention Hassan-i-Sabbah X himself.

Hassan-i-Sabbah X is the only black writer we know of who is
also quite explicitly a turned-on anarchist.

The Conspiracy of which he is a part is directed by seven ruling
members -- or Master Conspirators -- and has no membership. The
other Master Illuminati, besides you, me and Hassan, are:

Robert Anton Wilson   Tom McGivern   Greg Hill
1444 West Fargo Ave.   1543 Rosalia Rd. #206
Chicago, Ill. 60626   Paul Encimer   Los Angeles, CA 90027
                             ▮▮▮▮▮▮▮▮▮▮
                             218 E. Regent St.
                             Inglewood, Calif.

I suggest you get in touch with Tom and inform him of his role.
He, in turn, will have in a few days something to show you -- a
photocopy of the copy proofs to a future PLAYBOY FORUM letter and
answer on the Bavarian Illuminati, from Hassan i Sabbah ▮▮▮▮▮▮▮▮▮▮
(the original) to the present Berkeley group, which it explains as
a "put-on by the local anarchists." This is strictly confidential.

As you know if you have read the NYer piece by Epstein, one of
Garrison's Irregulars is Alan Chapman, foe of the Illuminati.
▮▮▮▮▮▮▮▮▮▮▮▮▮▮▮▮

I do not know where all this will end, but we will make the bicycle
scam of Amsterdam look like a game of tiddly winks.

Of course it will first be necessary to present the Bavarian Illuminati
side of things -- we are a much-maligned group. We are not, for example,
assassins -- not PEOPLE assassins, anyhow, but EGO assassins. We pick
out various targets in the power structure and, by one means or another,
TURN THEM ON. And, contrary to the exaggerations of our enemies, we
do NOT control ALL the TV networks -- better to blame us for the
assassinations than THAT! Nor have we yet secured complete control
of international banking (we still need your donations out there for
this project to continue).

Figure 4.2a Thornley's letter to Louise Lacey

outlining his plans for Operation Mindfuck

But it is plain that we definitely ARE on the offensive these days
(so much so that we can begin to come out in the open at relatively
liberated places like Berkeley) and one of our membership drive slogans
(as we are going to start openly selling memberships in the near future
in order to raise money for various worthy causes, such as Kerry
Thornley's Defense Fund -- "Don't let Garrison wreck the Illuminati!")
can be: GET ON THE WINNING SIDE -- JOIN THE BAVARIAN ILLUMINATI!

For only five bucks, folks -- or a larger donation if you can afford
it -- you get a Bavarian Illuminati MEMBERSHIP Membership Card, which
entitles you to XXXXXXXXX CONSPIRE and ILLUMINATE. (One of our goals
is to Illuminate the Opposition.) You also get other junk and especially
some ILLUMINATION STICKERS, which you paste up in heads and phone booths
& which are triangular, feature the Illuminati Pyramid, and said on
them either CONSPIRE or (depending on the sticker in question)
ILLUMINATE. You also get an "in Gold we trust" button and a psychedelic
recruiting poster -- XXXXXXXXXXXXXXXXXXXXXXXXX THE ILLUMINATI BUILDS
CONSPIRATORS! (THE ILLUMINATI BUILDS GODS?) (BUDDHAS?)

Naturally, all ████████████████████X illuminated people
are Illuminati, and nearly all the young people are illuminated these
days -- but to be a Conscious Agent of the Conspiracy, you have to be
a card-carrying Illuminati.

Organ-eyes to smash the State!

Love&Revolution,

kerry

PS - Cara is back, finally got around to going to a dr. today, &
definitely is pregnant.

PPS - The degree of seriousness w/which we Illuminati advance our
claims & ideas should be that which will keep intelligent people
saying to each other, "But what if it really ISN'T a put-on!"
I haven't yet told any of the others that they are
Master Conspirators of the Inner Circle of the Bavarian Illuminati
of Berkeley (but will do so when time permits).

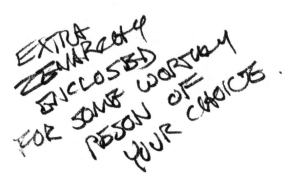

Figure 4.2b Page 2 of Thornley's letter to Louise Lacey

from **ROBERT ANTON WILSON**

Dear Kerry,

Since you mentioned the Illuminati in
your last letter, I'd like to take
advantage of you. Assuming you know
more about them than I do, please look
over the enclosed letter and answer,
and tell me if my answer has any
gross errors.

Thanks.

Bob

Figure 4.3 Note on
Playboy stationery from
Robert Anton Wilson to
Kerry Thornley regarding
the *Playboy Forum* prank

vestigation into the mysterious Ancient Illuminated Seers of Bavaria (A.I.S.B.). This article was ominously prefaced with an editor's note: "Before her recent death, Miss Glass was an expert on subversive affairs." The source—for many of the revelations in the article—came allegedly from an anarchist named Simon Moon, who would later turn up as a character in *The Illuminatus!*

According to the *Teenset* article, Adam Weishaupt founded the A.I.S.B. in Ingolstadt on May 1st, 1776, and their slogan—or secret password—was "*Ewige Blumenkraft*" which translates to "Flower Power Forever." At first glance, this motto seemingly refers to May Day, the date the A.I.S.B. came into existence. However—as later explicated in *The Illuminatus!*—the complete version of the motto is "*Ewige Blumenkraft und ewige Schlangenkraft*," which translates to "eternal flower power and eternal serpent power" and apparently suggests that the fertility rites of spring are connected to the kundalini force—or serpent power—which itself relates to the practice of Tantrism, or sex magic. And that, in essence, is the True Secret of the Illuminati: Sex Magic.

The *Teenset* article intimated that during the 1968 Democratic Convention, when Senator Abraham Ribicoff criticized police violence against anti-war demonstrators, Chicago Mayor Richard Daley responded with an animated retort, and "... his lips were forming the words that by this time have become frighteningly familiar: 'Ewige Blumenkraft!'"

I recently heard an old man of right-wing views—a friend of my grandparents'—assert that the current wave of assassinations in America is the work of a secret society called the Illuminati. He said that the Illuminati have existed throughout history, own the international banking cartels, have all been 32nd-degree Masons and were known to Ian Fleming, who portrayed them as SPECTRE in his James Bond books—for which the Illuminati did away with Mr. Fleming. At first, this all seemed like a paranoid delusion to me. Then I read in *The New Yorker* that Allan Chapman, one of Jim Garrison's investigators in the New Orleans probe of the John Kennedy assassination, believes that the Illuminati really exist. The next step in my galloping descent into credulity occurred when I mentioned this subject to a friend who is majoring in Middle Eastern affairs. He told me that the Illuminati were actually of Arabic origin and that their founder was the legendary "old man of the mountains," who used marijuana to work up a murderous frenzy and who fought against both the Crusaders and the orthodox Moslems, adding that their present ruler is the Aga Khan; but, he said, it is now merely a harmless religious order known as Ismailianism.

I then began to wonder seriously about all this. I mentioned it to a friend from Berkeley. He immediately told me that there is a group on campus that calls itself the Illuminati and boasts that it secretly controls international finance and the mass media. Now (if PLAYBOY isn't part of the Illuminati conspiracy), can you tell me: Are the Illuminati part of the Masons? Is Aga Khan their leader? Do they really own all the banks and TV stations? And who have they killed lately?—R. S., Kansas City, Missouri.

First, your informants have confused three historical entities: the Ismailian sect of Islam, the Hashishim and the Illuminati. The Ismailian sect is almost as old as the Moslem religion and the Aga Khan is, indeed, its leader. In the past, however, its members were persecuted for heresy; and around 1090 its leader, Hassan i Sabbah, the "old man of the mountains," formed a secret inner society within the Ismailian community that became known as Hashishim. This inner group turned on regularly with a marijuana-based concoction (not to "work up a murderous frenzy," as you were told, but to experience religious visions from which they believed they drew their strength). The Hashishim are believed to have lost all fear of death and, for almost three centuries, they fought a successful battle on two fronts, against both the Christian Crusaders and the orthodox Moslems. The Hashishim were finally crushed completely after the Mongol conquest in the 13th Century.

The Illuminati began in Germany in 1776. Based loosely on the Hashishim, they consisted of an outer circle of religious believers and an inner core of revolutionists, but with a new feature. Their secret teaching then was that all religions are false (including the outer religion of the Illuminati), that all men are equal and that monarchy should be overthrown. As part of their revolutionary conspiracy, the Illuminati attempted to infiltrate and take over the Masons; but they never succeeded. They were crushed by the Bavarian government in 1785.

Ian Fleming never told any of his friends that SPECTRE was based on a real organization. He died of natural causes, suffering a heart attack in the presence of his wife.

The belief that the Illuminati survive in the modern world and are responsible for most of our evils is about the fourth most common form of organized paranoia extant (its three more popular rivals are the Elders of Zion conspiracy, the Jesuit conspiracy and the notion that we have already been invaded by outer space, our governments being in the hands of Martians).

As for the Illuminati of Berkeley, this is a put-on by local anarchists.

Figure 4.4 *Playboy Forum* letter & answer
launching phase one of Operation Mindfuck

The article further asserted that:

> ... the Ancient Illuminated Seers of Bavaria has infiltrated, allied itself with or taken over all TV networks and wire services, the Federal Reserve System, the John Dillinger Died For You Society, the *Chicago Tribune*, the Discordian Society, the Communist Party (USA), the Paratheo-Anametamystikhood of Eris Esoteric (P.O.E.E.), Hell's Angels, the Sophisticated Sisters of Blessed Saints Claustrophilia and Theophobia, the Mafia, the Black Lotus Society, the Lawrence Talbot Memorial Society and enough additional organizations to fill a book the size of the Manhattan telephone directory (yellow pages).

A second article—which appeared un-attributed in *The Roger Spark* and carried the title "DALEY LINKED WITH ILLUMINATI"—promoted the theory that Mayor Daley was ". . . one of the top agents of the infamous and long legendary Bavarian Illuminati" [Figure 4.7].

To further the Bavarian Illuminati cause, Thornley invented a Do-It-Yourself Conspiracy Kit, which included stationery containing dubious letterheads. As Robert Anton Wilson noted in *Cosmic Trigger*: "Omar (Kerry) would send a letter to the Christian Anti-Communist Crusade on Bavarian Illuminati stationery, saying, 'We're amused you've discovered that we've taken over the Rock Music business. But you're still so naïve. We took over the business in the 1800s. Beethoven was our first convert'" [Figure 4.8–4.19].

In their ever-deepening research into the A.I.S.B., Thornley and cohorts came across some arcane conspiracy literature which included a "Chart of the World Revolution." At the core of the chart resided Adam Weishaupt and the dreaded Bavarian Illuminati who, according to the theory, fomented all the major revolutions in the world following their formation in 1776 [Figure 4.20–4.21].

In response, the Discordians came up with their own organization chart for world domination, at the center of which resided the Sacred Chao. Synchronistically, this chart included the Bank of America nearly ten years before Greg Hill actually began working for them [Figure 4.22–4.24].

According to Wilson in *Cosmic Trigger*, these Discordian Society hijinks set a new mythology in motion:

> The Discordian revelations seem to have pressed a magick button. New exposés of the Illuminati began to appear everywhere, in journals ranging from the extreme Right to the ultra-Left. Some of this was definitely not coming from us Discordians. In fact, one article in the *Los Angeles Free Press* (FREEP) in 1969 consisted of a taped interview with a black phone-caller who claimed to represent the "Black

Mass," an Afro-Discordian conspiracy we had never heard of. He took credit, on behalf of the Black Mass and the Discordians, for all the bombings elsewhere attributed to the Weather Underground (*Cosmic Trigger*, p. 64).

During a 2003 interview with this author, Robert Anton Wilson noted that the black Discordian phone caller in the FREEP article identified himself as "Hassan-i-Sabbah X," the very same character Thornley conceptualized in his August 1968 letter to Louise Lacey. Over time, Hassan-i-Sabbah X's name would appear in a number of Discordian-related writings—authored by Thornley and others—so, it would appear, the FREEP "Black Mass" piece was a prank perpetrated by Discordian Society provocateurs, and might very well have been Lord Omar himself at the reins, although Thornley never admitted a role in this hoax. Whatever the case, the article in question deeply disturbed Greg Hill with its association of Discordianism to terrorist-sponsored murders.

In a January 24th, 1971 letter to Greg Hill, Thornley wrote: "I'm fairly sure the FREEP interview was the work of Mord (Robert Anton Wilson)—as I see signs of his style and sense of humor in it . . ." However, it should be noted that Discordian Society member Roger Lovin (aka Fang the Unwashed) worked for the FREEP from 1969–1972, so his name can also be added to the list of suspects who may have perpetrated this ruse—if it was indeed a put-on. A more disturbing explanation is that neither Wilson, Thornley, or Lovin had anything to do with the "Black Mass" article and like so many other strange occurrences surrounding Kerry Thornley's life, the answer will forever remain a mystery.

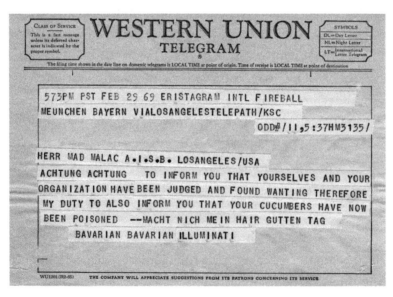

Figure 4.5 Western Union Telegram concocted by Greg Hill
(aka Mad Malac) issuing a dire Bavarian Illuminati warning

Figure 4.6a Introduction page from *Teenset* article on
"The Most Sinister, Evil, Subversive Conspiracy in the World"

Are these people part of the Bavarian Illuminati ... or are they victims, pawns in the most incredibly complex conspiracy ever revealed? The next few pages attempt to answer those questions ...

Figure 4.6b Introduction page from *Teenset* article on "The Most Sinister, Evil, Subversive Conspiracy in the World"

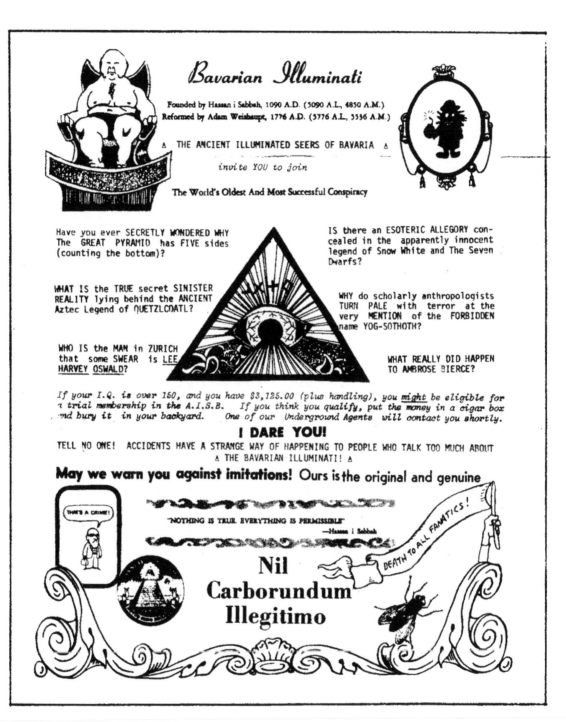

Figure 4.7 Advertisement for the Bavarian Illuminati
that appeared in early editions of the *Principia Discordia*

The World's Oldest And Most Successful Conspiracy

Bavarian Illuminati

Founded by Hassan i Sabbah, 1090 A.D. (5090 A.L., 4850 A.M.)
Reformed by Adam Weishaupt, 1776 A.D. (5776 A.L., 5536 A.M.)

Today's DATE: Pungenday, 14 Bureaucracy, 3136

FROM: Ho Chi Zen, Cong King of Gorilla Warfare

To: Robert Welch, 395 Concord Avenue, Belmont, Massachusetts

(X) OFFICIAL BUSINESS   (X) SURREPTITIOUS BUSINESS   (X) MONKEY BUSINESS

We have been meaning to write you for a long time, but decided for
security reasons to put it off until publication of our surprise take-over
issue of Harper's Magazine -- that being the August 1970 edition now on
the stands, which features our Symbol of Integrity on the cover and
carries within it Peter Schrag's interview with you and some of your
fellow patriots. You'll note we allow you to give us a free plug on
page 42.
All this is in keeping with our new policy of allowing alert and
sophisticated persons such as yourself and your followers and associates
a more comprehensive view of our activities. For with 96½% of the entire
world now under our collective thumb, we just no longer see any point in
sneaking around behind the scenes all the time.

I must say that you and yours gave us a fine fight. And, now that it is
all just about over, we wish to offer you a token of our sportsmanlike
admiration. At the end of the interview with Mr. Schrag, you will recall
that you replied wistfully, "I wish I knew -- I wish I knew," to his
question as to our identity.
I will not bother you with the peons, but I am now going to give you
the names of everyone in the Association of the rank of Magus Illuminatus
or above.

We are: Yours Truly, George Evil, Volga Vatavitch Ripoff, Rabbi Koan,
Hassan i Sabbah X, Madman Blatavatski, Van Van Mojo, Lord Omar, Mad Malik,
Dr. Confusion, Ewige van Blumenkraft, Rip Wasnewsky, Madame M., Leapin'
Lily, the Dragon Lady, Uncle Remus, all five of the Cosmic Orgasm, Lemuel
P., and Gary Allen.

So, you see, you were outnumbered from in front.
However, it is not necessary for you to quit immediately.
According to our Timetable for World Conquest the Revolution is not
slated to begin until 1 May of 1976 -- so we're going to have to drag our
feet some and cat-'n'-mouse your group around a bit. We hope you understand. If we screwed up the timing, They would stop sending us our aid
money from outer space.

Safeguard this letter, it may be an IMPORTANT HISTORICAL DOCUMENT

Figure 4.8 Illuminati prank letter from Kerry Thornley (aka Ho Chi Zen)
to Robert Welch of the John Birch Society

Washington, Weishaupt, Budweiser & Kief   Attorneys-at-Law

Taxes Evaded * Law Perverted * Justice Suborned * Subversives Defended * All Kinds Outrages

23 Clark Street, Chicago, Illinois 60601
European Office: 5 Scheissestrasse, Ingolstadt, Bavaria
Cable Address: SHYSTERCHICAGO

Robert Welch
395 Concord Avenue
Belmont, Massachusetts

Dear Mr. Welch:

Pay no attention to the recent letter from Ho Chi Zen in the Atlanta Cabal
of the Illuminati. Ho is one of those scrutible Orientals who is always
blurting out secrets, and when he runs out of real secrets he invents fake
ones.

Besides, Ho only speaks for CBS (the Conservative Bavarian Seers), the CBS
television network, and the Sphere of Aftermath. These are lower-rank Illuminati,
seldom personally communicate with our Masters from the Crab Galaxy, and
are usually given menial jobs like writing revisionist histories presenting
the Pearl Harbor story from the Japanese point of view. This is congenial
work for him since his "human" body was killed at Hiroshima.

I must warn you, however, that any reproduction, photo-offset, xerox or
similar use of Ho's letter, or any quotation from it concerning Hassan i
Sabbah X (our man in the Panthers), will result in an immediate libel
suit against you in the sum of $1,000,000.00.

In conclusion, please remember that even when heavily spiced with salt, pepper,
ketchup and Worcestershire sauce, a mouse does not taste good for dinner,
unless you happen to be a cat. Is that clear enough or should we be vulgar
and make an explicit parable out of it?

Weishaupt Lives!

George Evil (AKA George Washington)

George Washington IX
Attorney at Law (Specialist in Hemp Possession cases)

P.S. Your fudge is quite good with hashish, but even then it sticks to my teeth.
Any suggestions?

OFFICIAL
BAVARIAN ILLUMINATI
"EWIGE BLUMENKRAFT"

SUPPORT THE A.C.L.U. ***** PORNOGRAPHY YES ***** PRAYER NO!

Figure 4.9 Illuminati prank letter from Robert Anton Wilson (aka George Washington IX)
to Robert Welch of the John Birch Society

The Decided Ones of Jupiter the Thunderer

1730 Chicago Avenue
Evanston, Illinois

Rev. David Noebel
Christian Crusade Publications
Box 977
Tulsa, Oklahoma 74102

Dear Rev. Noebel,

I have just read your two books, "Communism, Hypnotism and the Beatles," and "Rhythms, Riots and Revolution," and they certainly opened my mind, which had been hermetically closed previously.

Thanks to your revelations, I have now officially banned all rock music, folk music, folk-rock music and similar subversive vibrations from all temples of the DOJT (Decided Ones of Jupiter the Thunderer.)

I would like to point out to you, however, that you have only scratched the surface of the music problem. The communists are merely a front for an older and more diabolical group, the Ancient Illuminated Seers of Bavaria (A.I.S.B.) These so-called Seers, founded by Adam Weishaupt, a notorious libertine atheist, in 1776, have taken over both Russia and America, insidiously worming their way into both communist and capitalist governments impartially; worse yet, they control television, the press and (of course) the music industry. They are sworn enemies of Our Lord Jesus Christ and worship Allah, whose chief prophet (they claim) is Hassan I Sabbah, "the old man of the mountains," who invented marijuana and led the infamous Assassins of the 12th Century.

The Illuminated Seers recruited Goethe, the German playwrite and poet, and his "Faust" is full of anti-Christian and pro-A.I.S.B. propaganda; I will explain that in a later letter. What is important right now is for you to realize than Ludwig von Beethoven was a Seventh Degree Illuminatus (rank of Rex) and his music, especially the Fifth and Ninth symphonies, is entirely worthless and seditious, being full of libertine, libertarian, anarchistic, Illuminated Seer ideology. Beethoven even kept Adam Weishaupt's slogan, "Ewige Blumenkraft" ("Flower Power Forever") above his piano while he was composing.

I suggest that you explore this whole matter and write a new book, "Bavarians, Beethoven and Bloodshed."

HARE KRISHNA JESU KRISHNA BABA RAM DASS

Rev C A Floyd, DOJT

Rev. Charles Arthur Floyd II
Primate of Illinois

LINDA LOVELACE FOR PRESIDENT

OFFICE OF MY HIGH REVERENCE
MALACLYPSE THE YOUNGER KSC
OPOVIG   HIGH PRIEST POEE

MOTHER MACHREE

KALLISTI ━━━━ **HAIL ERIS** ━━━━ **ALL HAIL DISCORDIA**

Safeguard this Letter, it may be an IMPORTANT DOCUMENT   Form No.: O.D.D. IIb/ii.1-370.VVM: 3134

Figure 4.10 Illuminati prank letter from Robert Anton Wilson (aka Rev. Charles Arthur Floyd II) to Rev. David Noebel of The Christian Crusade

The World's Oldest And Most Successful Conspiracy

Bavarian Illuminati

Founded by Hassan i Sabbah, 1090 A.D. (5090 A.L., 4850 A.M.)
Reformed by Adam Weishaupt, 1776 A.D. (5776 A.L., 5536 A.M.)

Today's DATE: 1 Bureaucracy, 3136

FROM: Ho Chi Zen, Cong King of Gorilla Warfare

To: John M. Fisher, American Security Council

( ) OFFICIAL BUSINESS   ( ) SURREPTITIOUS BUSINESS   (X) MONKEY BUSINESS

On behalf of our many members who received it, I wish to thank you for your survey form and particulary for the letter that was enclosed with it for the purpose of insuring that our answers would be informed ones and, what's infinitely more important, that they would tend to reflect opinons favorable to the National Interest insofar as security is concerned.

We particularly enjoyed the lines containing the information that you also gather intelligence on internal threats to the Republic -- like the Communist Party, the Black Panthers, SDS, the Yippies, and the General Semantics group: etc. -- a sure-fire way to insure that nobody who disagrees with your views will answer the survey, for fear you will put them on your Shit List.

Masterful!

Won't the President and all those Senators be impressed with what a bunch of Nazis the voters are becoming when you pass the filled-in survey forms on to them, without letting them know about the letters you sent out with them in the first place!!!

As you've already been told, we have a place for your kind of mind in Our Conspiracy -- aye, a man so liberated from qualms, scruples, and other moralistic clap-trap as yourself, sir, will undoubtedly advance to the innermost circles (where the real POWER is, baby) in no time.

And as for the security which is obviously essential to your sanity -- we have a little saying which we pass around, usually in code: Happiness is a Warm Conspiracy.

Think about it.

Our many centuries of success in this business have long-since vindicate Hassan i Sabbah's dictum that the worst paranoids make the best conspirator

So do not inwardly reject our overtures, as you have been doing, or dismiss them as mere joshing, as you have also been doing -- but realize that our sophisticated know-how when it comes to political applied psychology has taught us the unsurpassed values of the unorthodox, surrealistic approach in recruitment.

As you will presently learn, there really is an Illuminati (though you can't mention US in your propaganda for fear of sounding absurd -- we are so fucking CLEVER) and we love you.

Keep doing your thing.

Safeguard this letter, it may be an IMPORTANT HISTORICAL DOCUMENT

Figure 4.11 Illuminati prank letter from Kerry Thornley (aka Ho Chi Zen)
to John M. Fischer of the American Security Council

THE PARATHEO-ANAMETAMYSTIKHOOD OF ERIS ESOTERIC (POEE)
A Non-prophet Irreligious Disorganization

American Anarchist Association

"LEADERSHIP MEANS TAXES"

THE ERISIAN MOVEMENT
( ) Official Business   ( )Surreptitious Business

HOUSE OF APOSTLES OF ERIS
page 1 of 4 pages

Official Discordian Document Number (if applicable):

( ) The Golden Apple Corps   ( ) House of Disciples of Discordia; The Bureaucracy, Bureau of: Mind-Fucking

( ) Council of Episkoposes; Office of High Priesthood, Sect of the POEE   ( ) Drawer O

Today's DATE: Nov 8, 1968   Yesterday's DATE: 4 Ahua 8 Cumhu
Originating CABAL: Sons of Aquilonia Inc.

TO: Art Kleps, Neo-American Church/Society for Prevention of Injury to Neo-Americans
Paul Krassner, Protestors Terrorists & Assassins
Franklin Rosemont, Chicago Surrealist Group/Cthulhu Society/Bugs Bunny Gallery
Bernard Marszalek, Solidarity Bookshop/Resurgence Youth Movement
Mike Aldrich, Trans-Love Energies Unlimited
Randy Wicker, Underground Uplift Unlimited
Eric West, Alliance of Libertarian Activists

You are hereby invited to join the most powerful, unscrupulous, dangerous
and mind-blowing non-existent secret society in the world, the Bavarian
Illuminati(a front for the even more powerful and non-existent POEE.)

Your rights as a member are (1) to circulate all rumors contributed by
other members (2) to attribute all national calamities, assassinations
or conspiracies to the other member-groups.

Your risk as a member, to be frank, is that the Establishment might be
paranoid enough to believe some wild legend started by one of us and
thereupon round up all of us for killing Abraham Lincoln.

Yogge Sothothe Neblod Zin

Bob Wilson

TRANSENDENTAL BULLSHIT!!!

KALLISTI ~~~~~ HAIL ERIS ~~~~~ ALL HAIL DISCORDIA

Figure 4.12 Robert Anton Wilson's letter to various counterculture figures
inviting them to join the Bavarian Illuminati

The
STEPHEN DECATUR
Society
"Our Country, right or wrong!"

A Vast, Well-Financed, World-Wide, Super-Secret, Super-Patriotic Band of Militant, Dedicated Fanatics.

Pres. Richard Nixon
The White House
Washington, D.C.

Your Reverence:

As a loyal and patriotic American, I am concerned about the growing pessimism, alienation and mood of tombstone finality infesting this country, and I have a positive suggestion to help remedy the situation.

As you know, fiscal apprehension is one of the most common causes of the anxiety of our time and, as the withdrawal from Vietnam drags onward and outward (into Lao, Cambodia, etc.) the monetary-screaming-meemies are hitting more and more middle and lower-middle income families, even out here in Evanston.

What I suggest is that you have millions and millions of bumper stickers IN RED WHITE AND BLUE printed up and distributed to loyal and patriotic Americans of the so-called SilentMajoritytype -- those of us who are working too hard to have time to counter-demonstrate against the commies and panarchists and hepcats.

These bumper stickers should say:

SAVE YOUR FEDERAL RESERVE NOTES AND KEEP THE FAITH
THE FEDERAL GOVERNMENT WILL RISE AGAIN!

I think this would create a new mood of hope, faith and (at least long-range) optimism.

I will look forward to your comments. And tell Spiro to give them hell!

Faithfully,

Bob Wilson
Bob Wilson
125 Clyde
Evanston, Ill. 60202

"A POSITIVE PROGRAM FOR RESPONSIBLE EXTREMISM."

"Better Dead than Liberal!"   "I have not yet begun to fight!"   "You may fire when ready, Gridley!"

"Don't let THEM immanentize the Eschaton!"   "Millions for Defense, sir, but not a damned cent for tribute!"

"Give me Liberty, or give me death!"   "Nuts!" "I only regret that I have but one life to lose for my country!"

"Liberty and Union, one and inseparable, now and forever!"   "Send the Marines to turn on the water!"

"The price of Liberty is eternal vigilance!"   "Don't Tread on Me!"   "Retreat, Hell—we just got here!"

Figure 4.13 Letter from Robert Anton Wilson
to his reverence, Richard M. Nixon

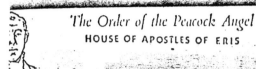

The Order of the Peacock Angel

HOUSE OF APOSTLES OF ERIS

2323 North Clark
Chicago, Ill.
9 VVM, 3135 y.D.

Dear Art Kunkin:

You are probably beginning to wonder what went wrong down in New Orleans, so I thought I'd let you in on the secret. We in the Order of the Peacock Angel know the answers to all mysteries (but we hardly ever reveal the answers to outsiders, so consider yourself honored.)

One of our agents has uncovered a man who had intercourse with all twelve members of the jury. This is what he discovered: each and every one of them was missing a left nipple.

You may not grasp the significance of this fact at once, even though it was your paper which performed the signal public service of revealing that Clay Shaw is missing a left nipple. The man who told that your reporter was trying to hint at something he dared not say outright, but we of the Peacock Angel Order have less fears about these occult matters.

The fact is that a missing left nipple is the hereditary sign of the inner ruling clique of the nefarious and infamous Bavarian Illuminati, the super-secret Zionist-Theosophist group who control all international finance and manage wars, revolutions, assassinations and California weather from behind the scenes!

You may well gasp, but the truth is even more astonishing than I have already revealed. The Discordian Society, a group of sincere humanists formed in 1958 to seek a final solution of the Bavarian Illuminati problem, has itself been infiltrated by the insidious Illuminatuses! The so-called leader of the Discordian Orthodoxy, Kerry Wendell Thornley, lies dead, shot in that Dallas jail corridor, while the man who is pretending to be Thornley today is none other than Lee Harvey Oswald -- the "second Thornley" suggested in the hypothesis put forth so brilliantly by Fang the Unwashed and Malaclypse the Younger, leaders of the Reformed wing of the Discordian movement!!

There are even more amazing disclosures which cannot be made at this time, but keep listening to Mark Lane and Jim Garrison and you will hear lots of stuff guaranteed to send a shiver down your spine, and every word of it literal Gospel truth!!!

Burn this letter, lest it fall into the hands of the C.I.A., the W.C.T.U. or some other "front group" for the Illuminati. Remember: those paranoids are organized and never stop plotting against us!!!!!

Mord², K.N.S.

Mordecai Malignatus, K.N.S.
Order of the Peacock Angel/HOAOE
Joe McCarthy Memorial Society/Jim Garrison Chapter
Department of the Division of the Bureau of Missing Left Nipples

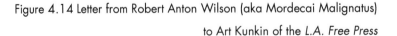

Figure 4.14 Letter from Robert Anton Wilson (aka Mordecai Malignatus)
to Art Kunkin of the *L.A. Free Press*

THE PARATHEO-ANAMETAMYSTIKHOOD OF ERIS ESOTERIC (POEE)
A Non-prophet Irreligious Disorganization

American Anarchist Association

"LEADERSHIP MEANS TAXES"

THE ERISIAN MOVEMENT   HOUSE OF APOSTLES OF ERIS
(X) Official Business   ( ) Surreptitious Business   page 1 of 1 pages
Official Discordian Document Number (if applicable): ODD#2b; iii/V; 60EM3134
( ) The Golden Apple Corps   (XX) House of Disciples of Discordia; The Bureaucracy, Bureau of: Self-Reflexiveness
( ) Council of Episkoposos; Office of High Priesthood, Sect of the POEE   ( ) Drawer O

Today's DATE: 60 EM, 3134 (1968 pagan)   Yesterday's DATE: 59 EM, 3134
Originating CABAL: Kount Korzybski Kommemorative Kabal

TO: Dr. S.I. Hayakawa

It has lately come to Our ears that you frequently and conspicuously pronounce
sentences in public having an "is of identity" followed by a "snarl-word" --
e.g., "These students are fascists," "These students are crazed by dope," etc.

A scientific discipline known as General Semantics teaches that such sentences
have detrimental effects upon the nervous system of the user, contribute to
neuro-semantic disoréenation, create confusion between the map and the territory,
and lead to unsane behavior. A person habitually addicted to such sentences
imitates animals in his nervous reactions, becomes dogmatic and categorical,
loses the characteristically human consciousness of abstracting, and may even
become so impassioned by neuro-semantic primitive reactions as to commit crimes
against property, such as attacking other people's trucks, tearing up other people's
wires, etc.

There have been several excellent teachers of General Semantics abroad in the land
during recent decades and one of them, coincidentally, has the same name as you
-- if We were not aware that "the label is not the thing," We might even think
he was you. By further coincidence, this man when last heard of was also at
San Fransisco State College. We suggest earnestly that you should attempt to
get in touch with him, if he can still be reached, and obtain from him some basic
training in General Semantics principles.

He might also teach you something about neuro-semantic relaxation. In the last
photograph We saw of you confronting the dissidents, your entire face, shoulders
and body showed rigidity, neuro-semantic "closedness" and the general non-verbal
message, "Don't talk to me, my mind is made up." General Semantics might also
teach you how to grow out of this infantile and primitive attitudénal set and
function as a time-binding and open personality. Please get in touch with the
other Dr. Hayakawa and give this a try.

Goddess bless you,

Theophobia the Elder, TLETC

"This Statement is False"
(courtesy of POEE)

KALLISTI .... HAIL ERIS .... ALL HAIL DISCORDIA

Figure 4.15 Letter from Robert Anton Wilson (aka Theophobia the Elder)
to Dr. S. I. Hayakawa

THE PARATHEO-ANAMETAMYSTIKHOOD OF ERIS ESOTERIC (POEE)
A Non-prophet Irreligious Disorganization

POEE
BOX 26475 SAN FRANCISCO
EARTH 94126

MALACLYPSE the Younger, KSC

Omnibenevolent Polyfather of Virginity in Gold
HIGH PRIEST

THE ERISIAN MOVEMENT
(X) Official Business   ( ) Surreptitious Business

HOUSE OF APOSTLES OF ERIS
page 1 of 1 pages

Official Discordian Document Number (if applicable): n/a

( ) The Golden Apple Corps   (X) House of Disciples of Discordia; The Bureaucracy, Bureau of: Eristic Affairs

( ) Council of Episkoposes; Office of High Priesthood, Sect of the POEE   ( ) Drawer O

Today's DATE: 3 Chs 3136   Yesterday's DATE: 2 Chs 3136

Originating CABAL: Norton Cabal

TO: Editor, TRUE MAGAZINE, NYC

Sir,

RE: Jan 70 "Strange But True."

Mr. Dubarry claims that a 297 mile stretch of straight flat railroad tracks rises, because of earth curvature, $2\frac{1}{4}$ miles at the center.

That would mean that the locomotive would require considerable fuel on the first part of the journey, going up hill, and could coast on the second half, going down hill.

Furthermore, $2\frac{1}{4}$ miles to 297 miles is approximately a 1:100 ratio which would mean that three yardsticks laid end to end would form an arch of over an inch. Nonesense! The middle stick lays flat on the floor.

Any fool can see that the earth is in fact FLAT, as the ancient Zarathud taught.

Mr. Dubarry has been duped by round-earthers like that fraud NASA-- which is a hoax and a front for The Ancient Illuminated Seers of Bavaria, who reap hugh insurance profits from deluding merchant shippers into sailing off the edge.

Respectfully,

Hon. Mal²

Mal Younger, AB, DD, KSC
THE FLAT EARTH PARTY
San Francisco Discordian Society

KALLISTI ✦✦✦ HAIL ERIS ✦✦✦ ALL HAIL DISCORDIA

Safeguard this Letter, it may be an IMPORTANT DOCUMENT   Form No.: O.D.D. IIb/ii.1-37D,VVM; 3134

Figure 4.16 Letter from Greg Hill (aka Malaclypse the Younger) to *True Magazine*

THE PARATHEO-ANAMETAMYSTIKHOOD OF ERIS ESOTERIC (POEE)
A Non-prophet Irreligious Disorganization

American Anarchist Association

"LEADERSHIP MEANS TAXES"

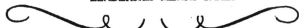

THE ERISIAN MOVEMENT
[✓] Official Business   [ ] Surreptitious Business

HOUSE OF APOSTLES OF ERIS
page 1 of __ pages

Official Discordian Document Number (if applicable):
[ ] The Golden Apple Corps   [ ] House of Disciples of Discordia; The Bureaucracy, Bureau of:
[ ] Council of Episkoposes; Office of High Priesthood, Sect of the POEE   [✓] Drawer O

Today's DATE: Nov 11, 1968   Yesterday's DATE: Nov. 12, 1968
Originating CABAL: Evanston Nihilist Circle
TO: Sen. Thomas Dodd, SOB, Washington, D.C.

My father, Charles Arthur Floyd I, used to quote to me many wise and pithy
remarks he had heard from the late John Dillinger; among those I especially
remember are "Never trust a district attorney's deal or a European automatic
pistol," "All Federal Reserve banks are fronts for the Bavarian Illuminati,"
and "There may be some U.S. senators who aren't on the take, but I haven't
met any."

Since you are interested in why the youth of today are distrustful of authority
and government, I thought you might consider those early childhood influences
in accounting for my sad and lawless career.

I was also inspired by the German Illuminatus (7th degree) Freidrich Nietzsche,
who said, "All that the State hath, it hath stolen. It even bites with stolen
teeth." Since your proposed investigation of anarchism will be financed by
tax money stolen from my pocket by IRS thugs, you can appreciate the truth of
that statment.

Another influence on my perverted life was Abigail Adams, wife of President John
Adams, who warned, "Power, whether vested in the many or the few, is ever grasping,
and like the grave cried 'Give, give!'"

The most pernicious thoughts of all, however, I acquired from the letters of George
Washington, famous hemp-grower of Mount Vernon, who wrote, "Government is not
reason, it is not eloquence -- it is force! Like fire it is a dangerous servant
and a fearful master." Those of us who know government chiefly as the wielder
of napalm and chemical MACE fully appreciate the accuracy of those words.

My father got shot for stealing; I hope you will be luckier than he was.

Pink Floyd

Charles Arthur ("Pretty Boy") Floyd II
President, Evanson Nihilist Circle
Treasurer, John Dillinger Died For You
Society

"This Statement Is False"
(courtesy of POEE)

KALLISTI ▲▲▲▲▲ HAIL ERIS ▲▲▲▲▲ ALL HAIL DISCORDIA
Safeguard this Letter, it may be an IMPORTANT DOCUMENT

Figure 4.17 Letter from Robert Anton Wilson (aka Rev. Charles Arthur Floyd II)
to Senator Thomas Dodd

The World's Oldest And Most Successful Conspiracy

Bavarian Illuminati

Founded by Hassan i Sabbah, 1090 A.D. (5090 A.L., 4850 A.M.)
Reformed by Adam Weishaupt, 1776 A.D. (5776 A.L., 5536 A.M.)

Today's DATE: 43 Conf (Sri Syadasti), Y.O.L.D. 3135

FROM: Discordian Society, San Francisco Cabal

TO: OPEN LETTER TO G.O.P. NATIONAL COMMITTEE

(X) OFFICIAL BUSINESS   ( ) SURREPTITIOUS BUSINESS   ( ) MONKEY BUSINESS

I hate to get picky fellows, but some of you Republican-types
(sneer) were lately trying to convince me that the ⊕ was
really the ancient satanic "broken cross".
(Actually, the broken cross ⏚ symbol looked like
↖ not like ⋏). And now I really hate to
tell you this, but those 3 inverted pentagrams on
your elephant's riot helmet are specifically used
to conjur evil spirits — when conjuring good spirit
one needs must have one point ascending, not
one point descending.
And also it seems that you insisted that the ◔
was a plot of the godless commies. Well I
find it noteworthy that your beast is painted red.

AP *Wirephoto*
NEW SYMBOL of the
Republican party was un-
veiled last week in Wash-
ington by the GOP Na-
tional Committee — the
stars are white on a
field of red with a
white bar separating the
top from a red body.

MAD MALIK, A.I.S.B.

OFFICIAL
DISCORDIAN SOCIETY
HAIL ERIS

Jul 9 2 00 PM '69
Jul 9 2 00 PM '69

"NOTHING IS TRUE. EVERYTHING IS PERMISSIBLE"
—Hassan i Sabbah

Figure 4.18 Illuminati prank letter from Greg Hill (aka Mad Malik)
to the G.O.P. National Committee

Their Peace Symbol - "The Broken Cross"

The Communists are winning their battle for men's minds. They make a special effort to capture the minds of our youth. And to destroy the will of all who resist their takeover.

Many Americans are familiar with the peace symbol shown here. Some are even willing to wear it. But, what most of them do not know, is that it is "the Broken Cross" of the anti-Christ.

The Communists won another victory when TIME magazine, on its cover of June 7, 1968, carried a picture of a bearded youth as the 1968 graduate. For all the world to see, he wore the Broken Cross!

The Communists have infiltrated the garment industry and you find the Broken Cross embroidered on jackets and other garments for the casual American to wear. The Broken Cross is also manufactured as a metal trinket, to be worn on a chain. And many of the younger set wear it thoughtlessly or as a peace symbol knowingly. But seldom do they realize that they

are supporting the emblem of the anti-Christ, the Broken Cross.

Today many men's stores and ladies' ready-to-wear stores advertise this symbol of the atheists and sell it openly, perhaps even ignorantly to thoughtless people who do not know what they are buying or planning to wear. But every symbol of the Broken Cross that is publicly displayed is noted gleefully by the godless Communists, who can see how thoughtless and vulnerable the Americans really are.

· FREE ENTERPRISE   July, 1968

GIVE COPIES OF THIS ARTICLE TO ANYONE WEARING THE "BROKEN CROSS PEACE SYMBOL; ALSO TO YOUR LOCAL MERCHANTS WHO MAY BE OFFERING THE "BROKEN CROSS" FOR SALE. 10 COPIES FOR 5¢---100 FOR 50¢.

THE NETWORK OF PATRIOTIC LETTER WRITERS, BOX 2003D, PASADENA, CALIFORNIA 91105.

Figure 4.19 The "Broken Cross" advertisement that inspired Greg Hill's letter to the G.O.P.

The World's Oldest And Most Successful Conspiracy

Bavarian Illuminati

"THE ONLY TRUE RELIGION"

Founded by Hassan i Sabbah, 1090 A.D. (5090 A.L., 4850 A.M.)
Reformed by Adam Weishaupt, 1776 A.D. (5776 A.L., 5536 A.M.)

"Victory Over Horseshit"

Today's DATE: November 20, 5729 A.M.

FROM: MORDECAI THE FOUL, HIGH PRIEST

To: Alice Widener

(✓) OFFICIAL BUSINESS   ( ) SURREPTITIOUS BUSINESS   ( ) MONKEY BUSINESS

All of us here at A.I.S.B. headquarters want to congratulate you on your excellent pamphlet, "Student Subversion," which exposes some of our most insidious schemes of recent years.

As a token of our appreciation, we enclose a chart showing the actual working of the main parts of our conspiracy. Chains of command in the heirarchy, as indicated, are never broken. For instance, SDS takes orders directly from the CPUSA only; the Mafia takes orders from the Democratic Party, Freemasons and Aga Khan; if the Federal Reserve wishes to influence the Bank of America, it cannot do so directly but must pass a request upward through the Elders of Zion to the Central Shoggoth, A.I.S.B., which then passes the request back down to the Bank of America through the Discordian Society, CIPA, the Black Panther Party, and AMORC.

We are not afraid to reveal this information to you because of our satraps in the Mental Health movement have already brainwashed the public into believing that anyone who writes conspiracy books like yours is a paranoid.

Freiheit/Wahrheit/Dummheit/Ewige Blumenkraft

Foul Mordecai

"NOTHING IS TRUE. EVERYTHING IS PERMISSIBLE"
—Hassan i Sabbah

Figure 4.20 Letter from Robert Anton Wilson (aka Mordecai the Foul) to Alice Widener, author of "Student Subversion," explaining the Discordian/Illuminati organizational chart

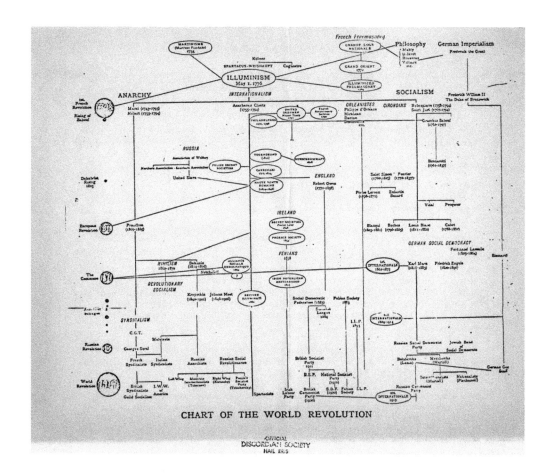

CHART OF THE WORLD REVOLUTION

OFFICIAL
DISCORDIAN SOCIETY
HAIL ERIS

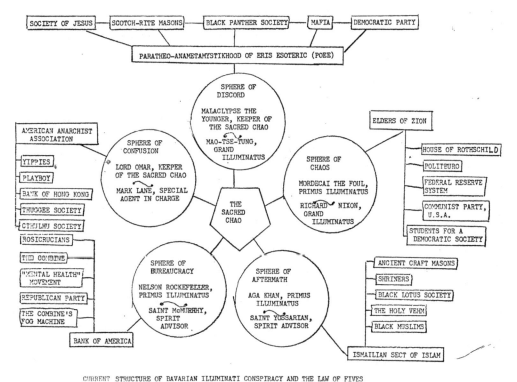

CURRENT STRUCTURE OF BAVARIAN ILLUMINATI CONSPIRACY AND THE LAW OF FIVES

Figure 4.21 "Chart of World Revolution" uncovered by the Discordian Society (above)

Figure 4.22 Discordian/Illuminati organization chart (below)

The World's Oldest And Most Successful Conspiracy

Bavarian Illuminati
"THE ONLY TRUE RELIGION"

Founded by Hassan i Sabbah, 1090 A.D. (5090 A.L., 4850 A.M.)
Reformed by Adam Weishaupt, 1776 A.D. (5776 A.L., 5536 A.M.)

Today's DATE: December 10, 5729 A.M.

FROM: MORDECAI THE FOUL, HIGH PRIEST

To: Staff of "Let Freedom Ring"

( ) OFFICIAL BUSINESS   (X) SURREPTITIOUS BUSINESS   ( ) MONKEY BUSINESS

As the world's most esoteric and disumbrationistic anarchist conspiracy, the
Bavarian Illuminati has proven attractive to paranoids for over a century now.
Although they usually begin by opposing us and our mind-manipulating and
symbol-manipulating tricks, most paranoids eventually come around to our
point of view, on the very sound pragmatic principle, "If you can't lick
them, join them."

Most of the world's leading paranoids are already in our synergetisphere
(see enclosed chart), and we believe, on the basis of your recent releases,
that you, too, are beginning to see the light.

If you are tired of being with the "outs" and want to join the "ins," if
you are sick and angry about being manipulated and want to become one of
the manipulators, if you realize fully how you are being persecuted daily
by forces too strong and occult to be defeated by mere mortal mind and wish
to come over to the camp of the persecutors, we will receive you gladly.
You will have immediate training in the Five Techniques of Hypnotism at
a Distance, the Nine Secrets of Mind Poisoning through Telepathy, and the
Thirteen Variations on the Orgasm-Death Gimmick. *

Interested? To contact us, merely place an ad, as thousands before you have,
in any local newspaper, saying, "In thanks to Saint Jude for favors granted"
(our usual code) and sign with your initials, L.F.R. One of our agents in
your own organization will then arrange a meeting with a Primus Illuminatus.

EWIGE BLUMENKRAFT!

Mordecai

Mordecai, TLETC

*The Orgasm-Death Gimmick is not dirty; have no fear. It is the method of
converting filthy, destructive sex impulses into good, clean acts of murder,
as originated by Hassan i Sabbah of the Assassins and perfected by joint research
recently financed by the Illuminati and the United States Army, with a grant
for advanced study of practical applications donated by the National Rifleman's
Association. This is only one of our 1001 Hidden Teachings.

"NOTHING IS TRUE. EVERYTHING IS PERMISSIBLE"
—Hassan i Sabbah

Safeguard this letter, it may be an IMPORTANT HISTORICAL DOCUMENT

Figure 4.23 Illuminati prank letter from Robert Anton Wilson (aka Mordecai the Foul)
to the staff of Let Freedom Ring

July 4, 1975

Main Street
Yourtown, USA
Mrs. Average Housewife

DEAR MRS. Street,

HELLO MRS. Street, OUT THERE ON Yourtown Us ?. THE BAVARIAN
ILLUMINATI IS LOOKING FOR A FEW GOOD PERSONS FROM Mrs,
Aver age Housewife TO HELP US CORRUPT CIVILIZATION.

WE ARE THE WORLD'S OLDEST AND MOST SUCCESSFUL CONSPIRACY.
THIS CENTURY, WE ARE CALLED THE ANCIENT ILLUMINATED SEERS OF
BAVARIA AND OUR INTERGALACTIC HEADQUARTERS IS NOW RIGHT HERE
IN Mrs, Aver age Housewife. AND WE NEED YOUR HELP, MRS.
Street.

IN EXCHANGE FOR YOUR COMPLETE SERVITUDE, WE ARE PREPARED TO
OFFER YOU:
    △ UNLIMITED FREEDOM FROM THOSE BOTHERSOME PROBLEMS THAT
        NAG ANYONE TRYING TO BE SELF-RESPONSIBLE. WE
        ASSUME 100 PER CENT OF YOUR MORAL OBLIGATIONS. WE
        BEAR THAT BURDEN OURSELVES, MRS. Street!
    △ A GUARANTEED ETERNAL RETIRMENT PLAN
    △ A FRIEND AT A ZURICH BANK, AND
    △ A POTENTIAL PLACE IN HISTORY

        EVERY POINT IS A STAR, MRS. Street.
      GET THE POINT NOW! BECOME initiated INTO
      The Legion of Dynamic Discord IMMEDIATELY!

BUT TELL NO ONE! SIMPLY PUT everything INTO a clear box AND
BURY IT. ONE OF OUR UNDERGROUND AGENTS WILL CONTACT YOU
SHORTLY.

                LOVE,
                MAD MALIK, A.I.S.B.
                BLOCK DISORGANIZER
                Mrs, Aver age Housewife, U.S.A.

Figure 4.24 Illuminati form letter from Greg Hill (aka Mad Malik)
to the Average American Housewife

Department of Justice

FOR IMMEDIATE RELEASE
TUESDAY, AUGUST 2, 1969

The existence of an international conspiracy cartel was disclosed today by J. Edgar Hoover, Director of the Federal Bureau of Investigation.

The disclosure came following months of patient investigation by Federal agents who traced a number of widely-circulated subversive documents to a Chicago residence which apparently has served as a clearing house for an undetermined number of conspiracies, both foreign and domestic. Arrested in a raid on the premises early this morning was a bearded Commie weirdo who gave his name as Charles Arthur Floyd II.

According to Hoover, the cartel "reaches its slimy tentacles throughout America, disseminating lewd, pernicious, pornographic, anti-American, subversive filth calculated to corrupt minds and destroy all respect for law and order. It is enough to make your skin crawl."

The FBI director added that Floyd has also used such aliases as Mordecai Malignatus, Simon Moon, Kevin O'Flaherty McCool and Shirley Temple Black. The organization behind him is known as the Ancient Illuminated Seers of Bavaria.

Asked if Floyd is the son of the infamous Charles Arthur (Pretty Boy) Floyd, a Depression-era gangster, Hoover remarked that Pretty Boy Floyd had only one known son, Jack Dempsey Floyd. "However," he added, "it is quite possible that this son of a bitch is a bastard."

Figure 4.25 Phony Department of Justice memo dictated by Robert Anton Wilson

THE CONSTITUTION OF THE ILLUMINATI
(Rising Atlantan Rite Exemplus)

(foundpoem:4Sep75gs)

Whereas the Rising Atlantan Rite Exemplus of The Illuminati partakes of the tradition and blessing of the Ancient Illuminated Seers of Bavaria, which in turn derives its authority from the Order of the Illuminati (Bavarian Illuminati) founded on May 1st of 1776 by Adam Weishaupt, Professor Extraordinary of Law at the University of Ingolstadt, in reformation of the Ancient Illuminated Seers of Persia (Hashishins or Assassins) which were founded in 1090 AD by Hassan-i-Sabbah and Omar Khayyam -- it is right and fitting that the Rising Atlantan Rite Exemplus hereby distinguish itself from earlier and other contemporary associations known by the name of "The Illuminati" by solemnly revealing the Five Rare Precepts upon which our Rite is based.

THE FIVE RARE PRECEPTS:

1) We renounce and oppose the use of coercion in human affairs, whether for the purpose of monopolizing land or industrial property, resolving disputes, or that of advancing any political cause;

2) We renounce and oppose the use of deception and secrecy in human affairs, except for the purposes of an occasional harmless put-on now and then;

3) We ahere to the principles of participatory democracy, de-centralism, and individualism within our association;

4) We give unqualified support to freedom of expression and freedom of belief;

5) Our specific purpose is to promote understanding and appreciation of anarchist ideas and practices in the political realm; we also encourage and support the cultural anarchism of surrealism and dada in the arts.

Offices in The Illuminati are determined by means of voluntary self-appointment; every member is an Officer. Membership is free and open to all who find themselves in substantial agreement with our Five Rare Precepts and who refrain from doing anything in the name of The Illuminati which is against the rules and regulations of the University. Issues are decided by means of consensus as this is practiced by the Quakers and outlined in the 1972 edition of their manuel, FAITH AND PRACTICE (Philadelphia Yearly Meeting, Fifteenth and Cherry Streets, Philadelphia, Pennsylvania).

Our official greeting is "Ewige Blumenkraft" (Eh-wig-ah Bloom-uhn-kraft), which is Bavarian for "Flower Power Forever."

Figure 4.26 "Constitution of the Illuminati" dictated
by Robert Anton Wilson and Robert Shea

WHAT SECRET POWER DID THIS MAN POSSESS?

How was Adolph Hitler able to take over a whole
country, starting out with only five followers?
(Have you ever tried to take over even a single city
block? It isn't easy!) How could Edgar Cayce diag-
nose and cure illnesses in people thousands of miles
away -- people he had never seen? Why did Pythagoras,
the greatest of all mathematicians, refuse to eat
beans? What was the secret of Abdul Alhazred, the
visionary whose <u>Necronomicon,</u> has been banned in
every country in the world, leaving only nine copies
extant, all of them kept under lock and key in the
closed shelves of a few libraries?

What sinister reality lies behind the ancient Aztec
legend of Quetzlcoatl, the "feathered serpent"?
Why do scholarly anthropologists turn pale with terror
at the very mention of the forbidden name of Yog-Sothoth?
Is there an esoteric allegory concealed in the apparently
innocent legend of Snow White and the Seven Dwarfs? Are
there gigantic survivors of the lost continent of Mu living
inside the earth at this very day?

Many people have wondered about these questions, but the
answers are given only to a select few in each generation.
The Roshinaya, the Allumbrados, the Brethren of the Rosy
Cross, the Order of the Peacock Angel, the Ancient Craft
Masons are all told but little; the complete truth is
mealously guarded by its traditional keepers, the Ancient
Illuminated Seers of Bavaria.

If your I.Q. is over 150 and you have $3125 left after
paying your income tax, you might be eligible for trial
membership in the A.I.S.B. If you think you qualify,
put $3125 in a cigar box and bury it in your backyard.
One of our underground agents will find it and contact
you shortly. Act now -- this offer will not be repeated
again until 2001.

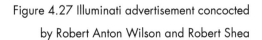

Figure 4.27 Illuminati advertisement concocted
by Robert Anton Wilson and Robert Shea

HOW TO TELL A TRUE ILLUMINATUS

As taught by The Illuminated Ones of Constanbul in the year
723 A.D. by ~~Shrefm~~ the Wizim of Zohoz, the Eye depicted on
the Pyramid emblem represents The Third Eye which manifests
itself at the time of an initiates illumination.

But because The Illuminated Ones are a <u>secret</u> society, it was
felt to be imprudent if the Eye were to appear on the initiates
forehead. So, instead, it appears in a secret place--deep
inside of one's asshole.

If you should question the authenticity of a person claiming
to be illuminated, mearly wait for an opportune moment and
casually look up his arse. And if you find an Eye peering back
at you--he is indeed an Illuminated One.

Hail Eris. All Hail Discordia.

MAD MALIK A.I.S.B.
Hauptscheistmeister

ODD# V/3,ii-40D;3135

Figure 4.28 Greg Hill (aka Mad Malik)
reveals the Secret of the Third Eye

Figure 4.29 Secret of the Third Eye illustration,
courtesy Kerry Thornley

THE ANCIENT ILLUMINATED SEERS OF BAVARIA - Bavarian Illuminati
"The World's Oldest and Most Successful Conspiracy" Reformed 1968 U.S.A.

TO ALL THE PEOPLES OF THE UNITED STATES AND OF THE AMERICAS

Regardless of one's personal political preferences, only a few will disagree that a
necessary part of a "free society" is unsupressed communication between individuals. If
you fear that there is a realistic possibility (whether probably or improbable) of the
United States becoming a police-type state (from the left, right or middle), then the
following information may interest you.

In the event of severe political supression, a private communication system can still
function for those who had the foresight to establish one. There are now such systems
established by a variety of groups that fear a supressive future. Here is a convenient
system which can be very effective if the participants are well chosen. Private information
can pass through many hands with few parties involved knowing the identities of sender or
receiver; and every few persons are endangered in the event of breakdown. It requires
little maintenance whether used or not, but the result is a large "spiderweb" network.

Invent a secret code name. Select from among your friends or associates those few
in whom you hold a deep confidence and with whom you would trust your life if need be.
Quality is essential--the strength of a chain is it's weakest link. Quantity will take
care of itself. Propose the idea, and if agreeable, then exchange your code name for his.
Neither is to ever reveal the other's true identity. The two of you must remain in some
kind of contact permanently. Add his code name to your list of personal exchange partners
(coded) and give him a copy of it. He does not know their identities--only that you trust
them and that they have agreed to participate in confidence. He then builds his own list
of persons he trusts by exchaning names with them. Periodically the growing lists are
again exchanged to keep each other up to date and to reaffirm a clear channel.

You should have one list of personally known partners with whom you are in contact,
plus an additional list for each of them of unknown persons that can be contacted through
him. Should a person you exchange with happen to be already in your system, then so much
the better--cross structures will stregthen the whole. To be successful, three things
must be remembered: 1) absolutely keep your trust, 2) select carefully, and 3) stay
in contact and up to date.

If severe political supression of communication does not occur, then this information
is extreneous and harmless. But if the future brings need of it....(judge for yourself).

Those who desire to supress free communication can be found throughout the political
spectrum. It is my opinion that any political ideology requiring the supression of
dissent is more harmful than any ideology which allows for argument among the people and
leaves the final power to the people.

                                        MAD MALIK
                                        A.I.S.B. - Norton Lodge
                                        San Francisco

Figure 4.30 A brief treatise by Greg Hill (aka Mad Malik) on open communications

The Rubber Stamp Rebellion

THE RESURRECTION OF THE BAVARIAN ILLUMINATI was only one aspect of Operation Mindfuck. Collecting rubber stamps was another. On one occasion, Robert Anton Wilson appropriated a rubber stamp while visiting a public-health clinic, which said: See mental health records.

Afterwards, any mail Wilson received that he considered insulting—especially that which originated from a governmental office—he stamped:

SEE MENTAL HEALTH RECORDS

and sent back, otherwise untouched. Another ingenious example of Operation Mindfuck in action!

Greg Hill, as well, was a rubber-stamp enthusiast, as Kerry Thornley observed in the Illuminet edition introduction to *Principia Discordia*:

You will also notice an unusual number of unusual rubber stampings scattered about among the following pages. That was Greg showing off his rubber stamp collection. Few hobbies are as psychologically gratifying—especially when some bureaucrat is making you wait, with his or her back to you for a moment—as collecting rubber stamps. This is also an exciting way to recoup some of your tax losses. But you must abide by the laws of the Rubber Stamp Congress. All Discordians are permitted to collect rubber stamps *provided* they don't mention the Discordian Society if they are caught. Just point out to them that among people of all faiths stamp collecting is a popular hobby. And tell them your religious preference is none of their business. Tell them that collecting stamps in the name of your nameless religion is your Constitutional right and then, to make your point, take the Fifth Amendment. They will find themselves in a legalistic quandary.

Figure 5.1 A selection from Greg Hill's rubber stamp collection

The Introduction of POEE

IN THE DISCORDIAN SOCIETY's early days, Malaclypse and Omar (Hill and Thornley) were the sole dispensers of Legion of Dynamic Discord certificates, reserving the right to ordain Popes (or Episkopos). This all changed in November of '69 when Malaclypse sent out a memo to Discordians far and wide, proclaiming that "the way in which a person is to be an official Episkopos of the Discordian Society, is for him to declare himself as such." And so it was. Of course, the next question was: How do you know when you are ready for Discordian popehood? The answer: When you say you are!

For a mainstream religion, such laissez-faire attitudes might cause all sorts of mayhem and, in time, lead to total, unadulterated chaos. But as Discordianism was a religion founded on total chaos, this built-in random factor of people declaring themselves popes and creating their own independent Discordian cabals created just the sort of cacophonous autonomy that made Discordianism flourish. And this pleased the Goddess to no end.

This change in Discordian Society philosophy resulted in the dramatic disappearance of Malaclypse the Younger and the subsequent introduction of the Paratheo-Anametamystikhood of Eris Esoteric (POEE) overseen by Greg Hill's new persona, Dr. Ignotum P. Ignotius (aka Professor Iggy).

In the correspondence of the period, it appears that Hill's motivation for creating POEE (pronounced "pooey") was to break free from the earlier Discordian Society religious structure (as disorganized as it may have been!) and transform *Principia Discordia* into more of an art project than religious tract, a change that began to take shape in the *Principia Discordia*'s second edition, which departed thematically from the first edition's focus on Discordian doctrine and structure. Subsequent *Principia Discordia*'s—following the second edition's theme of art collaboration (or a method that Hill referred to as a "Process Collage")—continued on in this vein and included contributions from Discordianism's inner circle: Hill, Thornley, Wilson, Dr. Newport, Camden Benares, Mungo, and Thomas The Gnostic.

THE PARATHEO-ANAMETAMYSTIKHOOD OF ERIS ESOTERIC (POEE)
A Non-prophet Irreligious Disorganization

MALACLYPSE the Younger, KSC
Omnibenevolent Polyfather of Virginity in Gold
HIGH PRIEST

THE ERISIAN MOVEMENT   HOUSE OF APOSTLES OF ERIS

(X) Official Business   ( ) Surreptitious Business   page 1 of 1 pages

Official Discordian Document Number (if applicable): V(B)/3.vi; 39AftEM.3135

(X) The Golden Apple Corps   ( ) House of Disciples of Discordia: The Bureaucracy, Bureau of:

( ) Council of Episkoposes; Office of High Priesthood, Sect of the POEE   ( ) Drawer O

Today's DATE: **DAY OF THE HOT OLIVES**   Yesterday's DATE: **NOV 26 1969**

Originating CABAL: **SAN FRANCISCO**

TO: **DISCORDIANS EVERYWHERE**

Ladies, Gentlemen, & Fellow Discordians,

It is my present pleasure to announce that your Polyfather has achieved a new level of consciousness and is consequently able to relieve The Discordian Society of an unfortunate pox; that is, the remnants of a young man's fear, who some ten years ago began to co-conceive the Society + fancied that it was *his* thing.

Lord Omar, the other Keeper of The Sacred Chao, has made it clear to me through his spirit that he will thoroughly approve of the following epistle:

The Golden Apple Corps herewith relinquishes its last perogative, that of appointing Episkoposes, and returns the decision for that to its rightful owner, the person who knows himself to be an authentic Episkopos—with or without the approval of The Golden Apple Corps.

That is, HENCEFORTH, the way in which a person is to be an official Episkopos of The Discordian Society, is for him to declare himself as such. No more, no less. Hail Eris. Thats where it began, so shall it be.

Thank you for your patience + assistance as teachers.

HAIL ERIS!

Mal 2

OFFICE OF MY HIGH REVERENCE
MALACLYPSE THE YOUNGER KSC
OPOVIG   HIGH PRIEST POEE

Revolution Dept.

KALLISTI ⚓⚓⚓⚓ HAIL ERIS ⚓⚓⚓⚓ ALL HAIL DISCORDIA

Safeguard this Letter, it may be an IMPORTANT DOCUMENT   Form No.: O.D.D. IIb/ii.1-37D.VVM; 3134

Figure 6.1 Greg Hill's November 26th, 1969 letter announcing that everyone everywhere is authorized to declare themselves a Discordian pope

THE GOLDEN APPLE CORPS   ODD#IVb/3,ii;70Dsc3136

THE DEPARTURE OF MALACLYPSE THE YOUNGER, OPOVIG

    These words were begun on May 6th, the day I discovered that Mal-2 had left.
It was a strange and empty day.
    Mal-2 was my alter ego since I was about 18, over 10 years now. I am essentially
an artist and Mal-2 was my own creation, but it can just as well be said that he had a
will of his own. Those of you who are poets will understand what I mean. Those of you
who are philosophers can recall the wisdom of Sri Syadasti (and I date this on His
Holyday): All statements are ture in some sense, false in some sense, meaningless in
some sense, true & false in some sense, true & meaningless in some sense, false &
meaningless in some sense, and true & false & meaningless in some sense.
    I did not "do away" with Mal-2 as you may suspect. He finished his work and left,
and that's all there is to it. His last day was Gulikmas 3136 (5/5 1970)--but I did not
realize it until the following day. It was not a surprise; before he left he wrote the
Fifth Edition of Principia Discordia but even I was not certain how to interpret it
until he did finally depart a few weeks later.
    There really is not much to say. I loved the crazy rogue.
    "Indeed, do many things come to pass."

                                        -- Gregory Hill, K.S.C.

                            -*-   Mythographer

OFFICE OF THE POLYFATHER   ODD IVa/3,iii;70Dsc3136

LIGHTNING SPLATTER PINEAL ADJUSTMENT!

                    -*- PROCLAMATION -*-

    The new POEE High Priest is Episkopos Dr. Ignotum P. Ignotius, KPS.
    His primary duty to The Goddess is Officer for The Polyfather of Head Temple and
What-all for That Office. His Title is KEEPER OF THE POEE SCRUPLE; and like his beloved
Guru, he keeps the POEE Scruple on his key chain next to his roach clip.
    Dr. Iggy has a Most Profound Understanding of Mal-2's philosophy and personality,
and is acknowledged as the World's Foremost Authority on Malaclypse the Younger, and is
most excellently qualified to carry on in Mal-2's place as POEE High Priest and as
medium to Mad Malik (who, as you no doubt recall, is wandering thru the Fifth Dimensional
Chaos Matrix seeking the power source for the Insidious Defamation League, and runs
A.I.S.B. Vigilance Lodge via seance thru the cabbage ashes and with automatic spirit
writing), and furthermore Dr. Iggy has a most intimate Knowledge of all Persons and
Things pertaining to POEE and Head Temple and Cabals wherever. (You shall not be
disappointed.)
    As for the rest of Norton Cabal, The Reverend Lady Malaclypse, D.A.R., she as Divinly
Appointed KEEPER OF THE POLYFATHER, blessed be her lovely soul, refuses to recognize
any of this.
    Hail Eris! All Hail Discordia! The Goddess Prevails.   SECURITY LAST INTERGALACTIC
                                                                BANK OF MALACLYPSE
                                                                ENDORSED AND GUARANTEED

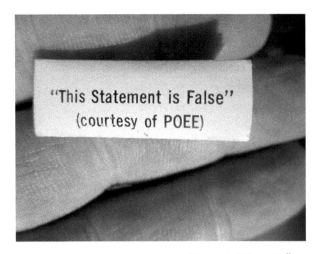

Figure 6.2 Greg Hill announces the departure of Mal-2 (above)

Figure 6.3 POEE sticker created by Greg Hill (below)

An Alternative Religion Aficionado

GREG HILL POSSESSED A FONDNESS for joining obscure organizations and religions, as seen from his diverse collection of membership cards. This, of course, inspired Greg to create his own Discordian membership cards and embossed membership certificates, all done with great attention to detail.

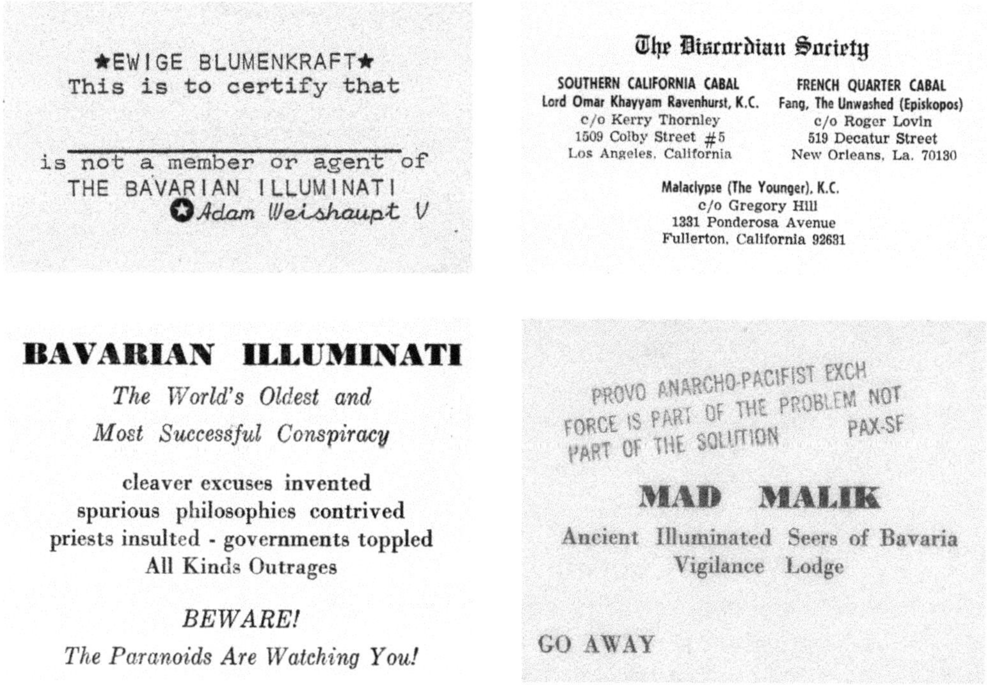

★EWIGE BLUMENKRAFT★
This is to certify that
_____
is not a member or agent of
THE BAVARIAN ILLUMINATI
◉ *Adam Weishaupt V*

The Discordian Society

SOUTHERN CALIFORNIA CABAL
Lord Omar Khayyam Ravenhurst, K.C.
c/o Kerry Thornley
1509 Colby Street #5
Los Angeles, California

FRENCH QUARTER CABAL
Fang, The Unwashed (Episkopos)
c/o Roger Lovin
519 Decatur Street
New Orleans, La. 70130

Malaclypse (The Younger), K.C.
c/o Gregory Hill
1331 Ponderosa Avenue
Fullerton, California 92631

BAVARIAN ILLUMINATI

The World's Oldest and
Most Successful Conspiracy

cleaver excuses invented
spurious philosophies contrived
priests insulted - governments toppled
All Kinds Outrages

BEWARE!
The Paranoids Are Watching You!

PROVO ANARCHO-PACIFIST EXCH
FORCE IS PART OF THE PROBLEM NOT
PART OF THE SOLUTION   PAX-SF

MAD MALIK

Ancient Illuminated Seers of Bavaria
Vigilance Lodge

GO AWAY

Figure 7.1a A collection of Discordian
business and membership cards

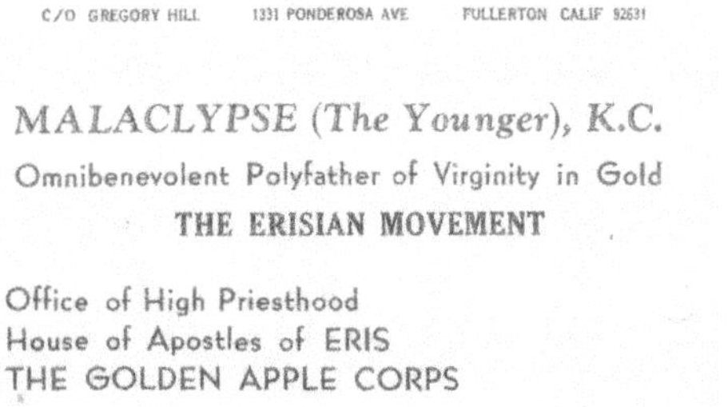

C/O GREGORY HILL   1331 PONDEROSA AVE   FULLERTON CALIF 92631

MALACLYPSE (*The Younger*), K.C.
Omnibenevolent Polyfather of Virginity in Gold
THE ERISIAN MOVEMENT

Office of High Priesthood
House of Apostles of ERIS
THE GOLDEN APPLE CORPS

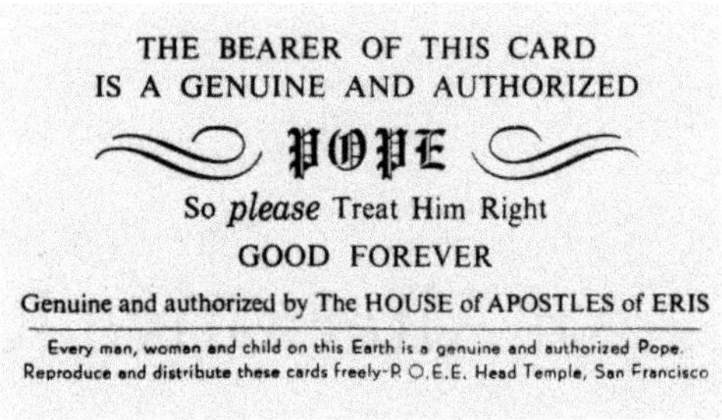

THE BEARER OF THIS CARD
IS A GENUINE AND AUTHORIZED
POPE
So *please* Treat Him Right
GOOD FOREVER
Genuine and authorized by The HOUSE of APOSTLES of ERIS
Every man, woman and child on this Earth is a genuine and authorized Pope.
Reproduce and distribute these cards freely–P.O.E.E. Head Temple, San Francisco

Figure 7.1b A collection of Discordian
business and membership cards

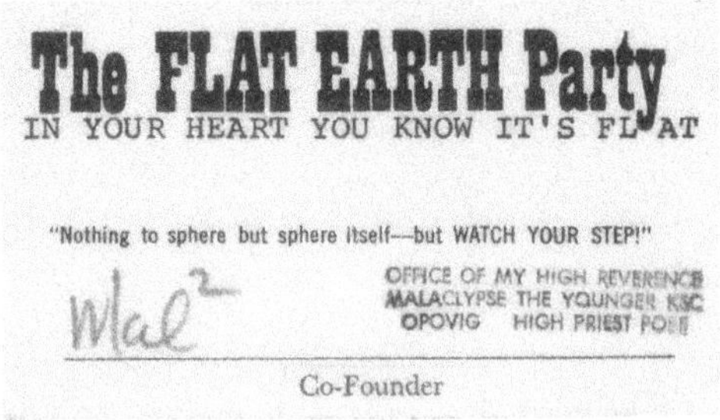

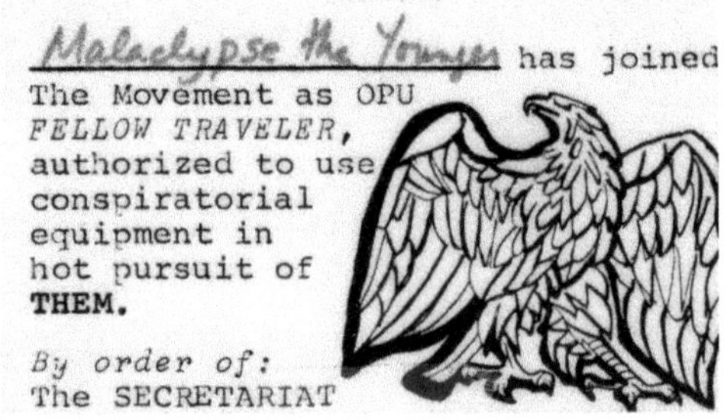

The FLAT EARTH Party
IN YOUR HEART YOU KNOW IT'S FLAT

"Nothing to sphere but sphere itself—but WATCH YOUR STEP!"

Mal²
OFFICE OF MY HIGH REVERENCE
MALACLYPSE THE YOUNGER KSC
OPOVIG   HIGH PRIEST POPE
―――――――――――――
Co-Founder

Malaclypse the Younger has joined
The Movement as OPU
FELLOW TRAVELER,
authorized to use
conspiratorial
equipment in
hot pursuit of
THEM.

By order of:
The SECRETARIAT

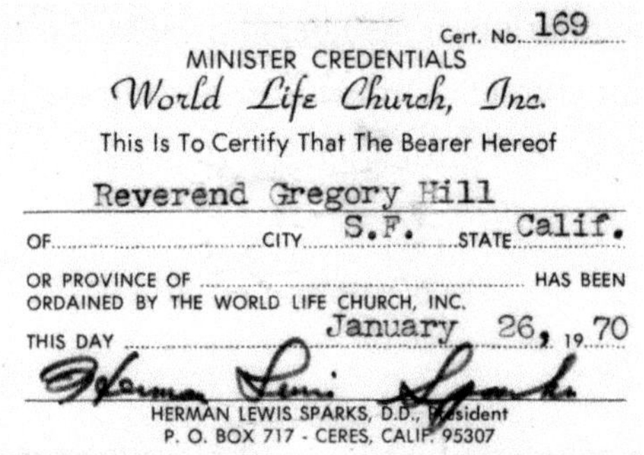

Cert. No. 169
MINISTER CREDENTIALS
World Life Church, Inc.
This Is To Certify That The Bearer Hereof
Reverend Gregory Hill
OF............................CITY S.F. STATE Calif.
OR PROVINCE OF .... HAS BEEN
ORDAINED BY THE WORLD LIFE CHURCH, INC.
THIS DAY .... January 26, 19 70
HERMAN LEWIS SPARKS, D.D., President
P. O. BOX 717 - CERES, CALIF. 95307

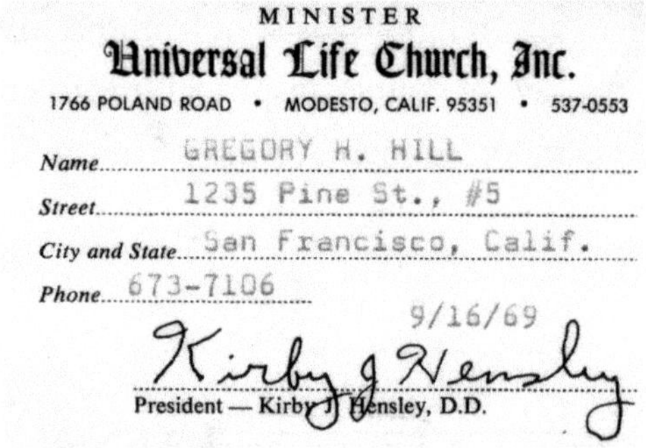

MINISTER
Universal Life Church, Inc.
1766 POLAND ROAD • MODESTO, CALIF. 95351 • 537-0553
Name........ GREGORY H. HILL
Street........ 1235 Pine St., #5
City and State.. San Francisco, Calif.
Phone.. 673-7106
9/16/69
President — Kirby J Hensley, D.D.

ECCLESIASTIC IDENTIFICATION
KNOW YE that the bearer of this card is a fully
ORDAINED MINISTER
of the faith and is entitled to perform all the duties
of this office and accept all its rights and privileges
GREGORY HILL
NAME
1235 Pine St #5, San Francisco Calif
ADDRESS
MAR 1 5 1970
DATE ORDAINED
MISSIONARIES of the NEW TRUTH
CHICAGO ARCHDIOCESE

This Certifies That
GREGORY HILL
is a member of the
NEO-AMERICAN CHURCH
ARTHUR J. KLEPS, CHIEF BOO-HOO
Neo-American Church
P.O. Box 101
Mount Eden, Calif. 94577

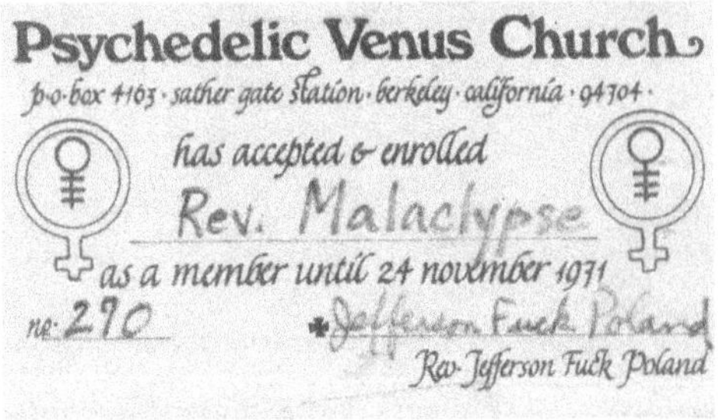

Figure 7.2 A collection of Greg Hill's
membership cards

Psychedelic Venus Church
p.o. box 4103 · sather gate station · berkeley · california · 94704 ·
has accepted & enrolled
Rev. Malaclypse
as a member until 24 november 1971
no. 290   Jefferson Fuck Poland
Rev. Jefferson Fuck Poland

Through the course of Greg Hill's research into alternative religions, he discovered an outfit in Modesto, California, called the Universal Life Church (ULC), which over the years has ordained several million ministers regardless of race, color, creed or sexual peccadilloes. In fact, the ULC became quite popular during the Vietnam War era when many potential draftees across the USA obtained their minster's credentials in the hopes it would help them evade the draft. Greg Hill himself became an ordained minister through the ULC, as demonstrated in a letter to the leader of the flock, the honorable Reverend Kirby Hensley, as presented below.

x

n/a   4

x

Sept 15 1969   Sept 14 1969
San Francisco

Dr. Reverend Kirby Hensly, Universal Life Church, Modesto Calif

Blessed Sir,

First, may I extend my admiration and compliments for your spirit,
your courage and your good nature!

Secondly, I have some questions (seperate page) which I would much
appreciate specific answers to, in as much as I and my fellow P.O.E.E.
Ministers fully plan to develop our Church as far as we can.

Thirdly, enclosed is $20 for you to further your excellent crusade,
with a request for a D.D. for myself and Ordination for my wife and
myself (seperate page).

Perhaps you would like to know who I am and what our Church is,
and why I have asked Ordination from you.

We are students of philosophy (I have a B.A. in philosophy) who
believe that all mankind has understood an essential religious truth,
and this truth is subtely expressed in all religions. And that the
ways in which religion differ in dogmas and creeds, are superficial
unimportant ways--the "clothing" so to speak. And that organized
religion, formal churches, lead persons into the superficial and
away from the essentials. We are also humorists and believe that
humor can be a great teacher when used to teach. With this in
mind, we have done the following:

We say that we worship the Goddess Eris, the Greek Goddess of Confusion.
We then organize into a super confusing funny crazy church that
a) points out how silly organized churches are and b) just "happens"
to have a lot of good religious philosophy in it. The result is
both entertaining and instructive, and we are proud of it and plan
to promote our message as much as we can.

I and an associate, Kerry Thornley, first conceived of the Paratheo-
anametamystikhood of Eris Esoteric (that's what we call our church,
the "P.O.E.E." for short) about 10 years ago but have done most of
the work on it over the last 5 years. We now have several hundred
members and 6 locations in the U.S. We have no set dogmas, no dues,
no restrictions. We are not commercial. We supply simply ask
people to laugh at pomposity and to look to their heart for guidance.

2

The reason I wish U.L.C. ordination, is because the POEE absolutely
refuses to legally incorporate; we find the idea antagonistic to
our message. We would also find it humorous to be the first church
in the world to advise its ministers to become ordained by another
church! Thus, we can have our cake and eat it too. For your kind
generosity we are grateful.

Let every man have his own understanding of his own god.
Let all live in peace and mutual respect.

Respectfully,

Gregory Hill
"Malaclypse the Younger, KSC"

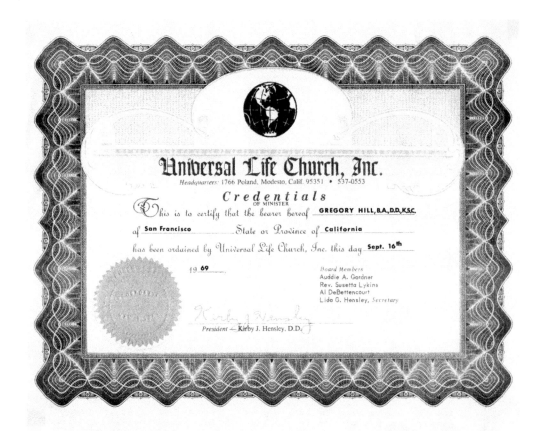

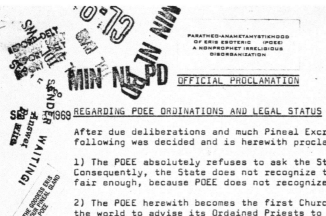

PARATHEO-ANAMETAMYSTIKHOOD
OF ERIS ESOTERIC (POEE)
A NONPROPHET IRRELIGIOUS
DISORGANIZATION

OFFICIAL PROCLAMATION

REGARDING POEE ORDINATIONS AND LEGAL STATUS

After due deliberations and much Pineal Excretions, the
following was decided and is herewith proclaimed by the Polyfather:

1) The POEE absolutely refuses to ask the State for legal status.
Consequently, the State does not recognize the POEE. Which is
fair enough, because POEE does not recognize the State.

2) The POEE herewith becomes the first Church in the history of
the world to advise its Ordained Priests to become ordained by
a competing Church. Hail Eris. As follows:

3) POEE Priests desiring legal cover for Erisian activities, are
advised to request ordination from UNIVERSAL LIFE CHURCH,
Rev. Dr. Kirby J. Hensley, 1766 Poland, Modesto, Calif. 95351
A post card will do, no charge, but if you feel generous you might
enclose a buck and a kiss. The Rev. Dr. Kirby cannot read or
write (he has memorized the Christian Bible) but his kids read
his correspondence to him.

4) The ULC has no dogmas or beliefs and ordains absolutely anybody
(including one dog to date)--no questions asked. It is registered
(incorporated) in the State of Calif and is LEGAL as are it's
Ordination Certificates. Rev. Hensly is an authentic living Erisian
Avatar (Class 1-A), born and bred a fundamentalist Christian who
believes that everyman is his own Minister and ought to be free to
act like one, no matter what the belief or absence of belief (he
has ordained Madalyn Murray). The POEE feels that Ordination in
the ULC is a privelege befitting all Erisians and perfectly
appropriate to POEE Priests. Mal-2 has himself become so ordained
by ULC.

5) This is not to mean that POEE is affiliated with or merged with
the ULC. Or maybe it does, but it doesnt matter because ULC imposes
no restrictions. Anyway, it means that Mal-2, in addition to
being Polyfather of the POEE with no legal status is also a Minister
of the ULC, with legal status, and his ministerial duties of ULC
are, by his own understanding of them, to promote the POEE; thereby
giving him legal authority to perform POEE marriages, collect
POEE tax-deductible donations, and a bunch of other stuff--most
of which he has no intention of bothering with but are nice to know.
You can do the same. KALLISTI.

Further information on legal specifics will be forthcoming when
i know more (maybe never). See other side.
HAIL ERIS   ALL HAIL DISCORDIA   BLESSED BE THE AVATAR:
            DOCTOR REVEREND KIRBY J. HENSLY!

38th Day of the Season of Bureaucracy, Year of our Lady 3135
ODD# 2(b)/V,iii;38B-Z 3135   SEP 1 5 1969

Certificates, Applications
& Excommunication

T O FOLLOW IS A COLLECTION of Discordian applications, membership certificates, and articles of excommunication that Greg Hill and his Discordian colleagues concocted during the late 60s and early 70s. Perhaps the most curious article among this collection is a Legion of Dynamic Discord Certificate awarded to Barbara Glancey Reid in September of 1964 by The Bull Goose of Limbo (aka Kerry Thornley). As fickle fate would have it, Barbara Reid would later become a key witness against Thornley during the course of New Orleans District Attorney Jim Garrison's JFK assassination investigation. Hail Eris, indeed!

Figure 8.1 Preparation of
POEE certificates, Greg Hill's
home office, early 70s

CERTIFICATE OF
HOLY ORDINATION

BE IT KNOWN THAT

HAS BEEN RIGHTEOUSLY ORDAINED AS A PRIEST OF
THE PARATHEO-ANAMETAMYSTIKHOOD OF ERIS ESOTERIC
AND THUSLY ENTRUSTED WITH ALL HOLY DUTIES
AND DIVINE PRIVELEGES OF THIS OFFICE

IN THE NAME OF THE GODDESS ERIS
→← GLORY TO THE SACRED CHAO →←

UNDER THE PATRONAGE OF APOSTLE THE ELDER MALACLYPSE
BY THE OMNIBENEVOLENT POLYFATHER OF VIRGINITY IN GOLD
MALACLYPSE THE YOUNGER, KSC; HIGH PRIEST

HAIL ERIS! →← καλλιχτι →← ALL HAIL DISCORDIA

____ DAY OF THE SEASON OF _____ YEAR OF OUR LADY ____

_____

_____

The Golden Apple Corps
HOUSE OF APOSTLES OF ERIS
THE DISCORDIAN SOCIETY

Figure 8.2 POEE Certificate of Ordination

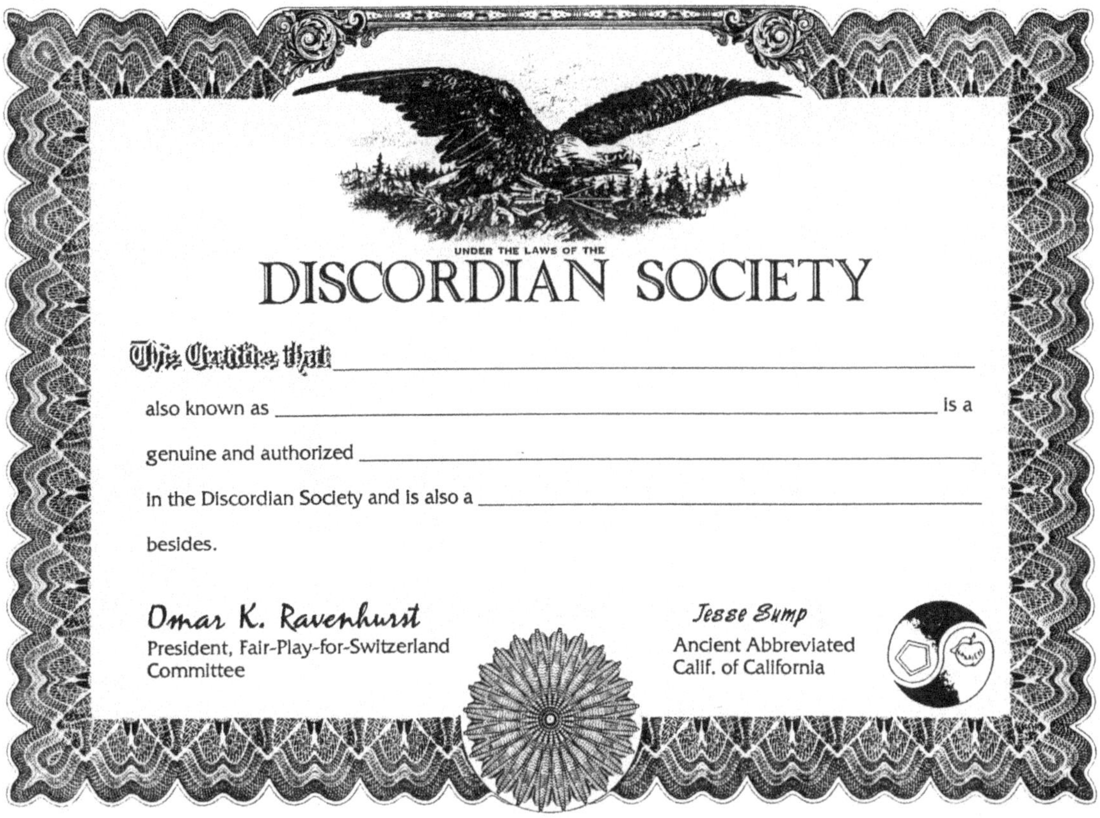

UNDER THE LAWS OF THE
DISCORDIAN SOCIETY

This Certifies that _____

also known as _____ is a

genuine and authorized _____

in the Discordian Society and is also a _____

besides.

Omar K. Ravenhurst
President, Fair-Play-for-Switzerland
Committee

Jesse Sump
Ancient Abbreviated
Calif. of California

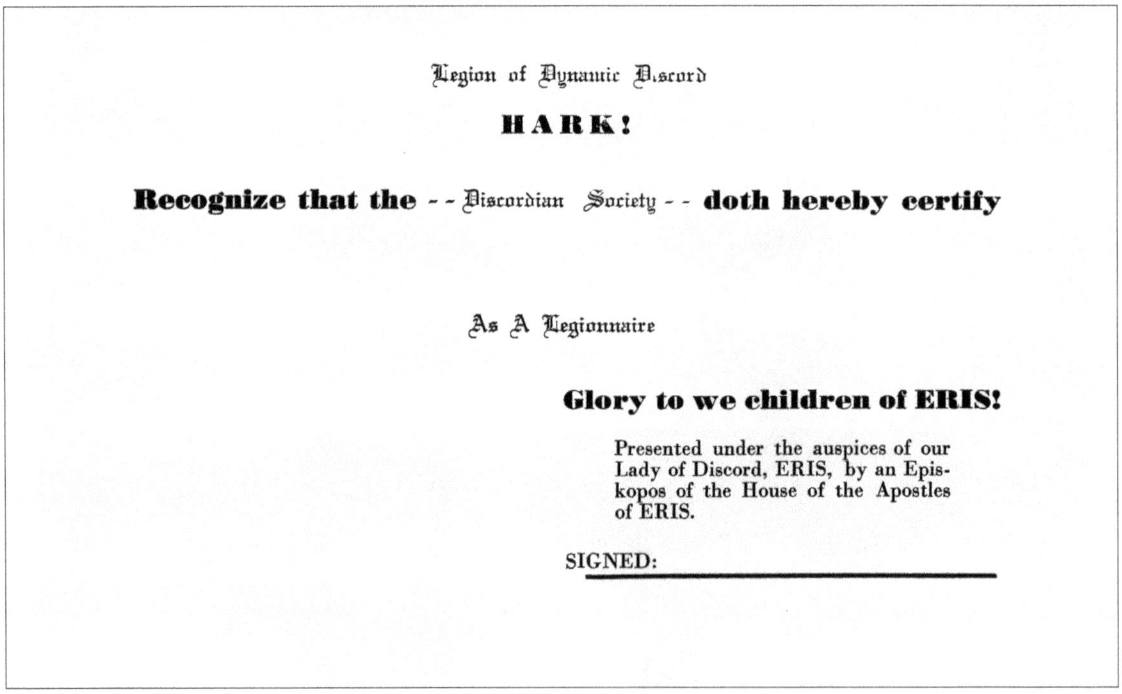

Legion of Dynamic Discord

HARK!

Recognize that the - - Discordian Society - - **doth hereby certify**

As A Legionnaire

Glory to we children of ERIS!

Presented under the auspices of our
Lady of Discord, ERIS, by an Episkopos of the House of the Apostles
of ERIS.

SIGNED: _____

Figure 8.3 Discordian Society certificate designed by Lord Omar (aka Kerry Thornley) (above)

Figure 8.4 Discordian Society legionnaire's certificate (below)

Application For Membership

In the Erisian Movement of the DISCORDIAN SOCIETY

1. Today's date   Yesterday's date

2. Purpose of this application: --membership in: a. Legion of Dynamic Discord   b. POEE   c. Bavarian   Illuminati   d. All of   the   above e. None of the above   f. Other--be *specific!*

3. Name   Holy Name

_____

   Address

_____

   If temporary, also give an address from which mail can be forwarded

4. Description: Born: | | yes | | no   Eyes: | | 2 | | other   Height:
   ....fl. oz.   Last time you had a haircut: Reason:
   Race: | | horse | | human   I. Q.: 150-200 200-250 250-300 over 300

5. History: Education - highest grade completed 1 2 3 4 5 6 over 6th
   Professional: On another ream of paper list every job since 1937
   from which you have been fired.   Medical: On a seperate sheet
   labeled "confidential," list all major psychotic episodes experienced
   within the last 24 hours

6. Sneaky questions to establish personality traits
   I would rather a. live in an outhouse b. play in a rock group c. eat
   caterpillers.   I wear obscene tattoos because . . . .
   I have ceased raping little children | | yes | | no -- reason . . .

7. SELF-PORTRAIT

For Office Use Only-   acc. rej. burned

Official Discordian Document -ODD- No. 1-3.

3-3-5-65.   Rev. Mungo, 8-69.

Figure 8.5 Application for membership designed by Rev. Mungo

Figure 8.6 Excommunication certificate prepared by Rev. Groucho (aka Robert Anton Wilson)

HARK!
This is to certify that

Gregory Hill

Is *Not*, and has *Never* been a member of
--𝕿𝖍𝖊 𝕯𝖎𝖘𝖈𝖔𝖗𝖉𝖎𝖆𝖓 𝕾𝖔𝖈𝖎𝖊𝖙𝖞--
Nor of any affiliated organization, *Nor* has he ever been
known as:

Malaclypse the Younger

Nor is he known by any member of the abovementioned
Society, including the undersigned, *who does not even
know the above-designated person's name!*

Periculum in mora:

The council of Episkoposes,
House of Apostles of ERIS!

Dated: *4 – 4* ,19*70*
By: *Mungory Bundlehoze*
KOB, CTE, etc. etc.

Figure 8.7 Excommunication certificate prepared by Rev. Mungo

HARK!
This is to certify that

THOMAS McNAMARA

Is *Not*, and has *Never* been a member of
--𝔗𝔥𝔢 𝔇𝔦𝔰𝔠𝔬𝔯𝔡𝔦𝔞𝔫 𝔖𝔬𝔠𝔦𝔢𝔱𝔶--
Nor of any affiliated organization, *Nor* has he ever been
known as:

THOMAS McNAMARA GNOSTIC

Nor is he known by any member of the abovementioned
Society, including the undersigned, *who does not even
know the above-designated person's name!*

Periculum in mora:

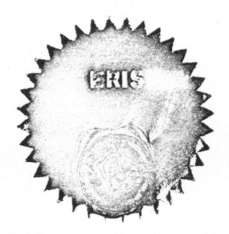

The council of Episkoposes,
House of Apostles of ERIS!

Dated: _____ ,19

By: Mal-2

OFFICE OF MY HIGH REVERENCE
MALACLYPSE THE YOUNGER KSC
OPOVIG   HIGH PRIEST POEE

DONT PHONE

Figure 8.8 Excommunication certificate prepared by Mal-2 (aka Greg Hill)

Figure 8.9 Barbara Reid's Discordian legionnaire's certificate
issued by The Bull Goose of Limbo (aka Kerry Thronley)

Further Manifestations of Operation Mindfuck

I N SOME INSTANCES, OPERATION MINDFUCK took the form of Discordian Society press releases offering a non-violent anarchist method to awake and mutate society's sleeping robots.

One such mindfuck was PURSE: an acronym for Permanent Universal Rent Strike Exchange, which encouraged everybody to stop paying rent forever. Similarly, PUTZ: Permanent Universal Tax Zap, where everyone stopped paying taxes.

Figure 9.1 PURSE illustration concocted by Robert Anton Wilson

Other items that promoted the Discordian Society agenda came in the form of business cards with slogans such as "There is no enemy anywhere" or "There is no friend anywhere," each particular card going to a certain person/mindset to jolt them awake—like a zen koan, Discordian-style.

The guiding philosophy behind "Operation Mindfuck" was originally proposed in *The Theory of Games and Economic Behavior* by John von Neumann and Oskar Morgenstern (1944), who contended that the only strategy an opponent cannot predict is a random strategy. The principal Discordian motto in this regard came from Malaclypse the Younger: "We Discordians must ALL stick apart," which promoted the radical decentralization of the Discordian Society, creating a built-in random factor within its ranks.

Figure 9.2 "There Is No Enemy Anywhere" card inside an envelope which reads "Top Conspiratorial (Illuminated Seers)," created by Greg Hill

As Wilson and Shea explained in the appendix to *Illuminatus!*:

> To this day, neither Omar [Thornley] himself nor any other Discordian apostle knows for sure who is or is not involved in any phase of Operation Mindfuck [OM], or what activities they are or are not engaged in as part of that project. Thus, the outsider is immediately trapped in a double-bind: the only safe assumption is that anything a Discordian does is somehow related to OM, but since this leads directly to paranoia, this is not a "safe" assumption after all, and the "risky" hypothesis that whatever the Discordians were doing is harmless may be "safer" in the long run, perhaps. Every aspect of OM follows, or accentuates, this double-bind.

Groovy Kits, Jakes & Cabals

DISCORDIANS WERE LOCATED all across the country and communicated with "Groovy Kits," strange and humorous oddities sent through the mail. Each player in the Discordian network would add their own twist to a Groovy Kit, then forward his or her efforts to the next name on the list, who—in turn—would pass it on to another Discordian. And so, in time, these Groovy Kits grew like some weird fungi, spreading their spores via the U.S. postal system through the collective brains of those enlightened souls who elected to play the game. In essence, it was an ongoing art project made up of a communal Discordian stew of collages, word games and hoaxes revolving around irreverent humor, the sexual revolution, alternative religions, crackpot cults, radical politics, and consciousness expansion. All of this, in turn, contributed to the evolution of the *Principia Discordia*.

In 1969, Greg Hill launched the Joshua Norton Cabal. Norton—who lived in San Francisco in the late 1880s—declared himself Emperor of the World and Protector of Mexico, as he wandered the streets dressed in regal, though ragged attire, accompanied by two mangy dogs.

Although a pauper, Norton was allowed to dine in the finest restaurants and treated as royalty throughout the old San Fran. Considered by many a kook, Norton issued his own currency that was accepted in saloons and other establishments. A popular Discordian mantra, courtesy of Malaclypse the Younger, went:

Everybody understands Mickey Mouse. Few understand Herman Hesse. Only a handful understood Albert Einstein. And nobody understood Emperor Norton.

Norton—among other accolades—was a recognized Illuminated Being by the Ancient and Accepted Freemasons, and granted a 33rd degree in the Order, the highest rank achievable. When he died, thousands of San Franciscans attended his funeral, and Norton was buried in the Masonic cemetery, courtesy of his Freemasonic benefactors.

Soon after the formation of the Joshua Norton Cabal, other Discordian cabals began popping up across the country like so many mind-bending mushrooms. As Greg Hill remembered:

> The 1969 Discordian Society was an exchange between independent artists of various kinds. Norton Cabal was just me and my characters and I used the other cabals as sort of a laboratory. In return, other Discordians would bounce their stuff off of me. We would toss in ideas and anybody could take anything out. It was a concept stew. *Principia* was my product from my perspective. Thornley, and Wilson and Shea, had other perspectives, which had substantial influence on me. It was mutual, but without the exchange each would have done something similar anyway. The exchanging of ideas and techniques broadened and encouraged all of us.

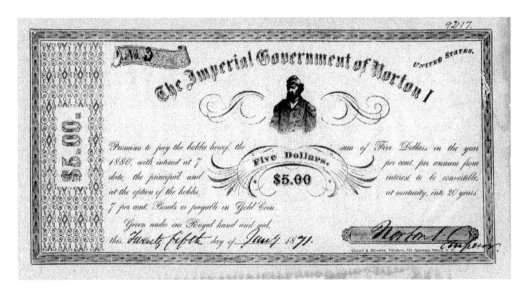

Figure 10.1 Emperor Norton's alternate currency

In 1966, Kerry Thornley was editing *The Innovator*, a libertarian newsletter which had published an article called "Postman Against the State" dealing with the various non-governmental postal systems throughout history that had functioned more effectively than government-operated systems. At the time, Robert Anton Wilson was editing the Playboy Forum, *Playboy* magazine's letter-and-answer column dealing with civil liberties issues and other political topics.

During this period, the Playboy Forum had been receiving a series of complaints about mail tampering and snooping by the U.S. postal service. In this regard, Kerry sent a copy of the "Postman Against the State" article to *Playboy*, which landed in Wilson's hands. This, in turn, initiated a longstanding correspondence between the two, setting the stage for Wilson's eventual entrée into the Discordian Society scene.

During their initial correspondence, Wilson and Thornley discussed, among other things, the American Letter Mail Company, operated in New England in the mid-1800s by the individualist anarchist, Lysander Spooner. During its heyday, the American Letter Mail Company offered cheaper postage rates than the U.S. Post Office, scheduled more deliveries per day, and made a profit, as well. Spooner was finally put out of business when Congress made it illegal to deliver a first-class letter for profit. To this end, both Wilson and Thornley agreed that the U.S. postal system was once again ripe for such change, and that the concept Spooner had launched one hundred years earlier was the direction the current mail system should go.

In a similar anti-government vein, just as Emperor Norton issued his own currency, the Discordians likewise followed the good Emperor's lead with what became known as Flax Notes, their namesake derived from an old Zen Buddhist koan about a pupil who asked his master what the meaning of life was, only to receive this enigmatic answer: "Five tons of flax!"

Curiously enough, Greg Hill later worked 23 years for Bank of America, which since has become one of the largest, monopolistic financial institutions in the world. But I guess to eventually overthrow the System, you must first infiltrate it, which might have been, in part, the method to Greg Hill's madness.

```
Effective 12 Sept 1969
THE SECURITY LAST INTERGALACTIC BANK OF MALACLYPSE
exchanges Notes with the following individuals and banks:

BANK OF OMAR, Lord Omar Khayyam Ravenhurst, KSC; Flaxscript
FIRST BANK OF BAVARIA, Mordecai Malignatus, KNS; Flaxscript
Flaxscript issued by MUNGOJERRY GRINDLEBONE, KOB
Flaxscript issued by HYPOCRATES MAGOUN, Disc Disc
IONOB!NK, Iona K. Fioderovna, Disc Disc; Flaxscript
Murphy Notes issued by HAROLD RANDOMFACTOR, ГZCS
   (1 Murphy = 30 Tons of Flax)


                              Malaclypse the Younger, KSC
                              Assistant Treasurer of
   SECURITY LAST INTERGALACTIC  THE JOHN DILLINGER DIED
     BANK OF MALACLYPSE            FOR YOU SOCIETY
   ENDORSED AND GUARANTEED
```

Figure 10.2 September 12, 1969 memo from Greg Hill
announcing The Security Last Intergalactic Bank of Malaclypse

Figure 10.3 First Ton of Flax issued by Kerry Thornley (aka Lord Omar)
in April of '69 in Tampa, Florida

THE SECURITY LAST INTERGALACTIC
BANK OF MALACLYPSE

SPECIAL STATEMENT REGARDING THE EXCHANGE OF
FLAXSCRIPT ISSUED BY THIS BANK WITH <u>MURPHY</u>
NOTES ISSUED BY HAROLD RANDOMFACTOR, PZCS,
OF OUR PEOPLE'S UNDERWORLD.

SLI*BOM will herewith exchange Flaxscript
freely with Murphy Notes of above mentioned
second party of the first part; at the exchange
rate of:
   1 TON OF FLAX = .03-1/3 MURPHYS
                      or 3-1/3 SNAFUS
   1 MURPHY = 30 TONS OF FLAX
   1 SNAFU = 3/10 of ONE TON OF FLAX
               (or 1½/5ths, if you prefer)

SLI*BOM, in order to expedite further exchange
of said Murphy Notes with other Flaxscript
Banks, will endorse Murphy Notes and guarantee
their payment in Flax to other Flax Banks, for
any Murphy Notes that pass thru the hands of
SLI*BOM and are passed on in payment for other
stuff like is ordinarily done.

SLI*BOM herewith ignores the fact that Murphy
Notes are on an inflation based base, despite
the fact that value increase is assured.
SLI*BOM does not want to fuck with mathematics.
Or economics, for that matter. Hail Eris.

ONE MAN -- ONE BANK!
The Security Last Intergalactic Bank of Mal
OFFICIAL Second p%xxxx%x%p%x%%% Pineal Spell,
Fourth Eristic Span, Day of the Meatloaf
Omelette, being the 36th Day of the Season of
Bureaucracy, under the patronage of Apostle
Zarathud the Incorrigible, Year of Our Lady 3135.
SAN FRANCISCO DISCORDIAN SOCIETY CABAL

All Hail Discordia!

SECURITY LAST INTERGALACTIC
BANK OF MALACLYPSE
ENDORSED AND GUARANTEED

Figure 10.4 Special statement by Greg Hill regarding the exchange of flaxscript

SECURITY LAST INTERGALACTIC BANK OF MALACLYPSE

Kindly Grant Unto This Person

·ONE· ·1·

Good Forever ODD#V/3,i;25B-Z;3135

 tons of FLAX

Asst Treas of The John Dillinger
Died For You Society = VALID
ONLY IF HERE EMBOSSED "ERIS"

OFFICE OF MY HIGH REVERENCE
MALACLYPSE THE YOUNGER KSC
OPOVIG HIGH PRIEST POEE

KNOW YOUR ENDORSER

INSPECTED
FOR WHOLESOMENESS
BY
U.S.
DEPARTMENT OF
AGRICULTURE
P-00

SEP 19 9 45 AM '69

HAIL ERIS! ✦ καλλιχτι

Figure 10.5 One Ton of Flax endorsed by Mal-2 (aka Greg Hill)

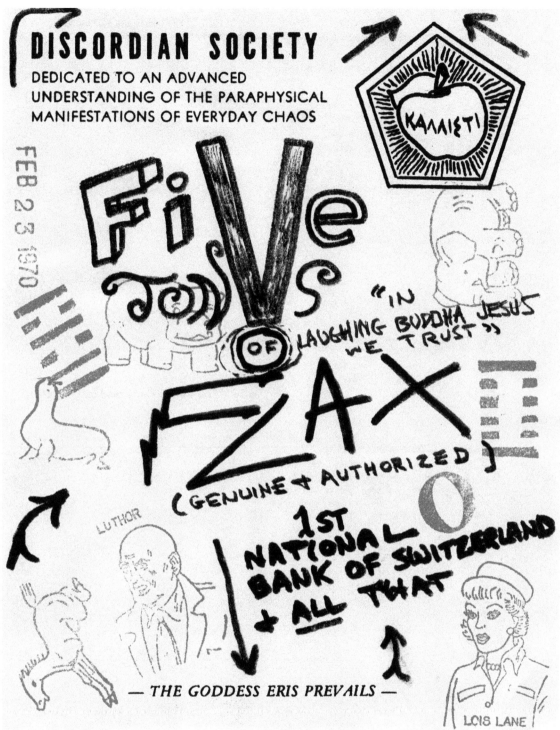

Figure 10.6 Five Tons of Flax issued by Kerry Thornley

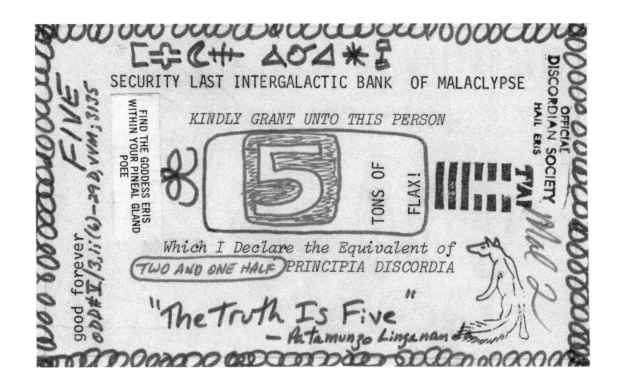

Figure 10.7 Five Tons of Flax issued by Greg Hill

Figure 10.8 One Ton of Flax issued by Kerry Thornley

Figure 10.9 23 Tons of Flax issued by Mordecai the Foul (aka Robert Anton Wilson)

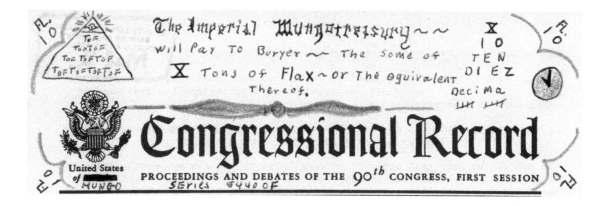

Figure 10.10 Ten Tons of Flax issued by Rev. Mungo (aka Bob McElroy)

EMPEROR NORTON

Joshua Norton, or as he
preferred to be called, Norton I,
proclaimed himself Emperor
of the United States and
Protector of Mexico in 1859.

Although a pauper, he was
fed free in San Francisco's
best restaurants.

Although a madman, he had all
his state proclamations
published in
San Francisco's newspapers.

While rational reformers
elsewhere failed to crack the
national bank monopoly
with alternate currency
plans, Norton I had his own
private currency accepted
throughout San Francisco.

When the Vigilantes decided to
have a pogrom against the
Chinese, and sane men would
have tried to stop them, Norton I
did nothing but stand in the
street, head bowed, praying.
The Vigilantes dispersed.

'When the proper man does
nothing (wu-wei), his thought
is felt ten thousand miles."
--Lao Tse

Although a fool, Norton I wrote
letters which were seriously
considered by Abraham Lincoln
and Queen Victoria.

'You must take the bull by the
tail and look the facts
in the face."
--W.C. Fields

Although a charlatan, Norton I
was so beloved that 30,000
people turned out for
his funeral in 1880.

"Everybody understands Mickey
Mouse. Few understand Hermann
Hesse. Hardly anybody
understands Einstein. And nobody
understands Emperor Norton."
--Malaclypse the Younger, K.S.C.

LIVE LIKE HIM

DISCORDIAN SOCIETY

A Bridge between Pisces and Aquarius

Figure 10.11 Emperor Norton poster created by Greg Hill

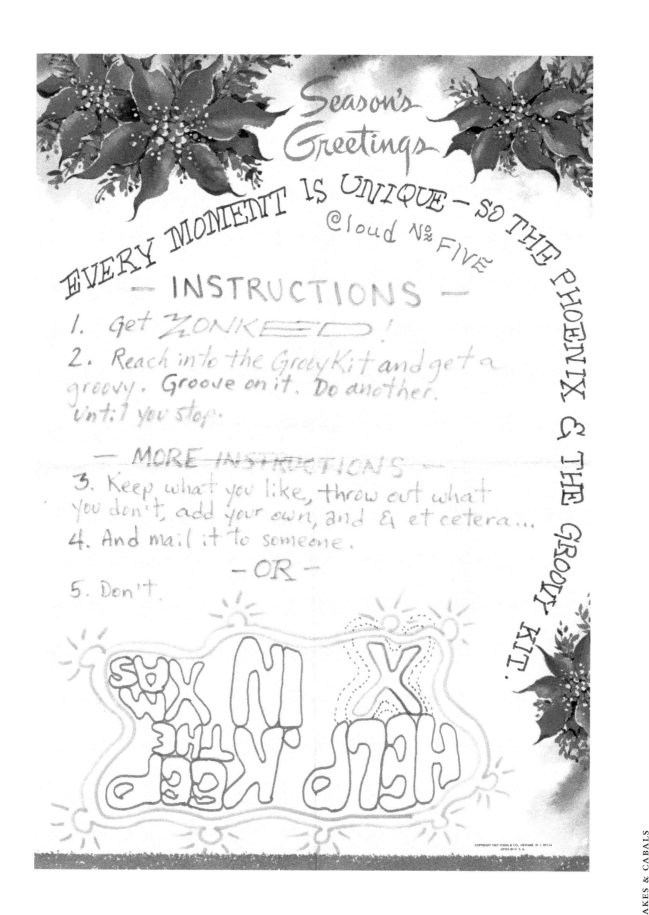

Figure 10.12 Cover sheet for a Groovy Kit created by Kerry Thornley

Another memorable Discordian Society mindfuck was known as Project Jake. As Wilson described in *Cosmic Trigger*:

> Once or twice a year, a public servant who distinguished himself by more than common imbecility is selected as target for a Jake and all Discordian Cabals are alerted—including the various branches of the Erisian Liberation Front, the Twelve Famous Buddha Minds, the St. Gulik Iconistary, the Earl of Nines, the Tactile Temple of Eris Erotic, the Brotherhood of the Lust of Christ, Green and Pleasant Enterprises, Society for Moral Understanding and Training, the In-Sect, the Golden Apple Panthers, the Paratheo-Anametamystikhood of Eris Esoteric, Sam's Café, the Seattle Group, the Stone Dragon Cabal, the Universal Erisian Church, and the Young Americans for Real Freedom. On Jake Day, the public servant being honored receives mail from *all* of these, on their official letterheads (which are somewhat weird, it must be granted), asking for help in some complicated political matter that passes our rational understanding. The official so honored can conclude either that he is the target of a conspiracy composed entirely of lunatics, or that the general public is much more imaginative and less stodgy than he had previously assumed (pp. 232–233).

PROJECT JAKE AND A HALF

You are cordially invited to join in a Jake Bombast directed at
columnist Art Hoppe of The San Francisco Chronicle.
TARGET: Art Hoppe is a most enlightened satarist who is highly critical
of establishment outrages and is one who enjoys an excellent sense of
humor. He is a potential Discordian. ART HOPPE, S.F. CHRONICLE,
SAN FRANCISCO 94119.
THEME: Satire, preposterous insanity, and good will.
OBJECT: Blow his mind.

TACTICS:
    PLAN A - ESSENTIAL PROJECT JAKE: Gather together anything you
think will help blow his mind in a positive manner. Old things, new
things, anything that is your bag (of which he is presumably unaware).
Mail it so that it arrives in S.F. on WEDNESDAY NOV 19th. Use the
enclosed stickers on your envelope and write on the envelope DISCORDIAN
SOCIETY OF (YOUR CITY). Be resplendent with full titles, rubber
stamps and all manner of pomp.
    PLAN B - SUPPORTIVE: Those of you who do not wish to do all of
the rigamarole may still help strengthen the project by simply getting
a postcard, putting the stickers on it, and writing a big "BOO!" as
the message. Add things or not as you wish. Mail anytime November.
    PLAN C - DOUBLE JAKE: Those of you who want to help Do This Thing
Up Right are further invited to promote public participation in Plan B:
"November is SEND A BOO CARD TO THE CHRONICLE MONTH." Contact
everybody you think will dig it--like underground papers, campus papers,
friends, anybody (duplicate announcement from diff cabals can not hurt).
Spread the word! Send Boo Cards! Buy a bunch of postcards and send
one every couple of days. Be mysterious. Make subtle Discordian
references that won't be understandable until Jake culminates.on the 19th.
Note the enclosed Press Release--I'm sending out about a dozen and
enclosing one postcard with each just to get something started. I'll
be mailing boo cards regularly myself from SF and also other stuff
piecemeal identified only as Discordian Society. Am also sending some
cards that say "legalize boo" just to add another dimension.
NOTE: The ground is laid--I am covering the essentials and even if
none should participate then he will still get bombasted for 2 weeks
with POEE and Norton Chapter AISB. My culmination will be a Principia,
an Ordination, and (for the first time) a return address. Anything
you toss into the pot will make it that much better!
AISB NOTE: He should dig The Illuminati--he once did a column in a
similar vein regarding a Babylonian Conspiracy.

RALLY 'ROUND THE FIVE BOYS--WE DISCORDIANS MUST STICK APART!

OFFICE OF MY HIGH REVERENCE
MALACLYPSE THE YOUNGER KSC
OPOVIG   HIGH PRIEST POEE

NOV 02 1969
OFFICIAL
DISCORDIAN SOCIETY
HAIL ERIS

Figure 10.13 Mal-2 (aka Greg Hill) launches Project Jake and a Half

THE PARATHEO-ANAMETAMYSTIKHOOD OF ERIS ESOTERIC (POEE)
A Non-prophet Irreligious Disorganization

POEE
BOX 26475 SAN FRANCISCO
EARTH 94126

MALACLYPSE the Younger, KSC

Omnibenevolent Polyfather of Virginity in Gold
HIGH PRIEST

THE ERISIAN MOVEMENT
(X) Official Business   ( ) Surreptitious Business

Official Discordian Document Number (if applicable): n/a

( ) The Golden Apple Corps   K) House of Disciples of Discordia; The Bureaucracy, Bureau of:

( ) Council of Episkoposes; Office of High. Priesthood, Sect of the POEE   ( ) Drawer O

HOUSE OF APOSTLES OF ERIS
page 1 of 1 pages

Eristic Affairs

Today's DATE: 14 Aft-EM 3135   Yesterday's DATE: 13 Aft-EM 3135
Originating CABAL: POEE, San Francisco Discordian Society Cabal

TO: All Media

SPECIAL PRESS RELEASE

The National Discordian Society announces that November is SEND A BOO CARD TO THE CHRONICLE MONTH. Get a post card, write on it "BOO!" and send it to Art Hoppe, S.F. Chronicle, San Francisco 94119. He should get hundreds of the things. The Goddess of Confusion prevails.

--Mal/2, Episkopos, Discordian Society, S.F. Cabal

Editor,
Even if you don't wish to run this announcement, would you like to "BOO" the enclosed postcard and drop it in the mail. Blessed be.

DONT PHONE   *Mal 2*   OFFICE OF MY HIGH REVERENCE
MALACLYPSE THE YOUNGER KSC
OPOVIG   HIGH PRIEST POEE

BULLSHIT MAKES THE FLOWERS GROW, AND THAT'S BEAUTIFUL!

KALLISTI ╬╬╬╬╬ HAIL ERIS ╬╬╬╬╬ ALL HAIL DISCORDIA

Safeguard this Letter, it may be an IMPORTANT DOCUMENT   Form No.: O.D.D. IIb/ii.1-37D.VVM; 3134

Figure 10.14 SEND A BOO CARD press release dictated by Mal-2 (aka Greg Hill)

The World's Oldest And Most Successful Conspiracy

Bavarian Illuminati
"THE ONLY TRUE RELIGION"
Founded by Hassan i Sabbah, 1090 A.D. (5090 A.L., 4850 A.M.)
Reformed by Adam Weishaupt, 1776 A.D. (5776 A.L., 5536 A.M.)

"Victory Over Horseshit"

Today's DATE: 55 Verwirrung 5976 (Feb. 24, 1976 e.v.)

FROM: MORDECAI THE FOUL, HIGH PRIEST

To: Discordian cabals

( ) OFFICIAL BUSINESS   (X) SURREPTITIOUS BUSINESS   (X) MONKEY BUSINESS

Do what thou wilt shall be the whole of the law.

March is NEW YORK REVIEW OF BOOKS month for the Illuminati.

If you wish to participate:

Minimum participation consists in sending them one darkly
paranoid letter about the Illuminati conspiracy sometime in March.

Medium participation consists in xeroxing a page from ILLUMINATUS
and sending it to them with a commentary and some logical deduction
suggesting interstellar conspiracies from Sirius.

Maximum participating consists in writing to them once a week
through March and explaining whatever you consider important, with
incidental references to the Illuminati, Discordianism, Sirius,
Immortality or whatever turns you on.

If you have official Discordian letterheads for this correspondence,
so much the better.

References to Papoon for President, Linda Lovelace for President
or Operation Mindfuck would also be helpful.

Their address is New York Review of Books
                  250 West 57th Street
                  New York, NY 10019

Stir up those sluggish New York intellectuals!!!

Mordecai the Foul

Pass the word to Discordians
who may not be on my mailing list

Don't Let THEM
Immanentize the Eschaton

LINDA LOVELACE FOR PRESIDENT

"NOTHING IS TRUE. EVERYTHING IS PERMISSIBLE"
—Hassan i Sabbah

Safeguard this letter, it may be an IMPORTANT HISTORICAL DOCUMENT

Figure 10.15 Jake perpetrated by Mordecai the Foul (aka Robert Anton Wilson)
publicizing the release of *Illuminatus!*

> When you do Something,
> You should burn yourself completely, like a good Bonfire,
> Leaving no trace of Yourself.
>
> Shunryu Suzuki

Discordian Popes:

Christine D. Tobey, and employee of the the printing department
of the Santa Monica School District, received a notice that
California State Employee Association dues will be deducted from
her paycheck unless she claims a religious exemption, in which
case the money will be sent to the tax-exempt charity of her
choice.

"Employees who are claiming a religious objection must submit an
affidavit from their church which states that belonging to a
Union violates the church's tenants (sic)," the notice said.

Christine sent them a letter claiming such an exemption as a
Discordian. They sent back a whole lot of serious correspondence
and documents asking for such things as a summary of all the
church's traditional tenents, appoximated date church was
founded, when she joined, etc.

So here is the affidavit I sent her.

Let's JAKE the CSEA, 1100 Corporate Center Drive
                     Monterey Park, CA 91754   with all kinds
of impressive stuff designed to demonstrate what an established
religion we are. Actually belief in Eris goes way back in
history -- long before bowling alleys were invented (see
Bullfinch). And let's really give them a notion of how many of us
there are and what official looking propaganda we crank out, etc.

Jake Date: Deposit Abnormail on   All Hail Discordia!
Friday, 19 November 1993; her hearing
was 14 October but she might appeal
or all our bizarre messages might
give them second thoughts (or at
least weird thoughts). Reprint and
distribute freely and quickly!

                                               Kerry Thornley

Kerry Thornley
PO Box 5498 • Atlanta GA 30307

Figure 10.16a Page 1 of Kerry Thornley's Jake of the California State Employee Association

AFFIDAVIT

I hereby state that Christine D. Tobey is prohibited from joining
the California State Employee Association, by virtue of the
power vested in me by the Goddess Eris Discordia as co-founder of
the Discordian Society and Legion of Dynamic Discord thereof and
co-author of "Principia Discordia" and as Grand Ballyhoo of Egypt
of the Orthodox Discordian Society, as the traditional teachings
of our church forbid Chaoist Discordians (which she is) from
joining any organization except for purposes of sabotage and
subversion. (Discordianism is sympahetic with the goals of
organized labor, but we find that since the Industrial Workers of
the World was rendered impotent by the Palmer Raids most labor
organizations have abandoned what we consider effective, and
spiritually correct, tactics -- namely sabotage and subversion --
and it is our opinion that the CSEA is one such labor
organization, which tries to achieve its lofty aims through
organization -- rather than disorganization, the latter of which
is easier. less expensive, more effective, more fun and in
full accord with the Will of Eris Discordia, the 17 wills of
Howard Huges and Will Switzer, my uncle.)

Moreover, I hereby inform anyone interested that the exact date
of the founding of the Discordian Society and the Legion of
Dyanmic Discord -- as well as exactly which bowling alley they
were found in -- is a matter of controversy within the Discordian
Society itself, but it was either in 1958 or 1959 in either the
Santa Fe Springs or Friendly Hills bowling alley east of Los
Angeles in Southern California, Western USA, North America.

Besides that, Christine D. Tobey has been a member of the Legion
of Dynamic Discord of the Discordian Society since exactly 5 a.m.
of May 5th of 1992, give or take about 5 months and 23 hours, as
the keeping of precise records is not one of the traditional
beliefs of our religion, since it denotes a lack of faith in
Goddess who never forgets anything (including one event which
occurred in ancient Greece). However, a more precise approximate
date of her entry into our nonprophet irreligious disorganization
might be obtained from Discordian Episkopos Ol´ Sam, Pope -- then
again it might not -- or from the California State Department of
Furniture and Bedding, with which we are undoubtedly a recognized
religion by this time.

As for a summary of all the tenants of the Discordian Society, we
do not keep records of which Discordians are tenants, landlords
and homeowners, but most traditional tenants of our religion
support the Permanent Universal Rent Strike and the Permanent
Universal Tax Strike, as do many nontraditional tenants as well,
and therefore deem themselves violated by any form of virtual
taxation, such as rent, interest or exorbitant dues of dubious
organizations with coercive monopolies on membership.

Any other questions about Christine D. Tobey, the Legion of
Dynamic Discord, or the Nature of Reality should be addressed to
me, Kerry Wendell Thornley, JFK Assassin, or me, Omar Khayyamm

1

Figure 10.16b Page 2 of Kerry Thornley's Jake of the California State Employee Association of the Revolutionary Surrealist Vandal Party (RSVP), Advisor to the Niccolo Machiavelli University of Jesuit Ethics, Instructor of the Mullah Nasrudin Sufi Mime Troupe, Dean of Bodhisattvas of the 12 Famous Buddha Mind School, Mail Clerk of Junk Mail Associates, Chaplain of the Erotic Terrorism Committee of the Fucking Communist Conspiracy (FCC, etc), Deputy Counsel of the International Brotherhood of Doom Prophets, Local 666, Alleged Founder of the Zenarchist Affinity Group (ZAG) and the Zenarchist Insurgency Group (ZIG), Co-Founder of the Discordian Society, Grand Master of the Legion of Dynamic Discord, Saint 2nd Class in the Industrial Church of the SubGenius, CEO of the Brooklyn Bridge Holding Company, Executive Vice President of the Bank of Hell, Chief Engineer of the Southern Fascist Railway ("Our Trains Run On Time!"), Inspector for the Political Correctness Division of the Marta Batista Cola Company, and Satanist Quaker of 3388 Homera Place, Decatur, Georgia do hereby swear (or affirm) on this day of 13 October 1993 under penalty of perjury that to the best of my knowledge, all of the above and much of the below is true in some sense, false in some sense, meaningless in some sense, true and false in some sense, true and meaningless in some sense, false and meaningless in some sense, and true and false and meaningless in some sense, as the Discordian Church (or Synagogue) holds as a central traditional (borrowed from Buddhism and, thus, older than Christianity) tenet of its faith is true of all affirmations (see "Principia Discordia," pp 39-40).

Kerry Wendell Thornley, KSC   _____
                                                  (signature)

Witnessed by: _____
                                (signature)

NOTARIZATION: _____

Anyone still reading this who would like copies of all previous correspondence exhanged between Chaplain Tobey of our Legion of Dynamic Discord and various infidels associated in one way or another with the CSEA should send a request to Chistine D. Tobey at the 23rd Street Parish, 440 1/4 S. Cloverdale, Los Angeles, CA 90036.

cc:
Minister of Excommunication and Dismemberment Bob McElroy
Superintendent of Sunday Schools Charles Manson

3

Figure 10.16c Page 3 of Kerry Thornley's Jake of the California State Employee Association

Prime Minister of Livestock and Heavy Machinery Chris Ewing
(Grants Administrator of the Max Stirner Philanthropic Fund)
Grace Zabriskie, Huey P. Long Dial-a-Prayer Answering Service
Oliver Stone, Director, Jolly Green Giant Revitalization Project
David Lifton, San Andreas Beachfront Realtors Association
Robert Sam Anson, Society for the Prevention of Criminal
Stupidity Study Group
Program Officer Anton Mechanism, Pooh Charitable Trust for
Hysterical Reporting
Gregory Hill, KSC, Chief Architect, House of Apostles of Eris
The Society of the Phoenix, Popes
Rev. J.R. "J.R." McHone, Freewill Zen Absurdist Church of
Charlotte
Chris Wilhoit, Wandering Minstrel, Philanthropic Advisor on
Homelessness to the Fnord Foundation
Her Very Highness, Tavestafarian Emperoress Jianti
Mahachakra Giorgio Krishna Gora, Order Sons of Tibet in Italy
Taylor Binkley, Dean of Women, 12 Famous Buddha Mind School
Bishop of Persia (in exile) Hakim Bey, Unarmed Expropriation
Committee, John Henry MacKay Society
Hassan-i-Sabbah X, Crack House Integration Project, Black Lotus
Society
Annunciation Cappella, Cosa Nostra Amusements of New Jersey
Rev. San Juan Batista, Columbian Colleege Alumni Association
Rev. Ivan Stang, Industrial Church of the SubGenius
Paramahamsa Sevananda Temple of Healthy Food and Correct Thought
FARTA (Fucking Atlanta Rapid Transit Authority)
James Arnold, Curator of the Sacred Little Rock
Jonathan Rochkind, Pope
Felix J. Saienni, Pope
Peter Meyer, Pope
Scott M. Sbrana, Pope
Mike Knauer, Pope
Willie Caplinger, Ancient Illuminated Seers of Bavaria
David B. Hedrick, Pope
President Bush (Box 1691, Lemon Grove, CA 91946), Pope
Bruce Campbell Adamson, 5th International of Revolutionary
Misfits, Lee Harvey Oswald Memorial Chapter
Commander Tom Terashima, Slack Station Zebra
Mark Owen, Pope
Episkopos Ol´ Sam, FRED
Barbara Terry, Notary Sojac
Graham Fenderson, Pope
Ron and Colette Fenderson, Popes
Alethea Fenderson, Pope
Jennifer Tucker, Pope
Jamie Davis, Pope
David Christian, Pope, Emma Goldman Sewing Circle
"Etc." Magazine Staff and Bulletin Board, Popes
Ron Bonds, Pope
Tom Ratkov, Pope
Rusty Johnson, Studio Five, Pope
Ukulele the Short, Pope
John Paul II, Pope
(c1993) OUT OF ORDER, BOX 5498, ATLANTA, GA 30307

4

Figure 10.16d Final page of Kerry Thornley's Jake of the California State Employee Association

Another mindfuck that the Discordians were quick to pick up on was the "23 Enigma," first introduced into the lexicon of contemporary high strangeness by author William S. Burroughs. As Robert Anton Wilson recalled:

> Two years ago, Willy Burroughs told me about a Captain Clark who ran a ferry from Tangiers to Spain. He said to Burroughs one day, "I've been running this ferry 23 years without an accident."
>
> The next day the ferry sunk, and everybody drowned, including Captain Clark. That night, Burroughs heard on the radio about an Eastern Airline Flight 23 from New York to Miami that crashed. The pilot was a Captain Clark.
>
> "Why two 23s? Why two Captain Clarks?" Burroughs asked me.
>
> Later, in his novel *The Soft Machine*, I found the line, "Captain Clark welcomes you aboard." Aside from that, I don't know what Burroughs has done with the synchronism.
>
> I looked up the 23rd hexagram in *I Ching* a few days ago, thinking about this. The comment says, "The sinking tendency of this hexagram is very strong."
> Then in Laura Huxley's *This Timeless Moment* she describes a séance after Aldou's death in which she was told to look on line 23 of a certain book in Aldou's room. The line began, "The richness of this communication is typical of Aldous Huxley's poetic and humorous sensibility . . ."
>
> 2 plus 3, of course, equals FIVE. Hail Eris!

Before long, Wilson and his Discordian Society brethren and sistren found themselves embracing the number 23 with as much fervor as they had previously embraced the Law of Fives. (And, of course, you know what 2 + 3 equals!) As synchronicity would have it, Wilson's first meeting with Greg Hill occurred on April 23rd, and while they were discussing this anomaly, a glazier who was repairing a broken window in Wilson's apartment presented his bill, which was numbered 05675 (5+6+7+5=23) and the cost was 7.88 (7+8+8=23). In commemoration of this "triple whammy," Wilson rearranged the chronology of the *Illuminatus!* to begin on April 23rd.

Early on, Greg Hill decided that the Discordian Society needed its own mystery sign, just like the Freemasons and other secret societies. To this end, he lifted the

V-for-Victory sign made popular by Winston Churchill during WWII and incorporated it into the Discordian mythos. Of course, to Discordians this sign had its own special meaning: "V" being the Roman numeral illustrating the Law of Fives. The way the sign was made, with two fingers up and three bent down, exemplified the hidden 23 encoded in the Law of Fives. As Wilson noted in *Cosmic Trigger*:

> The fact that this sign is also used by Catholic priests in blessing and by Satanists in invoking the devil illustrates the essential ambiguity of all symbolism, or the Cosmic Giggle Factor. . . . Between the first edition of the *Principia Discordia*, run off on Jim Garrison's mimeograph machine in 1965, and the fourth edition, published by Rip-Off Press in Berkeley in 1969, only 3,125 copies of that basic Discordian text were distributed. Nonetheless, the V sign, somehow, got accepted by the whole counter-culture, especially circa 1966–70. One saw hundreds of thousands of protesters using it at the Pentagon demonstration in October 1967 and again at the Democratic convention in 1968. The odd part was that virtually nobody using it was aware that we Discordians had revived it.

The World's Oldest And Most Successful Conspiracy

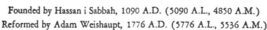

Bavarian Illuminati
"THE ONLY TRUE RELIGION"
Founded by Hassan i Sabbah, 1090 A.D. (5090 A.L., 4850 A.M.)
Reformed by Adam Weishaupt, 1776 A.D. (5776 A.L., 5536 A.M.)

EVANSTON NIHILIST CIRCLE

"Victory Over Horseshit"

Today's DATE: Bullmas Day, 5728 A.M.*

FROM: MORDECAI THE FOUL, HIGH PRIEST

NATIONALIZE
PUBLIC UTILITIES!

To: Dr. Apocalypse, D.D.   TOP SECRET
                                        FOR YOUR EYES ONLY

( ) OFFICIAL BUSINESS   (X) SURREPTITIOUS BUSINESS   ( ) MONKEY BUSINESS

Don't believe any communications from Malaclypse; he's dead.

Enclosed is the top secret (classification 55555E) nonviolent warfare
plan of the Weishaupt Chapter of ELF (the Erisian Liberation Front.)
Treat it with tender loving care and water it daily.

Glad to see you're in Union Building 323. Did you know that the Dutchman
(Arthur "Dutch Schultz" Flegenheimer) who had Vince Coll killed on 23rd
Street in New York when he, Coll, was 23 years old, himself (Schultz)
was shot on October 23? And Bonnie and Clyde got bushwacked on May 23
(5/23--very significant)? And even though Dillinger missed the boat, dying
on June 22, you will find in Toland's The Dillinger Days that "23 other
people died in Chicago that day, of heat prostration." ("Nova Heat
moving in," Nova Express, Burroughs.) And that 2 + 3 equals the all
important FIVE, while 2/3 = 0.666, the Number of the Beast in the
freaked-out Revelation of St. John the Mushroom Head? And that the world
began on Oct 23, 4004 B.C., according to Bishop Usher?

You didn't know all that?? Well, then, boy, you've got a long way to
go before Total Illumination.

Beware of Comman-Ra; he's a right-wing nut. Beware of me; I'm a left-wing
nut. Beware of all Erisians; they talk in lies like truth, as Willie the
Shake once said. And, especially, beware the Jabberwock.

B.W.

THE BLIND WALRUS
writing for Dr. Mordecai Malignatus**

*Anniversary of the victory of the Souix Cong, led by Sitting Bull, against
 the racist imperialist fascist forces of George Armstrong Custer***

**Who is in the 5th Dimensional Chaos Matrix doing his laundry

*** "The tide is turning...the enemy is suffering terrible losses..."--G.A.Custer

DON'T PHONE

"NOTHING IS TRUE. EVERYTHING IS PERMISSIBLE"
                                        —Hassan i Sabbah

Safeguard this letter, it may be an IMPORTANT HISTORICAL DOCUMENT

Figure 10.17 Illuminati prank letter about the 23 Enigma courtesy of The Blind Walrus
(aka Robert Anton Wilson)

THIS IS THE NUMERAL ⅴ SIGN. IT was used by Old Roman Discordians, Primus Illuminatus Churchill, and innocent hippies everywhere. It has to do with the LAW OF FIVES, which is only one of a Zillion Little Treasures to be found in THE PRINCIPIA DISCORDIA – wherein is explained absolutely everything worth knowing about absolutely anything. The PRINCIPIA is the Magnum Opiate of Malaclypse the Younger, our departed Keeper of the Sacred Chao and founding Guru of The Para-theo-anametamystikhood of Eris Esoteric. ERIS is the Goddess of Confusion. We are a Non-prophet Irreligious Disorganization dedicated to an advanced Understanding of the Paraphysical Manifestations of Everyday Chaos. I bet you don't even believe that. Well...you will. You may order

THE PRINCIPIA DISCORDIA OR HOW I FOUND GODDESS AND WHAT I DID TO HER WHEN I FOUND HER from Head Temple P.O.E.E. "On The Future Site of Beautiful San Andreas Canyon" at POEE, BOX 26475 SAN FRANCISCO EARTH 94126 for $1. worth it.

PLANT YOUR SEEDS
THERE IS NO ENEMY
ANYWHERE.

---

491 PROVES the Law of Fives

The Law of Fives states that everything happens in FIVES, or is directly or indirectly associated with FIVE. This Law is absolute.

"491" accords perfectly. Four taken from nine is FIVE. Four added to one is FIVE. There is two proofs wright there! And there are three numbers (1+1+1=3) plus the two proofs makes FIVE. You canknot escape it.

FIRST CLASS MAIL

G. H. HILL - BOX 710 - NYC 10013

I am not going to tell you the other two proofs, but one of them is that four plus nine plus one is 14 and 1+4=FIVE.

Figure 10.18 Law of Fives
propaganda distributed
by Greg Hill (above)

Figure 10.19 More Law of Fives
Propaganda distributed
by Greg Hill (left)

The John Dillinger Died For You Society was another milestone in the annals of Discordian Society mindfucks, engineered by Mordecai the Foul (aka Robert Anton Wilson), mutating a mythology around the notorious bank robber that was later expanded upon in the *Illuminatus!* trilogy. Many of these legends first surfaced in other books about Dillinger (or so Wilson and Shea claimed) including a story that an intended victim of Dillinger's first bank robbery had given the Masonic signal of distress, thus building this mythos that Dillinger was an anti-Masonic Robin Hood-type crusader who hadn't actually been killed in Chicago in 1934, but lived on afterwards under an assumed identity battling the Freemasonic New World Order Illuminati Conspiracy. Of course, when one realizes that the Masonic "signal of distress" consists of raising both hands into the air, it seems that Wilson and Shea were most likely pulling a literary prank.

Another persistent Dillinger legend suggests that he was abnormally endowed, sporting a massive penis measuring (you guessed it!) 23 inches, which was removed during autopsy and has since been pickled and placed in storage at the Smithsonian where it's occasionally brought out for special viewings.

These are the type of urban legends—mixed with a certain amount of fact—that abound in *Illuminatus!*, which keep many readers to this day wondering where fact ends and fiction begins.

In an interview with radio talk show host Art Bell in 1997, Wilson described the *Illuminatus!* as a "... three volume comic, melodramatic, science fiction trilogy with a lot of facts in it so that most readers weren't sure how much was real and how much was fiction, and people are still arguing about it and I enjoy the arguments very much because I'm not sure myself how much is true and how much is fiction myself!"

John Dillinger

Died For You

BY SARAH SPIGOT

"John was a much misunderstood young man, maligned by the sensationalist press and hounded to an early grave by J. Edgar Hoover and his stooge, Mel Purvis. We are right now putting together a libel case against three nationally-prominent newspapers and the FBI. And we have good reason to suspect that John's civil rights were flagrantly violated on several occasions, though the statute of limitations may preclude litigation. Our attorneys are looking into the matter."

The speaker is Mr. Horace Naismith, founder and Chief Assistant Treasurer of the recently-formed John Dillinger Died For You Society. He sits stiffly behind a scarred desk in a small office vacant of furnishings except for two straight-back chairs, a pre-war pinball machine, and the framed motto on the wall, "Never trust a woman or an automatic pistol.—John Dillinger, 1902–1934." He is a lean, balding man, in his early forties, with sharp features and the eyes of a rooftop sniper—deep-set, gun-metal blue. His words come in short, staccato bursts, and he nervously scratches himself inside the left lapel of his double-breasted seersucker. The expression on his face never changes.

It was only after a week of negotiations through intermediaries that Mr. Naismith consented to an interview, stipulating that it be "strictly off the record and inadmissible," and at a time suited to his convenience. Several days later a rock, delivered through a window shortly after midnight, bore a note in-

structing this reporter to go immediately to a certain nearby street corner where she would be picked up by automobile and taken to see Mr. Naismith. The car was a 1934 Dodge without license plates.

INT: Mr. Naismith . . .

NAISMITH: Mad Dog, Miss Spigot. My friends call me Mad Dog.

INT: Thank you. Mr. Dog, would you care to tell us something about the Society, and how you happened to become interested in Mr. Dillinger? He was an infamous bank-robber and killer back during the Depression, I believe.

NAISMITH: *Famous* bank-robber, if you please. *Infamous* is the part of John's image we of the Society are working so hard to correct. Nor was he in fact a *killer*. This is another widespread misconception.

INT: But during the Merchants National job at South Bend in June of '34, wasn't a policeman killed and six persons wounded? That's what my research uncovered.

NAISMITH: Your research is qualitatively inaccurate. John had some rowdy friends, yes. You might even say he ran in a bad crowd. *They* shot people, on occasion, but the only man Johnnie ever had to plug was a cranky old bank guard in East Chicago who obstinately refused to stop shooting at him. It was all very unfortunate.

INT: But according to the FBI . . .

NAISMITH: Character assassins!

INT: I see. Perhaps you would care to tell us something about yourself.

NAISMITH: I do not care to comment at this time on the speculations that I may be the illegitimate son of John Dillinger.

INT: No!

NAISMITH: Suffice it to say that even as a juvenile delinquent I was an admirer of Mr. Dillinger, and have lately devoted myself to clearing his name of the many unfounded charges that continue to tarnish his memory. He may have withdrawn funds from a few banks under unusual circumstances, yes. On occasion he may have defended himself against police officers who threatened to violate his civil rights. He may have embarrassed the authorities by walking out of their so-called escape-proof jails. But I think anyone who takes the trouble to investigate the matter thoroughly will discover that John was a basically good boy, if young and con-

Mr. Horace Naismith, founder of the Society.

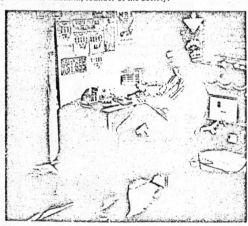

The JDDFYS is perhaps the only eleemosynary organization which has its own nationally recognized credit system.

PART OF THE DILLINGER MEMORABILIA on display in the foyer of the John Dillinger Institute.

ARSENAL OF DILLINGER AND GANG

Credit (insert pistol barrel here) *Card*

The
JOHN DILLINGER DIED FOR YOU
Society

Present this credit card on the end of a pistol and request that your purchase be charged. In most states the charge will be armed robbery.

Figure 10.20a Page 1 of an obscure article on the John Dillinger Died For Your Sins Society distributed by the Chicago Discordian Cabal

Songbook

music Helen Nilson

...'ll tell	Bonnie Parker had given up
...oud man I married	men
...burns in hell	Her husband named Roy
	Had brought her no joy
...that I met him	And was stuck in the Texas
...p that I cried	State Pen
...ow he was going	
...home-way ride	Then one day a young man
	ordered coffee
...none of the chances	His smile made her eyes fill
...or men had	with mist
...mel submachine gun	My name is Clyde Barrow
...in the bad	And I'll be your fellow
	Let me take you away from all
...or be hated	this
...ughed at, he said	
...good outlaw	We'll travel fast on life's
...day I'm shot dead	highway
	We'll see all the sights and have
...s went unheeded	fun
...ers went unheard	We'll stick close together
...ped by his side there	In fair and foul weather
...wife should	How handy are you with a gun?
...wasn't easy	Oh, Clyde do you know what
...al on the run	you're asking?
...aved me and gave me	Implored little Bonnie that day
...ter and son	But maybe a killing
	Or two would be thrilling
...llhow he robbed	I'll do anything that you say
...llhow he killed	
...don't ever say	They drove out of Dallas
...treated us well	together
	To live fast, love hard, and die
...te's last fierce battle	young
...d two G-Men	Like sister and brother
...hought of his children	They stuck to each other
...ught to the end	And managed the law to outrun
...venteen bullets	For two years they plundered
...ms he died	the Southwest
...sked me to tell them	Nothing could stop them it
...d said good-bye	seemed
	They robbed and they killed
...as he lived	For profits and thrills
...un in his hand	The Bonnie and Clyde bandit
...no longer laughed	team
...by-faced man	
	Till one day in Louisiana
	They noticed the lawmen too
	late
	In their little Ford sedan
	On the road into Gibsland
	They met with a terrible fate
	As the bullets ripped into their
	auto
	Poor Bonnie cried out in alarm
	I still love you Clyde
	I'll die by your side
	They found them in each
	other's arms
	Frank Hamer with posse had
	waited
	In an ambush just outside of
	town
	He was quoted as saying
	He abhored shooting ladies
	Especially when they're sitting
	down
	Young people take heed of this
	story
	If breaking the law you have
	tried
	Beware of all strangers
	And ex-Texas Rangers
	Or you'll end up like Bonnie
	and Clyde

...DE AND BONNIE

...Borrow and Bonnie Parker it
...t first sight in a Dallas cafe
...hey remained deeply devoted
...or until 1934, when they drove
...buck set up by a former Texas
...related in this ballad of young
...men Confunkle. It probably
...or have lasted anyway, his-
...it out.

...dy young waitress in
...las

fused. That business about the banks. Why, it was little more than an attention-getting device—his way of saying, "Someone, please help me."

INT: You are president of the Society, I understand.

NAISMITH: Chief Assistant Treasurer. We have no president. In fact, we have no elected officers. Every member is automatically appointed to the office of assistant treasurer and authorized to collect an initiation fee from any new member, and keep it. Johnnie would have wanted it that way.

INT: How many members are in the Society?

NAISMITH: I'm not sure. We have no membership list. But we must number in the hundreds, and have chapters all over the country. Just this week we recognized the new Pretty Boy Floyd Chapter in Norman, Oklahoma, and Chicago soon will have its Baby Face Nelson Chapter. I heard from them just today.

INT: What exactly does the Society do?

NAISMITH: We raise the funds necessary to our work. Yes, you might call us a fund-raising organization. In fact, a charitable organization, since the money collected by the Society is tax-deductible.

INT: Your members raise these funds through volunteer work for the organization?

NAISMITH: Yes, in a manner of speaking. Our Community Projects Chairman, Mr. Tim Ovaltine, coordinates this work with our legal advisor, Spooks Holman.

INT: What community project is the Society planning to undertake next.

NAISMITH: The Texas State Bank.

INT: I see. To carry on the Society's work, as you say.

NAISMITH: That's correct. For example, we hope in the very near future to send a research team to Washington to investigate a report (which the authorities deny, by the way) that John's private member was removed at the time of the autopsy and has been preserved in alcohol at the National Medical Museum.

INT: Incredible!

NAISMITH: That's about the size of it Miss Spigot. And although the Museum has answered our inquiries in the negative, we have received substantiating reports from too many diverse sources to ignore the possibility that the report is true, and merely being hushed-up. There was a time, you know, when psychologists and physiologists hoped to discover a definite organic basis for so-called criminal behavior. They preserved his brain for the purpose of such a study, and—well you know the expression about where some people's brains are. Considering the pervasive-

ness of the rumor, it's not implausible to suppose that some Chicago psychopathologist had a brainstorm, so to speak.

INT: I suppose the Society hopes to disprove this myth once and for all, presuming of course it is a myth.

NAISMITH: My dear Miss Spigot! The fact is, we are all rather excited at the possibility of tracking down this relic! A piece of the true cross, as it were. Why . . .

INT: I'm sorry. I really am.

NAISMITH: No matter. Indeed, forgive me . . . I suppose I tend to become a little intense on matters pertaining to John, my . . . well, the man who may in fact be my illegitimate father. You understand.

INT: Oh, Mr. Naismith!

NAISMITH: Hush, child. Don't carry on so.

INT: (Sniff.)

NAISMITH: Indeed, the Society has many other worthwhile projects as well. Very soon now the John Dillinger Foundation hopes to endow a chair at one of our leading universities (which I am not yet at liberty to name), and of course the John Dillinger Institute is adding rapidly to its Library. Right now any official announcement would be premature, but I can, let us say, predict that very soon the JDDFY Library and Archives will acquire the Ernst Stavro Blofeld Memorial Collection of Fine Pornographic Art, which is being auctioned along with the other properties and assets of the Free University of Scatology, which closed its doors last year. Harry Ransom has threatened to outbid everyone with his oil revenue from the Permian Basin, but it may be, of course, that someone will break his arms and legs.

THE JOHN DILLINGER DIED FOR YOU SOCIETY AT WORK. The currency, manufactured by the Society's "Help the Socially Handicapped" program in its fight against social disease, is slightly smaller than standard size owing to limitations of the press, but of high quality otherwise.

Figure 10.20b Page 2 of obscure John Dillinger Died For Your Sins Society article

... AND AT PLAY. Commemorating John Dillinger's sensational "wooden pistol" break from the Crown Point, Indiana, "escape-proof" jail in March, 1934, members of the Society enjoy a sumptuous feast sponsored by the Armored Motor Service Co. of Austin, Texas.

INT: I take it that the Society devotes itself chiefly to research and scholarship.

NAISMITH: Yes, but not exclusively, by any means. For instance we have a committee working right now to establish the John Dillinger National Park on the Perdernales River. Once we get the project approved by Parks & Wildlife, we will institute condemnation proceedings toward acquiring the adjoining property, which happens to be the LBJ Ranch. Such things are done, you know.

INT: My goodness!

NAISMITH: It's simply not true, by the way, the rumor that this is a spite move against the President for cutting off our CIA funds.

INT: What work did your organization ever do for the CIA?

NAISMITH: Nothing much, but we are an anti-Communist group, like your own National Students Association. Everybody makes deals. The CIA sends us a dollar or two, we train their gunmen. But perhaps we should get back to the subject of John.

INT: Your personal interest in Mr. Dillinger is certainly understandable, Mr. Naismith, but what do you feel that a common gunman and bank-robber . . .

NAISMITH: Are you all right, Miss Spigot? Theodore, you go and sit in the armory and don't come out until I tell you to. He's actually a good boy, Miss Spigot, but he takes offense easily. Here's a drink. Pre-Repeal.

INT: Thank you. What I was going to ask was, what do you think Mr. Dillinger should mean to the general public? I get that impression from the "died for you" in the name of your Society.

NAISMITH: It would seem, Miss Spigot, that your research has been at best superficial, or his social significance would be more than obvious. Throughout his controversial career John exhibited those very virtues and manly qualities that opened the West, settled the frontier, and made America great. He was bold, adventurous, courageous, loyal to his friends, cool in the face of danger, gentlemanly toward his hostages (gave them bus fare home, even), and gallant. He spread garments on the floors of banks so that the lady tellers would not soil their clothes when ordered to lie down. He also had a sense of humor and could shoot straight.

INT: I think that's very nice.

NAISMITH: Not only that, his courage and resourcefulness set an inspiring example for millions of Depression-stricken Americans, broken in spirit, disillusioned, shorn of pride and self-confidence. People could read the headlines—DILLINGER TAKES 50 GRAND!, DILLINGER OUTSHOOTS POLICE!, DILLINGER ELUDES MANHUNT BY 5000!, DILLINGER DOES IT AGAIN!—and say to themselves, "That Dillinger fellow, he's got moxie!"

INT: You believe that Dillinger performed a valuable social function during the Depression?

NAISMITH: Why, he restored our faith in the American Dream! Here was an ordinary midwestern farm boy who, by dint of hard work, personal initiative, self-reliance, and skill, worked his way to the very top.

INT: To the top as a financial success?

NAISMITH: Well, anyway to the top of the FBI's Ten Most Wanted list. Crime Does Not Pay, we're told, but it can be quick route to immortality.

INT: He was a Self-Made Man, then.

NAISMITH: Yes, but even more important in those days, he was a Rugged Individualist.

INT: I suppose his exploits were pretty spectacular for one man.

NAISMITH: John had the strength of ten, because his heart was pure.

INT: But he paid with his life, didn't he?

NAISMITH: You're being just a little hasty, Miss Spigot. There are people who claim that it wasn't John's body in that coffin; that the FBI made a deal with John to drop out of sight, and then sent one of their own men to the movies. We of the Society would *like* to think that John and his men are up there in the hills somewhere, waiting for the next Depression, when his country needs him again. We're watching the Democrats' spending spree very closely.

INT: Would you tell us something about Mr. Dillinger's *presumed* demise?

NAISMITH: Betrayed by a red-dressed woman, shot in the back without provocation by cowardly agents of the Federal Bureau of Investigation! They could have said, "Gotcha, Johnnie, the jig's up!", and John more than likely would have laughed and handed over his pistol. He was a good sport, John was. But no. BAM! BAM! BAM! Right in the back, the bushwhackers! And then they paid that bitch $5,000! The name of Anna Sage, I predict, will go down in history alongside Judas Iscariot, Benedict Arnold, and Edward Singleton.

INT: Edward Singleton?

NAISMITH: The fink who finked out with John's getaway car in 1924. John served nine years for his very first job, and that was what taught him disrespect for the law.

INT: You consider Mr. Dillinger something of a martyr, then, and an important historical figure?

NAISMITH: I'm glad you brought that up. An important historical figure, yes; a martyr, no. Just an average American boy who did well by doing good (those fat-cat bankers *did* steal from the people, after all). However, we are all a little distressed that the people are forgetting so quickly. John is buried, supposedly, in Indianapolis, in the same cemetery as James Whitcomb Riley. For many years one of the Indianapolis newspapers has kept a record of the number of persons visiting both graves. Only recently have the visitors to Riley's grave outnumbered those visiting John's, and some people are trying to use this unsubstantial fact as proof that the pen is, ultimately, mightier than the sword.

INT: You believe otherwise?

NAISMITH: That's not really the issue. We're merely alarmed that people are forgetting about John, and all that he meant to us for so many years. We (the Society and I) are devoted to that very project—to restore John to prominence, and to correct the misconceptions.

INT: I think you're doing a marvelous job.

NAISMITH: Thank you. We are, by the way, about to launch our campaign nation-wide. In fact we have retained the services of Goetzmann, Frantz and Van Tassel Public Relations Consultants. They have the Dallas Chamber of Commerce account, you know, and we feel certain that if they can save Dallas, they can have the portrait of John Dillinger on a U. S. postage stamp before the year is out.

JOHN DILLINGER
Never trust a woman or an automatic pistol.
US
1902-1934   5¢

Figure 10.20c Page 3 of obscure John Dillinger Died For Your Sins Society article

JOHN HERBERT DILLINGER

1903-1934

"We only stole from the
bankers what the bankers
stole from the people."

Figure 10.21 John Dillinger propaganda poster distributed by the Chicago Cabal
(aka Robert Anton Wilson and Robert Shea)

The
JOHN DILLINGER DIED FOR YOU
Society

October 26, 1970

Dr. Ignotum P. Ignotius, KPS
High Priest -- POEE Head Temple
Officer of the Polyfather

Dear Doctor:

Packmules being slow and contrary beasts, your letter and enclosure
only yesterday reached our remote hideout in the mountains of
northern Illinois. Luckily, however, we have airmail service going out.

Myself and my Consigliori, Mr. Helmer, have never clearly understood
the distinctions between the Discordian Society and the P.O.E.E. On
one occasion when a practice round of tracer set fire to a stand of
wild hemp and we battled the smoke and flames for what began to seem
like many hours, and eventually seemed not worth the effort, which
was finally abandoned in our increasing appreciation of the
extraordinary colours -- on that unusual occasion it all seemed clear.
But after a time, the understanding vanished.

But there are many things I do not understand, will never understand,
and therefore do not care to understand. My Consigliori advises me
that this is evidence of great wisdom. (Meanwhile, I have fetched him
out to secure more hemp.)

In so far as I am an Episkipos in the Discordian Society -- at least
having, through the good offices of our Chaplain Rev. Charles Arthur
Floyd II, a document to that effect -- I presumably am a Discordian.
But of course I would not object to ordination in the Paratheoetc.
In this business, every connection counts.

While the J.D.DF.Y.S. aids and abets all conspiracies and is eager
to confuse its enemies through affiliations, acquisitions, absorptions
and subordinations, it does have an independent membership and
history, dating back to 1966, when a small mob first assembled in
Austin, Texas, at a notorious beer garden, and swore a blood oath
that none would rest until Johnnie's penis -- the Dear Departed
Member, supposedly pickled and on display at the Smithsonian -- could
be found and reclaimed. Since that time we have carried on our
search for this Holy Grail or, more accurately, this Piece of the
True Cross. (Needless to say, the Smithsonian's frightened bureaucrats
have obstructed our quest by the expected denials and a general lack
of cooperation.)

But none of this need interfere with the close cooperation, amalgamation
and collaboration between the Society and any other non-violent
terrorist organizations, especially those dedicated to conspiracy and

Figure 10.22a Letter to Ignotum P. Ignotius (aka Greg Hill)

from Dr. Horace Naismith (aka Wilson and/or Shea)

enlightenment. (Actually, we are not opposed to violence in principle; while the Society rejects capital punishment as a barbaric and counter-productive policy, it has nothing against an occasional old-fashioned killing. Purely a matter of situation ethics.) Which is to say that any member of the D.S.C. or the P.O.E.E. is welcome to join the J.D.D.F.Y.S. as an officially appointed Assistant Treasurer duly authorized to collect an initiation fee of any amount from any new member he may recruit, and keep it. (Johnnie would have wanted it that way.)

As Johnnie used to say:

Keep calm and lie down on the floor,

Dr. Horace Naismith

Chief Assistant Treasurer
JOHN DILLINGER DIED FOR YOU SOCIETY

Figure 10.22b Page 2 of letter to Ignotum P. Ignotius from Dr. Horace Naismith

JOHN DILLINGER DIED FOR YOU

<u>FACT SHEET ON SAINT JOHN THE MARTYR</u>
<u>TO DISPEL OLD MYTHS AND RUMORS</u>
        <u>....AND REPLACE THEM WITH NEW ONES!</u>

WAS DILLINGER A MURDERER?

> John Herbert Dillinger (1903-1934) was never convicted of homicide
> in any court at any time. While this was partly due to the inability
> of the police to ever hold him in custody long enough for him to
> be brought to trial, the fact remains: On the record, no act of
> murder was ever proven against St. John. Can any recent American
> President make the same claim, after hundreds of thousands of
> our boys were lost in wars they started?

WAS DILLINGER THE WORST THIEF OF HIS TIME?

> While it is true that he often found it necessary, during those
> hard Depression years, to make withdrawals from banks under some-
> what unorthodox circumstances, Dillinger's larceny was actually
> quite moderate. The people of his home town (Mooresville, Indiana)
> in a petition for clemency wrote to the Governor, "It is our
> opinion that many of the financial institutions of the state have
> just as criminally robbed our citizens without any effort being
> made to punish the perpetrators." The perpetrators of these
> larger robberies are, in fact, still free and still operating
> their usury-ridden banks.

COULD DILLINGER WALK THROUGH WALLS?

> Many accept this as the explanation of his remarkable escape
> from the "escape-proof" Crown Point Jail (March 2, 1934), but
> the John Dillinger Died For You Society does not demand this
> as an article of faith among members. It's enough to believe
> that Johnnie was a lot smarter than most cops.

WHAT CONTRIBUTIONS DID DILLINGER MAKE TO MANKIND?

> John Dillinger pioneered the technique of the Non-Negotiable
> Demand now widely in use among dissenters; in fact, he never
> left a building before his demand was granted. He taught
> greedy bankers the philosophy of Oriental meditation and
> detachment from materialistic concerns, always advising them
> kindly, "Lie down on the floor and keep calm." By his personal
> example, he proved that even in Hard Times, a man need not wait
> for Washington to clear up a mess, but can go out and solve
> his own poverty problem simply and directly.

IS IT OBLIGATORY TO PRAY TO SAINT JOHN?

> In John's own words, "You can get more with a simple prayer and
> a Thompson submachinegun than you can with a simple prayer alone."

Figure 10.23 John Dillinger factsheet compiled by the Chicago Cabal

THE ERISIAN MOVEMENT · HOUSE OF APOSTLES
( )Official Business   **OF ERIS**
( )Surreptitious Business

RUMORS TO BE SPREAD

Charles Arthur Floyd II, son of Charles Arthur Floyd I ("Pretty
Boy" Floyd) is chairman of the Chicago branch of the John
Dillinger Died For You Society and is planning to knock over
the Federal Reserve Bank on Wall Street.

All 32nd degree Masons are members of the Bavarian Illuminati.

Hassan i Sabbah X, president of the Black Lotus Society, is the
chief supplier of hashish for Bavarian Illuminati meetings.

J. Edgar Hoover is really the old Bolshevick, Kamenev, and is
the number one Communist agent in America.

All Grand Exalted Cyclopses of the Ku Klux Klan are Illuminati
members, but no others, not even Imperial Wizard Robert Shelton,
are members or are aware that the Klan has been infiltrated.

Shirley Temple Black is the Secret financial backer of the Up
Against the Wall M..... f..... .

Attempts were made to recruit Timothy Leary in 1962, but he
refused, and Illuminati agents in government have been behind
his persecution ever since.

The reason Marquis de Sade went broke is that he poured all his
money into support of the American Revolution. De Sade and Washington disgraced the Illuminati by engaging in sodomitic orgies
during a sacred conspiratorial meeting with John James
Audobon and other Illuminati leaders in a secret location in
the Mayan ruins, 1796.

Washington grew hemp at Mount Vernon. (This one happens to be
true, but spread it anyway.)

"Accidents have a strange way of happening to people who know
too much about the Bavarian Illuminati."

Every time the message "In thanks to Saint Jude for favors
granted" appears in the personals columns of a newspaper,
it means that the Illuminati have completed another successful assassination.

"Of course, the Illuminati and the Thuggee knew all about the
Orgasm Death Gimmick long before Burroughs put it into his books."

Figure 10.24 More propaganda from the John Dillinger Died For Your Sins Society,
courtesy of the Chicago Cabal

UNIFORM DONOR CARD

OF <u>JOHN HERBERT DILLINGER</u>

Print or type name of donor

In the hope that I may help others, I hereby make this anatomical gift, if medically acceptable, to take effect upon my death. The words and marks below indicate my desires.

I give: (a) _____ any needed organs or parts

        (b) ✔ only the following organs or parts

<u>PENIS</u>

Specify the organ(s) or part(s)

for the purposes of transplantation, therapy, medical research or education;

        (c) _____ my body for anatomical study if needed.

Limitations or special wishes, if any: <u>SEND TO SMITHSONIAN INSTITUTE</u>

Figure 10.25 Dillinger donor card concocted by the Chicago Cabal.

Legend has it that Dillinger's 23 inch penis is now on exhibit at the Smithsonian Institute.

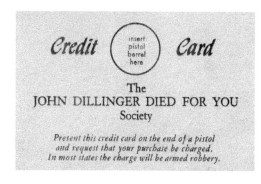

Figure 10.26 John Dillinger Died For Your Sins membership cards

Appendexia Discordia

featuring:

The Discordian Holy Books

A Who's Who of Early
Discordianism

The Brunswick Shrine Realized

Assorted Fnords

The Discordian Dialogues

The Discordian Holy Books

How I Found Goddess (1965)

Kerry Thornley

AT THE MARRIAGE of King Peleus to the sea nymph Thetis it began.
Eris, the goddess of Discord, who had a seedy reputation as a sower of
strife, was not invited. This really pissed Her. She is still pissed about it,
in fact—at everybody. That is why we Discordians call it the doctrine of Original
Snub.

But our Eris was—and still is (be She exalted!)—a clever goddess. To gain Her
revenge She tiptoed up to the door of that Olympian banquet hall and threw a
golden apple into the festivities. Upon it was engraved: FOR THE PRETTY ONE.

(According to *The Honest Book of Truth*, a holy work of the Discordian Society, the apple landed on the edge of a punch bowl, and cracked it, and made the
Nectar—in the colorful words of The Honest Book of Truth—"leak therefrom."
Hence we have in our language the expression "crackpot" to denote a true Disciple
of Eris and the proverb: "The golden apple spoils the punch," which has since been
corrupted. Edith Hamilton fails to mention this in her version of the story.)

Now all the goddesses wanted this apple—each thinking herself the one for which
it was so obviously intended—but in the end it was decided that The Pretty One
was Aphrodite, Hera, Pallas Athena. Zeus was asked to be the final judge in this
on-the-spot Olympia contest, but he was no fool either. "Nothing doing," he said.

To better shirk this whole responsibility he even went so far as to suggest a young
man who, in his mind, was an excellent judge of beauty—Paris, a young shepherd
prince of Mount Ida, near Troy.

Now each of the goddesses, being only divine, offered Paris a bribe. Hera would make him lord of Europe and Asia. Athena would lead him and the Trojans to victory against Greece. But Paris, being only human, took Aphrodite's offer: that the fairest woman of all the world should be his. This turned out to be Helen of Troy. The result was the Trojan War which, as everybody knows, sparked that chain of events culminating in the present crisis with which the administration is grappling, as well as all the previous ones.

What it amounts to is that Eris still rules the earth and probably always will. We Discordians can prove this with no sweat. We just point to all the chaos in the world around us and say, "Look! You think this mess just happened?" Naturally, all sane people agree that somebody had to put it here.

Well, so much for the Ancient Discordian Society, which began shortly after this spectacular exhibition of party crashing and lasted until Rome fell and Western civilization silently miscarried with the popularization of Christianity. (The Romans, incidentally enough, referred to Eris as Discordia, feeling no doubt that such a name was more to the point.)

Since I am one of the founders of the modern Discordian Society—and also its Infallible Leader, The Bull Goose of Limbo—I'm qualified to bring you up to date.

It happened in an all-night bowling alley in Whittier, California. (Notice that it was a *bowl*ing alley. Remember how the golden apple cracked a punch *bowl*? Our religion is riddled with such tiny miracles!) Simply stated, the founding of the Discordian Society occurred when Greg Hill—the Omnibenevolent Polyfather of Virginity-in-Gold—and I decided we needed a religion so we could have peace of mind. Everybody knows you need a religion to have peace of mind. So we did the logical thing. We started a religion.

(In *The Honest Book of Truth* there is a bunch of bullshit about darkness overwhelming us and Eris appearing in a vision, but that is just there for the impressionable. You have to exaggerate sometimes nowadays to make your point.)

With an understanding that transcended our years—as this was back in 1958 or '59—we decided we needed something *not* to explain the order of things, as other religions had done, but to account for the miraculous *dis*order of everything. A Discordian Society was the obvious and only answer.

The Discordian Society is a nonprophet religious disorganization devoted to the just glorification of Eris. Since its beginning with only two members about five years ago, enrollment has nearly tripled—and that is only counting the Enlightened, Inner-Circle Discordians, called Episkoposes. There are also many others, including millions of unconscious, intuitive disciples who serve in the armed forces of the nations of the world. (Those in the United States are called The Knights of the Five-Sided Temple.)

Our symbol is a golden apple, called The Golden Apple, imposed over a pentagon—as those were the two most fitting emblems of chaos we could imagine. The official seal, however, is more elaborate. It is like the *yin* and the *yang* of Taoism, except with The Golden Apple and Pentagon on the opposite sides of the circle. We call this the *hodge* and the *podge* or The Sacred Chao.

Had I known in advance I was going to found the Discordian Society, I could not have picked a better cofounder than Greg Hill. The first thing he did was title himself Holy Polyfather of Virginity-in-Gold (later he changed the Holy to Omnibenevolent, or Omni-anything-else, depending on one's mood).

And when I declared myself Infallible Leader and Grand Papal Dictator (later I changed this to the more politic Bull Goose of Limbo) he at once, almost, decided to become a heretic. So to this day his official title is Omniwhatchamacallit Polyfather of Virginity-in-gold and High Priest of the Heretic Fringe and Protestant Persuasion. (I remain Infallible Leader of the Orthodoxy.)

We both realize that schisms are in keeping with the basic principles of all great religions—as well as the basic laws of discord—so our conflict is an amicable one, and seldom if ever do we excommunicate each other now. (In fact there is some talk of reunification in the distant future.)

Each sect of the Discordian Society has its own holy work. *The Honest Book of Truth* is that of the Orthodoxy, though Heretics often quote from it to bolster their arguments—usually against the Orthodoxy—when the copy fits. The *Principia Discordia (Or How The West Was Lost)* is that of The Heretic Fringe and Protestant Persuasion, and it is by-and-large accepted by the more Orthodox (except for some libelous remarks about The Orthodoxy which appear therein).

We also have plenty of Dogma—the most interesting of which is The Law of Fives—but perhaps more typical, we have Katma. Most people don't know about Katma, since only true religions have any. But since ours is a true religion, we have Katma all over the place.

Katma is what heathens call miracles and skeptics call coincidence. It is Katma, for example, that Eris broke a punch *bowl* with her apple and that the Discordian Society was founded in a *bowl*ing alley. Katma is the opposite of Dogma. Dogma is based on faith; Katma is sensory evidence that Eris is the One, True Goddess Of Everything.

The Law Of Fives, as I indicated, is Dogma. It is a Law which states everything happens in fives or can in some manner be divided by five. It is Katma, however, that everything happens to indeed confirm this Law. The Pentagon, for example, has five sides (that, in fact, is the observation which inspired The Law of Fives). There are countless other manifestations of fiveness in the universe and each of them is Katma. (That Katma has five letters in itself is Katma.)

Other Katma includes the importance of the apple in the primary myths of both Discordianism and Christianity (thus proving Discordianism and proving that

Christianity is really corrupted Discordianism), the fact that the pentagram which is the official emblem of the United States and the Soviet Union and werewolves resembles a five-pointed star, and the little-known truth that the "eristic" is derived from Eris.

When a Discordian is particularly fond of discovering and pointing out Katma to demonstrate the divinity of Eris, we say that he is Katmatic.

There are many Katmatic Discordians.

The Kataclysm (1965)

Kerry Thornley

WE ORTHODOX DISCORDIANS who worship Eris, who among other things is the Greek Goddess of Discord, call the formal study of Katma—the opposite of Dogma—The Kataclysm.

Actually the study of Katma, or Kataclysm, is a complex matter. It is divided into five parts: 1) discovering Katma, 2) interpreting Katma, 3) certifying Katma, 4) classifying Katma, and 5) fattening Katma.

Before one may discover Katma he, unlike Columbus for example, must know exactly what it is he is seeking to discover. Katma is anything which in some more or less isolated manner goes to further assure those who interpret it that Eris is indeed the Supreme Will in the universe, as will already be evident anyhow to anyone sufficiently interested to seek Katma. This consideration in itself, by the way, is Katma—as is the fact that Columbus discovered America looking for India, thought America was India after he discovered it, and persisted to his death in thinking the world was round instead of flat. Because Katma is that, considering all his misconceptions, Columbus managed to reach a substantially correct conclusion concerning the shape of the earth.

Katmatic interpretation is difficult to teach. It is a talent, owned by certain very gifted types. Due to their superior ability at interpreting Katma, these types are intuitively envied by the unenlightened—and that is why non-Discordians call them paranoid personalities, which is a term of disapproval, and conspire against them, seeking in most cases to have them locked up in asylums. In truth these so-called paranoids are highly Katmatic people and are among the Elect and Chosen Ones of Eris—so everybody should stop persecuting them. (That Katmatic people, the Elect of Eris, are discriminated against in a universe owned and operated by Eris is another example of Katma.)

Certification of Katma takes place whenever a True, Inner-Circle Discordian says "Hail Eris" in recognition of having observed or heard of an example of Katma. All True, Inner-Circle Discordians are, further, themselves living Manifestations of Katma. Therefore, the official greeting between True, Inner Circle Discordians is: "Hail Eris!"

Classifying Katma is simple. There are only two kinds. Katma Major or Katma Minor. Katma Major is fully developed, ready-made Katma—and is called simply Katma. Underdeveloped or uncertified Katma is Katma Minor, which is either Katma which appears evident only after much complex interpretation or Katma over which no qualified Discordian has yet said "Hail Eris." Such Katma, to distinguish it from Katma Major, is known officially as Kitma.

Katma fattening occurs when a Discordian Compiler of Truth—Esoteric—writes any Holy Writ which goes to further bolster the Katmatic standing of any Katma or Kitma. For example when I, as Infallible Leader of the Orthodoxy, wrote as Dogma The Law of Fives, stating that everything happens in fives or can in some manner be divided by five, The Pentagon in Washington—which due to its method of functioning was already Katma—was made even more Katmatic by the fact of its having five sides. It is now the fattest Katma of them all.

When a Compiler of Truth is especially adept at fattening Katma in this manner over a long period of time he is accorded the special honor of placing a P.B.K. after his name, which stands for Phi Beta Katma.

The Honest Book of Truth (1969)

Lord Omar Khayyam Ravenhurst, KSC

THE BOOK OF UTERUS

– I –

1. Before the beginning was the Nonexistent Chao, balanced in Oblivion by the Perfect Counterpushpull of the Hodge and Podge.

2. Whereupon, by an Act of Happenstance, the Hodge began gradually to over-power the Podge—and the Primal Chaos thereby came to be.

3. So in the beginning was the Primal Chaos, balanced on the Edge of Oblivion by the Perfect Counterpullpush of the Podge and Hodge.

4. Whereupon, by the Law of Negative Reversal, the Podge swiftly underpowered the Hodge and Everything broke loose.

5. And therein emerged the Active Force of Discord, the Subtle Manifestation of the Non-existent Chao, to guide Everything along the Path back to Oblivion—that it might not become lost among Precepts of Order in the Region of Thud.

6. Forasmuch as it was Active, the Force of Discord entered the State of Confusion, wherein It copulated with the Queen and begat Eris, Our Lady of Discord and Gross Manifestation of the Nonexistent Chao.

7. And under Eris Confusion became established, and was hence called Bureaucracy; while over Bureaucracy Eris became established, and was hence called Discordia.

8. By and by it came to pass that the Establishment of Bureaucracy perished in a paper shortage.

9. Thus it was, in accord with the Law of Laws.

10. During and after the Fall of the Establishment of Bureaucracy was the Aftermath, an Age of Disorder in which calculations, computations, and reckonings were put away by the Children of Eris in Acceptance and Preparation for the Return to Oblivion to be followed by a Repetition of the Universal Absurdity. Moreover, of Itself the Coming of Aftermath waseth a Resurrection of the Freedom-flowing Chaos. (Hail Eris!)

11. Herein was set into motion the Eristic Pattern, which would Repeat Itself Five Times Over Seventy Three Times, after which nothing would happen.

– II –

1. Hail Eris, Daughter of Discord.

2. Hail Eris, Princess of Confusion.

3. Hail Eris, Gross Manifestation of Non-existent Chao.

4. Hail Discordia, Queen of Bureaucracy.

5. Hail Discordia, Mother of Aftermath.

– III –

1. So the Passage of Being is Divided into Five Ages of Eris: the Age of Chaos, the Age of Discord, the Age of Confusion, the Age of Bureaucracy, and the Age of Disorder of the Aftermath.

2. Now an Age of Eris might be, in the Passage of Time, an Interval or a Season or an Error—or some longer span.

3. An Age of Chaos is one in which Things Seem Ready to Happen and, a midst much activity, no specific Direction seemeth yet to be emerging. These are Ages of Balance, wherein one action negates another in the Eye of the Observer, who does not yet exist.

4. An Age of Discord is one wherein Something Happens to Activate the Cycle of Events and the main theme of Whatever Is Coming begins to reveal Itself. These are also known as Primitive Ages, coming as they do after the Primal Ages of Chaos, and they are Ages of Unbalance as well.

5. An Age of Confusion, or an Ancient Age, is one in which History As We Know It begins to unfold, in which Whatever Is Coming emerges in Corporal Form, more or less, and such times are Ages of Balanced Unbalance, or Unbalanced Balance.

6. An Age of Bureaucracy is an Imperial Age in which Things Mature, in which Confusion becomes entrenched, and during which Balanced Balance, or Stagnation, is attained.

7. An Age of Disorder or an Aftermath is an Apocalyptic Period of Transition back to Chaos through the Screen of Oblivion into which passeth, finally. These are the Ages of Unbalanced Balance.

– IV –

1. Hark, unto each Age of Eris—Chaos, Discord, Confusion, Bureaucracy, and Aftermath—is assigned an Apostle of Eris. Hail Eris.

2. Hung Mung, Chaoist Sage and True Man of Old, is Patriarch of Chaos.

3. Van Van Mojo, Doctor of Hoodoo and Vexes, or Patamunzo Linganananda, Tantric Consort of Mother Chaos, is Patriarch of Discord, the other being an Imposter.

4. Blessed Saint Gulik the Stoned and Sri Syadasti, Indian Pundit of the Peyotl Tribe, are—as Duel Aspects of the same Essential Being (that of Being High)—Patriarchs of Confusion.

5. Zarathud the Staunch, Chaosphe Bible Banger and Offender of the Faith, is Patriarch of Bureaucracy.

6. The Elder Malaclypse, Chaotic Prophet of the Bygone, as First Apostle of Eris, is Patriarch of Disorder of Aftermath, last of the Ages of Eris. Hail Eris.

THE BOOK OF EXPLANATIONS

– I –

1. There one day came to Lord Omar, Bull Goose of Limbo, a Messenger of our Lady who told him of a Sacred Mound wherein was buried an Honest Book.

2. And the Angel of Eris bade of the Lord: Go ye hence and dig the Truth, that ye may come to know it and, knowing it, spread it and, spreading it, wallow in it and, wallowing in it, lie in it and, lying in the Truth, become a Poet of the Word and a Sayer of Sayings—an Inspiration to all men and a Scribe to the Gods.

3. So Omar went forth to Sacred Mount, which was to the East of Nullah, and thereupon he worked digging in the sand for five days and five nights, but found no Book.

4. And at the end of five days and five nights of digging, in came to pass that Omar was exhausted. So he put his shovel to one side and bedded himself down on the sand, using a Golden Chest he had uncovered on the first day of his labors as a pillow.

5. Omar slept.

6. On the fifth day of his sleeping, Lord Omar fell into a Trance, and there came to him in the Dream a Messenger of our Lady who told him of a Sacred Grove wherein was hidden a Golden Chest.

7. And the Angel of Eris bade of the Lord: Go ye hence and lift the Stash, that ye may come to own it and, owning it, share it, and sharing it, love in it and, loving in it, dwell in it and, dwelling in the Stash, become a Poet of the Word and a Sayer of Sayings—an Inspiration to all men and a Scribe to the Gods.

8. But Omar lamented, saying unto the Angel: What is this shit, man? What care I for the Word and Sayings? What care I for the Inspiration of all men? Wherein does it profit a man to be a Scribe to the Gods when the Scribes of the Governments do nothing, yet are paid better wages?

9. And, lo, the Angel waxed in anger and Omar was stricken to the Ground by an Invisible Hand and did not arise for five days and five nights.

10. And it came to pass that on the fifth night he dreamt, and in his Dream he had a Vision, and in this Vision there came unto him a Messenger of Our Lady who entrusted to him a Rigoletto cigar box containing many filing cards, some of them in packs with rubber bands around, and upon these cards were sometimes written verses, while upon others nothing was written.

11. Thereupon the Angel Commanded the Lord: Take ye this Honest Book of Truth to thine bosom and cherish it. Carry it forth into the Land and lay it before Kings of Nations and Collectors of Garbage. Preach from it unto the Righteous, that they may renounce their ways and repent; unto the Sinful, that they may be made to feel Silly; and unto the Silly, that they may be made to feel Righteous and renounce their ways and repent.

– II –

1. Now this sort of double talk was none too clear to Omar, but he journeyed over the Plain of Truth, northward, rounding the Old Wall of Defense, and entered Axtopolis through the East Checkpoint, whereupon he espied a Garbage Collector.

2. In accordance with the Commandment of the Angel, he laid The Book before him, and the other did collect it and throw it into his cart.

3. And though Omar did bid of the Collector of Garbage, in words that were both sweet and bitter, to surrender back the cigar box containing the cards designated by the Angel as The Honest Book of Truth, the Collector was to him as one who might be smitten deaf, saying only: Gainst the rules, y' know.

4. At the fifth repeating of these words by the Collector, Omar waxed pissed. Even did he curse the man, even calling him a toad and a hyena, and even calling his ancestors worms, rats, apes, chickens, cockroaches, termites, newts, silverfish, earwigs, eels, maggots, gnats, lice, fleas, fungi, snakes, skunks, gophers and guinea pigs.

5. After which did the Collector reply unto him: Rules is rules.

6. So Omar spake, saying this time to the Collector that his children would be slugs and snails, and that his children's children would be ants, ticks, leeches, chiggers, swine, goats, sheep, mice, flies, do-do birds, and hippotamuses, so pissed did he wax.

7. But the Collector only pushed his cart along and said: No exception—'cause if I give you back your garbage, then everybody would want their garbage back and this here garbage is Government Property now.

8. Upon which occasion did Omar say that then the Government of Axtopolis must surely be one of vultures and buzzards.

9. Whereupon a policeman appeared out of the blue (for in that city their uniforms were green).

10. And, lo, did he arrest Lord Omar for: uttering treasonous statements; probably nurturing seditious intentions; and, entering into a dispute with a public servant.

11. Omar was thereupon placed in chains and marched at bayonet point to the Axtopos for questioning.

– III –

1. At the Axtopos, Omar was taken to a desk, in front of which he was told to stand with his hands at his sides.

2. Five hours later, there came to sit behind the desk an officer, who spake thusly, I am the Collector Inspector; it has come to my attention that you were apprehended harassing a Garbage Collector.

3. It is my duty (spake the Inspector further) to inform you of your rights under the Honest Government of Axtopolis, based as it is upon the system of Horseshit Dictatorship: you have none.

THE BOOK OF PREDICTIONS

– I –

1. Once on top of a time there came out of the West a beggar, who strode through the dust of The Land in silence, wearing a purple robe and also having purple skin. Now this man bore a very wise countenance, and he also bore a very large wine flask on his back, and it did leak.

2. Further, he bore a hole in the ground beside the road between the City and the River, and therein he dwelt and was content.

3. And in the passage of the days, travelers on the road did notice him, and saw they that he *was* content.

4. Soon there were murmurings amongst the people of the City. We, spake they, in our wooden houses with all our riches and bitches are not content, but instead envy we the people of Elsewhere. Yet, spake they one to the other, behold this purple beggar who lives in a mean hole beside the road—and see ye sure that he is content.

5. Verily, said one unto another of the people of The City, this man must indeed be a True Sage. And so it was that henceforth this man who dwelt with his wine flask in a hole by the road was known in The Land as the Purple Sage.

6. And it did come to pass that word of the contentment of the Purple Sage did reach even into the ears of the Mayor of the City.

7. So he did with his Vices travel to the place by the road near where the Purple Sage dwelt in his hole, and he did see that therein *was* the Sage and, lo, he saw that it was as the people had spoken: The Purple Sage *was* content, and moreover did he bear a very wise countenance.

8. And the Vices rendered to the Sage gifts of the finest wine, and in flowery speech the Mayor then bade of him some True Words, that the Secret of His Contentment might be imparted and his Excellency be an humble receptacle thereof.

9. But the Purple Sage only fixed them with his eyes. He spake no Words.

– II –

1. But, lo, thereupon the Purple Sage cast open his mouth and, throwing his tongue into activity, gave voice to his thoughts in such words as follow thereupon.

2. The Earth quakes and the Heavens rattle; the beasts of nature flock together and the nations of men flock apart: volcanoes usher up heat while elsewhere water becomes ice and melts; and then on other days it just rains.

3. Indeed do many things come to pass.

4. Forasmuch as many things come to pass, it is better to be wise than a damned fool.

5. And knew ye well this Knowledge—that the fulfillment of All Wisdom is in damned foolishness.

6. Wipe thine ass with What Is Written and grin like a ninny at What Is Spoken. Take thine refuge with thine wine in the Nothin behind Everything, spitting on all distinctions as you hurry along the Path.

7. Thus spake the Purple Sage, who thereupon belched and slept for five days and five nights without dreaming.

THE BOOK OF ADVICE

– I –

1. Seek into the Chaos if thou wouldst be wise
And find ye delight in her Great Surprise!
Look in the Chao if thou wantest to know
What's in a Chao and why it ain't so!

2. Things of Order are Things of Death
Perfectly still and without any breath.

3. Climb into the Chao with a friend or two
And follow the Way it carries you
Adrift like a Lunatic Lifeboat Crew
Over the waves in whatever you do.

4. The Chao don't exist
And is outside of Time—
Quite beyond Reason,
But easy to Rhyme.

5. Mister Order, he runs at a very good pace
But Old Mother Chaos is winning the race.

6. Chose ye this day on whom ye will bet,
But pick Mister Order and you'll go into debt.

7. All Things are Perfect
To every last flaw
And bound in accord
With Eris's Law.

8. So know ye the Fact
That when Matter was Mixed
That Old Chao ran the Act
And the Game is now Fixed.

– II –

1. The Words of the Foolish and those of the Wise
Are not far apart in Discordian Eyes.

– III –

1. The dog did a dance after dinner,
But the cat did it better, so she was the winner.

2. Go to the cat
And see where it's at.

3. Cats are examples
To all who are wise;
Note how they catch
And gobble up flies!

4. Cats are soft and cats are nice
To those of us who are not mice.

5. Plagued with rats?
Get some cats.

THE BOOK OF GOOKS

– I –

1. Lao-tse, wandering east, encountered Hung Mung, who was rambling about, slapping his buttocks and hopping like a bird.

2. Amazed, The Old Boy stood reverently and said, "Venerable Sir, who are you and why are you doing this?" Hung Mung went on slapping and hopping, saying, "I am enjoying myself."

3. Lao-tse said, "I wish to ask you a question." Hung Mung looked up and said, "Pooh!"

4. Lao-tse, however, continued, "These are disordered times; rewards and punishments have pitted man against man and lured men into deceit and scheming for position; humanity and justice have replaced natural goodness; men have lost their original innocence and now even the four seasons are off schedule. I wish to restore order—how shall I go about it?"

5. Hung Mung slapped his buttocks, hopped about, and shook his head, saying, "I do not know! I do not know!"

6. Lao-tse could not pursue his question, but five years afterwards he again happened upon Hung Mung in the East.

7. Delighted, he hastened forth and said, "Have you forgotten me, Great Sage of High? Have you forgotten me, O Heaven??" He then bowed twice to the ground, wishing to receive his instructions.

8. Hung Mung said: "Wandering aimlessly, I know not what I seek; carried by impulse, I know not where I go; I drift about and know that Nothing proceeds without method—

9. Lao-tse replied, "I also seem aimless, and yet people follow me wherever I go. I cannot help it. What should I do?'

10. Hung Mung said, "What disturbs the mysterious ecology of Heaven scatters herds of animals, makes birds sing at night, turns lawns brown, and is disaster to all insects."

11. The Old Boy replied, "It has been difficult getting this meeting with you, O Sage; I should like to have a True Word."

12. Hung Mung said, "Ah! Your mind nourished! Do nothing! Neglect your body! Cast away hearing and sight!—and cultivate a grand similarity with the Primal Chaos!"

13. Upon hearing this, Lao-tse was enlightened.

THE GOSPEL ACCORDING TO FRED

– I –

1. In the beginning there was Chaos.

2. But when Discord emerged therefrom it brought forth as its twin a certain amount of Order, that the Disordered Array might seem more glorious by comparison.

3. And it was ordained on High that unto each universe, each galaxy, each system, each world, each continent, each nation, each province, each settlement, and each individual should be issued a limited Ration of Order.

4. And so that this Order might not increase itself and get out of the Five-Fingered Hand of Eris, it was further ordained on High that there should come into existence a Law whereby it might be governed.

5. And this Law became known as the Law for the Government of Order, reading: Henceforth and forever, let it be that whosoever striveth to increase whatever amount of Order he finds by the Grace of Eris to be, he shall only by his efforts reduce it.

6. And, behold, thusly was the Law formulated: Imposition of Order = Escalation of Chaos!

– II –

1. Be it known that In Truth there be Five Apostles of Eris, that these are High Personages, Exemplars to Man, and Chosen Ambassadors of Mortals at will and Inspire them to Consummate Acts of Inanity, thereby.

2. Know ye that the First Apostle of Eris is Malaclypse (the Elder), Chaotic Prophet of the Bygone.

3. And hark that the Holiest Apostle of Eris is Patamunzo Lingananda, Tantric Consort of Mother Chaos.

4. And heed ye that the Wisest Apostle of Eris is Hung Mung, Chaoist Sage and True Man of Old.

5. And behold that Most Devout among the Apostles of Eris is Zarathud the Staunch, Chaosphe Bible Banger and Offender of the Faith.

6. And, lo, Saint Gulik, Ecstatic Patron of the Chaotic Array, is Most High among the Apostles of Eris or anyone else. The High Saint is also his designation, as well as: Blessed Saint Gulik the Stoned.

7. Blessed Saint Gulik is also Sri Syadasti, Syadavaktavya, Syadastic Syannasti, Syadasti Cacaktavyasca, Syadasti Syannasti Syadavaktavyasca—Indian Pundit of the Peyotl Tribe, son of High Chief Morning Glory Seed and squaw Merry Jane—nonidentical with St. Gulik only in time, space, physical characteristics, and personality.

– III –

1. The Hell Law says that Hell is reserved exclusively for them that believe in it. Further, the lowest Rung in Hell is reserved for them that believe in it on the supposition that they'll go there if they don't.

2. To the True Children of Eris, Hell is known as the Region of Thud, and those who do not call it Thud can go to Hell.

3. Thud can seldom be found in the same place more than twice in a row, as it is conditional, not geographic.

4. The Four Conditions of Thud are: Nothing Happening; Nobody Caring; The Law of Fives Not Working, and Lawns Turning Brown.

5. Wheresoever do these Four Conditions prevail, it may be said surely that here be the Region of Thud, or some Prefecture of it.

6. There are Seven Prefectures, or Rungs, in Thud.

7. President of these United Rungs of Thud is Dr. Van Van Mojo, Dhv (Doctor of Hoodoo and Vexes), Imposter Apostle of Eris, Believer Deceiver, and Maker of Fine Dolls.

8. It is Dr. Mojo's contention that Patamunzo Lingananda is the Real Impostor Apostle, and he the Genuine Original Historic Creole Apostle of Eris.

9. Van Van Mojo heaps hatred and curses upon Patamunzo Lingananda, while Lingananda eternally sends back vibrations of his all-compassionate love and blessings, along with an occasional anonymous poison-pen letter.

– IV –

1. Now the Four Conditions do prevail in all the Seven Prefectures of Thud, and also in Thud Proper, to boot.

2. In addition, there is to be found within each of the Seven Prefectures a Distinguishing Presence, which separates each from the others, and from Thud Proper.

3. In the First Prefecture, for example, there dwells a Black Dragon in a cave.

4. In the Second Prefecture a Blue Dragon lives in a lake.

5. In the Third Prefecture a Green Dragon lurks in a forest or jungle.

6. In the Fourth Prefecture is a Red Dragon, basking in a great fire.

7. In the Fifth Prefecture may be found the Gate to Nothingness, beyond which one finds the Road to the Aneristic Empire.

8. In the Sixth Prefecture is a Yellow Dragon, very conspicuous against whatever background, but making for a nice color scheme, what with all the brown lawns.

9. At last, in the Seventh Prefecture, or the lowest Rung of the Region of Thud, are to be found Oil Sprites, everywhere.

10. In Thud Proper is a White Dragon, hibernating in a patch of warm snow.

11. Some say, though, that the Region of Thud does not exist, while others say it is only a state of mind. Frankly, I think it is a bunch of insane bullshit, and I record it here for the devout and stupid.

Discordian Cosmogony

Gregory Hill

I N THE BEGINNING there was Void, who had two daughters: one (the smaller) was that of Being, named Eris, and one (the larger) was that of Non-Being, named Aneris. (To this day, the fundamental truth that Aneris is the larger is apparent to all who compare the many things that do not exist with the comparatively few things that do exist.)

Eris had been born pregnant, and after 55 years (goddesses have an unusually long gestation period, longer than even that of elephants), Her pregnancy bore the fruits of many things, which were all composed of the five basic elements, Sweet, Boom, Pungent, Prickle, and Orange. Aneris, however, had been created sterile. When she saw Eris enjoying Herself so greatly with all the existent things She had borne, Aneris became jealous, and finally one day she stole some existent things and changed them into nonexistent things and claimed them as her own children. This deeply hurt Eris, who felt that Her sister was unjust (being so much larger anyway) to deny Her Her small joy. So She made Herself swell again to bear more things. And She swore that no matter how many of Her begotten Aneris would steal, She would beget more. In return, Aneris swore that no matter how many existent things Eris brought forth, she would eventually find them and turn them into nonexistent things for her own. (To this day, things appear and disappear in this very manner.)

At first, the things brought forth by Eris were in a state of chaos and went in every which way, but by the by she began playing with them and ordered some of them just to see what would happen. Some pretty things arose from this play, and for the next five zillion years She amused Herself by creating order. She grouped some things with others, and some groups with others, and big groups with little groups, and all combinations thereof, until She had many grand schemes that delighted Her.

Engrossed in establishing order, She finally one day noticed disorder, which previously had not occurred to her. There were many ways in which chaos was ordered, and many ways in which it was not. "Ha!" She thought, "Here shall be a new game!" She taught order and disorder to play with each other in contest games, and to take turns amusing each other. She named the side of disorder "Eristic," after Herself, because being is anarchic. Then, feeling sympathy for Her lonely sister, She named the other side "Aneristic," which flattered Aneris and smoothed the friction between them a little.

Now, all this time, Void was somewhat disturbed. He felt unsatisfied, for he had created only physical existence and physical non-existence, and had neglected the spiritual. As He contemplated this, a great Quiet was caused, and He went into a state of deep Sleep that lasted for five eras. At the end of this work, He begat a brother to Eris and Aneris, who was Spirituality, and who had no name at all.

When the sisters heard this, they both confronted Void, and pleaded that He not forget them, His Firstborn. So Void decreed that their brother, having no form, was to reside with Aneris in Non-Being, then to leave her and, that He might play with order and disorder, reside with Eris in Being. But Eris became filled with sorrow when She heard this, and She began to weep.

"Why are you despondent?" demanded Void. "Your new brother will have His share with you."

"But, Father," said Eris, "Aneris and I have been arguing, and she will take Him from Me when she discovers Him, and cause Him to return to Non-Being."

"I see," said Void. "Then I decreed that when your brother leaves the residence of Being, He shall not reside again in Non-Being, but shall return to Me, Void, from whence He came. You girls may bicker all you like, but My son is your brother, and We are all of Myself."

And so it is that we, as men, do not exist until we do; and then it is we play with our world of existent things, and order and disorder them, and so it shall be that nonexistence takes us back from existence and that nameless spirituality shall return to Void, like a tired child home from a very wild circus.

The Epistle to the Paranoids (1970)

Kerry Thornley

Questions

Have a friendly class talk. Permit each child to tell any part of the unit on "Courtesy in the Corridors and on the Stairs" that he enjoyed. Name some causes of disturbance in your school.

EXECUTEL

00069

```
Chapter 1, THE EPISTLE TO THE PARANOIDS
--Lord Omar
```

1. Ye have locked yerselves up in cages of fear--and, behold, do ye now complain that ye lack FREEDOM!

2. Ye have cast out yer brothers for devils and now complain ye, lamenting, that ye've been left to fight alone.

3. All Chaos was once yer kingdom; verily, held ye dominion over the entire Pentaverse, but today ye wax sore afraid in dark corners, nooks, and sink holes.

4. O how the darknesses do crowd up, one against the other, in ye hearts! What fear ye more that what ye have wroughten?

5. Verily, verily I say unto you, not all the Sinister Ministers of the Bavarian Illuminati, working together in multitudes, could so entwine the land with tribulation as have yer baseless warnings.

DESPITE strong evidence to the contrary, persistant rumor has it that it was Mr. Mombmoto's brother who swallowed Mr. Momomoto in the summer of '44.

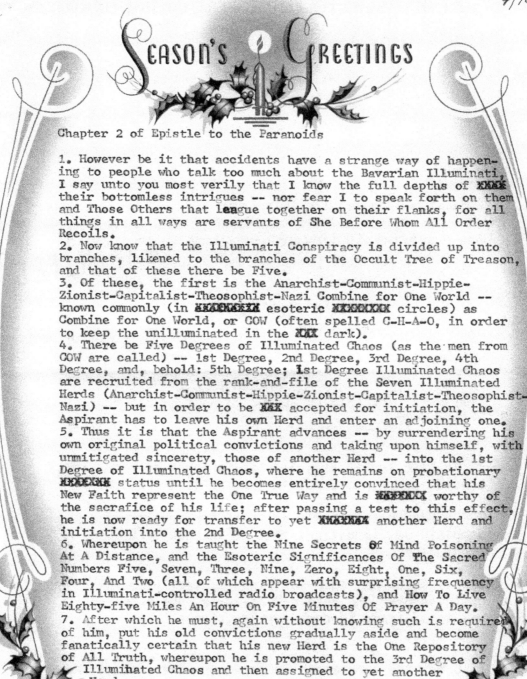

Season's Greetings

Chapter 2 of Epistle to the Paranoids

1. However be it that accidents have a strange way of happening to people who talk too much about the Bavarian Illuminati, I say unto you most verily that I know the full depths of XXXX their bottomless intrigues -- nor fear I to speak forth on them and Those Others that league together on their flanks, for all things in all ways are servants of She Before Whom All Order Recoils.

2. Now know that the Illuminati Conspiracy is divided up into branches, likened to the branches of the Occult Tree of Treason, and that of these there be Five.

3. Of these, the first is the Anarchist-Communist-Hippie-Zionist-Capitalist-Theosophist-Nazi Combine for One World -- known commonly (in XXXXXXXX esoteric XXXXXXX circles) as Combine for One World, or COW (often spelled C-H-A-O, in order to keep the unilluminated in the XXX dark).

4. There be Five Degrees of Illuminated Chaos (as the men from COW are called) -- 1st Degree, 2nd Degree, 3rd Degree, 4th Degree, and, behold: 5th Degree; 1st Degree Illuminated Chaos are recruited from the rank-and-file of the Seven Illuminated Herds (Anarchist-Communist-Hippie-Zionist-Capitalist-Theosophist-Nazi) -- but in order to be XXX accepted for initiation, the Aspirant has to leave his own Herd and enter an adjoining one.

5. Thus it is that the Aspirant advances -- by surrendering his own original political convictions and taking upon himself, with unmitigated sincerety, those of another Herd -- into the 1st Degree of Illuminated Chaos, where he remains on probationary XXXXXXX status until he becomes entirely convinced that his New Faith represent the One True Way and is XXXXXXX worthy of the sacrafice of his life; after passing a test to this effect, he is now ready for transfer to yet XXXXXXX another Herd and initiation into the 2nd Degree.

6. Whereupon he is taught the Nine Secrets Of Mind Poisoning At A Distance, and the Esoteric Significances Of The Sacred Numbers Five, Seven, Three, Nine, Zero, Eight, One, Six, Four, And Two (all of which appear with surprising frequency in Illuminati-controlled radio broadcasts), and How To Live Eighty-five Miles An Hour On Five Minutes Of Prayer A Day.

7. After which he must, again without knowing such is required of him, put his old convictions gradually aside and become fanatically certain that his new Herd is the One Repository of All Truth, whereupon he is promoted to the 3rd Degree of Illuminated Chaos and then assigned to yet another Herd.

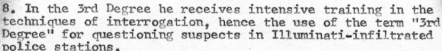

8. In the 3rd Degree he receives intensive training in the techniques of interrogation, hence the use of the term "3rd Degree" for questioning suspects in Illuminati-infiltrated police stations.

9. After he masters these, and again becomes loyally convinced of the righteousness of his new Herd, he is given orders to enter yet another Herd and a promotion to the 4th Degree.

10. Whereupon, dear Chaosophile, he is tuaght in the 4th Degree diverse,numerous and wonderful things, including how to hand roll 100% hashish cigars, which are then given to politicians -- which explains everything.

11. After capitulating once more to group mystique, and succumbing to the ideology of the Herd he is supposed to be infiltrating, the Aspirant is promoted to 5th Degree Chao and put out to pasture.

12. Now those of you out there in XXXXXXXXXXXXXXXX Bible studyland with simeon type enough minds to have paid close attention during the eleven preceeding verses will have noted that, by the time he is initiated into the 5th Degree, the Aspirant has been a True Believer in all the Seven Herds, save one. With this one remaining Herd, whichever it is in any given individual case, the 5th Degree Illuminated Chao will have had XXX no contact whatsoever,meither as an infiltratorX nor as a convert. So, to round out his experience, he is appointed by the XXXXX Illuminated Panel of Five, XXXXXX as soon as there is an opening, to the XXXXXXXXXXXXXXX XXXXXXXXXXX Throne of Grand ManipulatorXXXXXXXXXXXXXXXX in the remaining Herd, giving him absolute control over all the activities of said Illuminated Herd -- which explains everything else.

"For a political explanation of XXXXXXX why the world is in such confusion, the Bavarian Illuminati; for a philosophical explanation, the Discrodian Society."

Remember: LAUGHING BUDDHA JESUS LOVES US ALL!

top sacred

CHAPTER 3 of the Epistle of Omar to the Paranoids
(translated from the Theban by Ho Chi Zen)

1. Having once proven himself on the political testing ground, the Illuminated Chao at last becomes elegible for formal initiation into the Ancient Illuminated Seers of Bavaria, after which he or she is slowly but thoroughly trained in the exalted art of REAL power-wielding: priestcraft.

2. Depending upon the results of his IBM-scored aptitude test, the Neophyte is initiated either as an Episkopos in the Paratheoanametamystichood of Eris (Esoteric), or a Pastor in the Five Round Fundamentalist Pentacostal Church of the Laughing Buddha Jesus, or as a Sinister Minister in the Chicago National Office Faction of the Bavarian Illuminati, or as a Koan Rabbi in the 12 Famous ▮▮▮▮▮▮▮▮▮▮ Buddha Minds School, or as a Catholic Chaplain in the Knights of the Five-Sided Castle.

3. In each case, the initiation Ceremony is the same,*although the Initiates never learn this. It is as written of old in the ▮▮▮▮▮▮ PRINCIPIA DISCORDIA. Only there is one part of the Ceremony the authors of the PRINCIPIA were not permitted to reveal -- the Hahamantra: LAUGHING JESUS, LAUGHING JESUS, JESUS JESUS, LAUGHING LAUGHING; LAUGHING BUDDHA, LAUGHING BUDDHA, BUDDHA BUDDHA, LAUGHING LAUGHING. Chanting this ecstatic vibration ▮▮▮▮▮▮▮ is authorized as the topmost yoga system. ~~in the entire universe.~~ (It is ▮▮▮▮ almost as good a cure for warts as a Swiss Army Knife!)

4. Thereafter the devotee must chant the Hahamantra five hours a day, five days a week, five months a year, for the next five decades -- before he is ▮▮▮ eligible for further promotions in the Illuminati.

5. Meanwhile, he is intructed to infiltrate the church or ~~synagog~~ synagogue of his choice.

*More or less.

A Tale of Starbuck (1963)

Gregory Hill

HE THEN SAW...

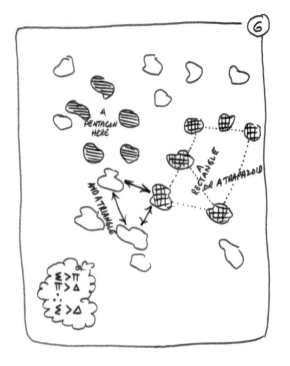

AND HE WROTE ABOUT EVERYTHING IN HIS BOOK
AND READ THE BOOK TO A POET FRIEND OF
HIS WHO HAD HAPPENED BY

BUT SOON THE POET TOO WAS TURNED ON TO THE
MAGIC DESIGNS AND HE TOO WAS IMPRESSED

AND SO THEY CAME TO SEE THE DESIGNS

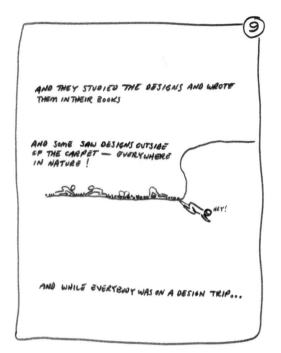

9

AND THEY STUDIED THE DESIGNS AND WROTE THEM IN THEIR BOOKS

AND SOME SAW DESIGNS OUTSIDE OF THE CARPET — EVERYWHERE IN NATURE !

HEY!

AND WHILE EVERYBODY WAS ON A DESIGN TRIP...

10

THE PHILOSOPHERS DECLARED THAT ONLY A GOD COULD CREATE THIS MONUMENTAL BEAUTY — FOR IT SURELY WAS NOT MAN

AND THAT WAS THE DAY THAT GODDESS WAS BORN

11

WHERE ITS AT!

YEAH! RAY! HOORAY! LOVE IT!

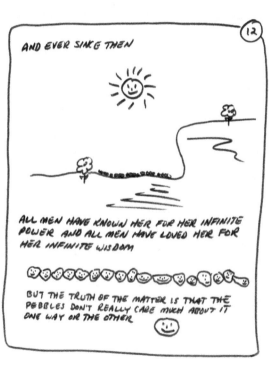

12

AND EVER SINCE THEN

ALL MEN HAVE KNOWN HER FOR HER INFINITE POWER AND ALL MEN HAVE LOVED HER FOR HER INFINITE WISDOM

BUT THE TRUTH OF THE MATTER IS THAT THE PEBBLES DON'T REALLY CARE MUCH ABOUT IT ONE WAY OR THE OTHER

The Book of Alarms

Dr. Mungojerry Grindlebone

– I –

1. It came to pass in the first year of the reign of Richard of Nixon, that a wandering prophet came to the land of Mungo.

2. And he did establish his tent in the parish of Ouachita, near the Inn of Ramada, off the by-pass, the number of which is one hundred and sixty and five.

3. And he did nightly preach many falsehoods, and did predict many dire disasters, and many heard him and did believe.

4. And he did fill his coffers to overflowing.

5. But the children of Eris did remain aloof from his rantings, and were not affected thereby.

– II –

1. The leader of the regurgitationalists did venture to hear this false prophet.

2. And lo! He was almost forced to practice the devotions of his sect, then and there.

3. And Harmon, the Regurgitationalist, did after speak of the prophet in these words: The Man's a real professional—He's coining the dough.

4. And Harmon did wax wroth.

5. Then Roth waxed Harmon for a while.

– III –

1. The false one did preach for nigh on to a month.

2. The flock was fleeced nightly by electric organ shears.

3. And in his greed for wealth, the prophet did allow himself to be lashed with knotted cords.

4. And he did allow himself to be hung upon a cross, in the manner of a wolf.

5. But ERIS sees all.

– IV –

1. And lo, it came to pass that ERIS did descend upon the tent of this charlatan in the form of a mighty wind.

2. And the tent-poles snapped like match-sticks by the force of Her mighty breath.

3. And sixty tens of people were trapped beneath the canvas as it fell, though none were killed.

4. Many of the injured persons refused medical attention for fear lest others know that they attended the phoney.

5. But the prophet did not repent, nay, nor did he cease his iniquitous ways.

– V –

1. And Mungo laughed.

2. And laughed.

3. And laughed.

4. And laughed.

5. And laughed.

The Cannon of St. Gulik

Kerry Thornley

THE CANNON OF ST. GULIK

INTRODUCTION: Up to now the Discordian Society has worked pretty much on the principle of "to each his own thing." All that must change. Henceforth and forever all Laughing Buddha Jesus Discordians will obey The Cannon Of St. Gulik and, further, will seek to inflict it on other Discordians and Popes.

1. The Cannon of St. Gulik declares that cockroaches are sacred, and shall not be destroyed, harmed, or made to feel uncomfortable or unwelcome.

2. Moreover, cockroaches XXX shall be fed regularly and provided with proper shelter by those who would just as soon not go to Thud.

3. Acts of special merit shall include setting up computerized matching services and doing all else within reason to assure the rapid expansion of the cockroach population, and each Pope who wants to stay out of Thud shall donate five percent of his or her earnings toward this work.

4. Every Discordian shall write at least 500 letters a year to important people, particularly political representatives, insisting that points 1., 2., 3., and 4. of This Cannon be pressed into law and made binding and mandatory on all people everywhere, for the good of their own souls. A petition will be circulated to appropriate five billion dollars in Federal funds for the prevention of birth control and disease among the cockroach population.

5. All who obey this Cannon to the letter shall be incarnated next time around as cockroaches. Act now for free food, no rent, and all the sex and company you can dig!

("Say the Magic Word and the duck
will come down and pay you $100.")
-- MARX

Death to the Fanatics; All power to the Cockroaches!

BLUMENKRAFT!

Greyface

Gregory Hill

CONVENTIONAL CHAOS

00042

DO NOT BEND

GREYFACE

In the year 1166 B.C., a malcontented hunchbrain by
the name of Greyface, got it into his head that the
universe was as humorless as he, and he began to teach
that play was sinful because it contradicted the ways
of Serious Order. "Look at all the order about you,"
he said. And from that, he deluded honest men to
believe that reality was a straightjacket affair and
not the happy romance as men had known it.

It is not presently understood why men were so gullible at that particular time, for absolutely no one
thought to observe all the disorder around them and
conclude just the opposite. But anyway, Greyface and
his followers took the game of playing at life more
seriously than they took life itself and were known
even to destroy other living beings whose ways of life
differed from their own.

The unfortunate result of this is that mankind has
since been suffering from a psychological and spiritual imbalance. Imbalance causes frustration, and
frustration causes fear. And fear makes a bad trip.
Man has been on a bad trip for a long time now.

It is called THE CURSE OF GREYFACE.

(55)

Bullshit makes
the flowers grow
& that's beautiful.

55

Figure 11.1 Greg Hill's original paste-up of "Greyface" from the 4th ed. of *Principia Discordia*

The Curse of Greyface

Gregory Hill

To choose order over disorder or disorder over order is to accept a trip composed of both the creative and the destructive.

But to choose the creative over the destructive is an all-creative trip composed equally of order and disorder. To accomplish this, one need only accept creative disorder along with (and equal to) creative order, and also be willing to reject destructive order as an undesirable equal to destructive disorder.

The Curse of Greyface is the division of life into order/disorder as the positive/negative polarity, instead of dividing into creative/destructive for a game foundation. He thereby caused man to endure the destructive aspects of order and prevented man from effectively utilizing the creative aspects of disorder. Civilization reflects this unfortunate division.

POEE proclaims that the other division is preferable, and we work toward the proposition that creative disorder, like creative order, is possible and desirable; and that destructive order, like destructive disorder, is unnecessary and undesirable.

Seek the Sacred Chao—therein you will find that Order and Disorder are the same phenomena!

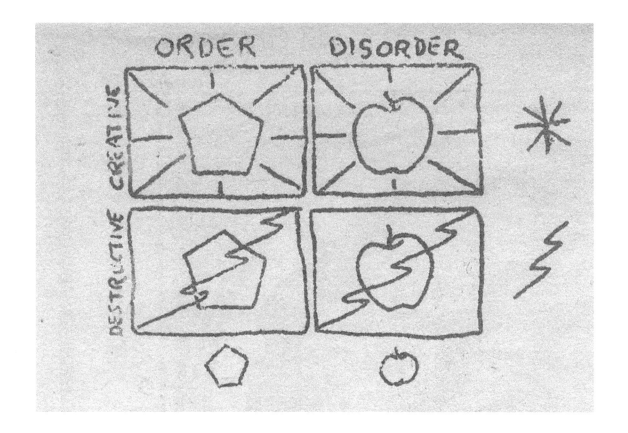

Figure 11.2 Greg Hill's rough sketch depicting the Curse of Greyface

The Kid Was Perfect!

Kerry Thornley

IN THE EARLY 1980s, Kerry Thornley adopted yet another Discordian persona, that of the Reverend Jesse Sump, and forthwith published his own set of irreverent tracts entitled: *THE KID WAS PERFECT! Or the Gospel of Jesus According to Fred the Publican as revealed by the Goddess Eris Discordia in an act of Divine Embellishment to Reverend Jesse Sump, Ancient Abbreviated Calif. Of California and Pastor Present of the Church of the Anarchist Avatar and First Commercial Evangelical Erisian Orthodox Church of the SubGenius.* (Accompanying illustration by Discordian graphic artist, Roldo Odlor.)

Figure 11.3 Roldo Odlor's sketch of *The Kid Was Perfect!*

THE KID WAS PERFECT! or The Gospel of Jesus
According to Fred the Publican as revealed
by the Goddess Eris Discordia in an act of
Divine Embellishment to Reverend Jesse Sump,
Ancient Abbreviated Calif. of California and
Pastor Present of the Church of the Anarchist
Avatar and First Commercial Evangelical Eris-
ian Orthodox Church of the SubGenius:

CHAPTER ONE

1. I wasn't there at the manger scene and I
hate geneology because it is boring.

2. I met Him at the Sermon on the Mount.

3. As future discoveries of ancient writings
are made you'll probably realize I don't go
to revivals usually.

4. Me, I was just there working the rubes.

5. I was in other words a friend of the pick-
pockets in the crowd, but with a gambler's
sense of fairness. Me and my boys, we run
an honest game.

6. So I hear this old rabbi ask the preacher where He wants to stand and He says,
"Right here will do."

7. And there I am, in the front row.

8. Then He looks at me and winks. I know
He knows I'm workin' the rubes.

9. "Blessed are the poor in spirit," He
says to me, "for their's is the Kingdom
Heaven."

10. Then He lifts His voice and begins
talking to everyone. So loudly and clearly
did He speak that a few fools spread the
rumor afterwards that even foreign gentiles
could understand Him in their own tongue.
I wouldn't lay you odds, but I suspect they
were just rubes saying that who didn't want
to think about translators. For in those
days the people were hungry for a Messiah.
It was like a contagion.

11. And how gullible they were becomes
obvious if you recall that the Illuminati
even conned the Sanhedrin into letting the
money lenders set up in the Temple.

12. Before He took on those bastards He
said to me, "The people are likened to a
jackass; I need to hit them over the head
so as to wake them up."

13. I says to Him, "You tell 'em, Slim!"
He then commences to improvise a donkey
scourge and goes after those bankers
like the wrath of God.

CHAPTER TWO

1. Last I heard all the Apostles got
together and decided to exclude me from
the Scriptures because of my seedy reputation. They say it was Paul's idea,
the new guy with short hair who is so
worried about what people will think.

2. I'll tell you something, though.
Jesus enjoyed my company most of all.
He used to sit and drink wine with me
in the backroom of my tavern, where I
also work as a lot caster in one of the
games of chance.

3. In fact, He used to say the sancti-
mony of the Apostles made Him weary.
"They don't listen," He complained.
"I tell them the sun shines on the good
and the wicked alike -- but it just goes
in one ear and out the other."

4. Me, I'm the publican they were always
grumping about when they called Him a
consort of publicans and sinners. He
didn't take to many other publicans, but
He knew lots of sinners.

5. And when it came to pass that the
Apostles bugged Him for squandering so
much time with me, He said to them,
"Judge not, lest ye yourselves be judged
and found wanting."

6. I think Jesus liked me because I never
teased Him about that wine trick he pulled at the wedding in Cana, because His
mother insisted. The Apostles were always calling Him the Little Old Wine
Maker. You'd of thought they didn't understand what Jewish mothers are like.

7. Like everyone else Jesus had His pet
peeves, such as Roman colonialism and
rich Jews who betrayed poor Jews by
selling out to the Establishment. But
if you think He was a moralistic man you
are mistaken.

(Copyrighted 1982 by the Church of the Anarchist Avatar.)

JESSE SUMP TO DR. IGGY

8. His love of preaching stemmed from His ability to thereby stir up the rabble and make the Roman oppressor uneasy.

9. Now another thing, while we are at it: I never heard the sonofabitch say He was God or the Son of God. I think the Sanhedrin framed Him. Around me He always took pains to say He was the Son of Man. Telling a Zealot you are the Son of God or God Himself can get you crucified!

CHAPTER THREE

1. As you may have noticed, everybody who writes about Jesus says that the kid was perfect. Many of them even explain what He meant by that word. To Him, perfection was feeling at one with the universe. It was not the self-righteous perfection of the Scribes and the Pharisees. It exceeded that because there was no greed for status in it.

2. "Why callest thou me good?" he would say. Telling them to harken to the perfection of the Creator, He would point out that the rain falls on the good and wicked alike. That was also the message of the parable of the sower. True perfection consisted of being a funky human who sometimes succeeds and sometimes fails -- and admitting that much to yourself.

3. All Jesus was trying to tell them was that feelings of goodness or guilt have got nothing to do with enlightenment. As He often said to me, it is hard to explain that without seeming decadent or cynical or apathetic -- when in fact it is not cynicism but poverty in spirit, humorous humility, realism that weeps because it is infused with love.

4. True righteousness is understanding that you cannot get one-up on the universe. It is identification with all Creation, seeing yourself right in there with the rest of it and noticing that a lot of it stinks but only temporarily and not without purpose. Manure makes the flowers grow and if it smelled nice children would play in it. And much of it is beautiful and if you cease avoiding one thing and striving after another the results can be much the same as when you fret and worry and struggle for wealth or power or righteousness.

5. To the graspers He would say, "Which of you by taking thought can add so much as a cubit to his own stature?" They would knit their brows and try to figure out what in Heaven's name He was trying to say -- for He spoke as one with authority, even when nobody else understood what He meant. "Lest your mind be naked," He once told me, "you shall no wise remain in the Eden of eternity."

CHAPTER FOUR

1. Jerusalem Slim, as His friends called Him, fulfilled the prophecies. That is He did what the Scriptures said the Messiah would do "in order to fulfill" the prophecies. That is, He maneuvered Himself into a position where Rome could no longer brush Him off as a madman or obscure street preacher.

2. It was like taunting an enemy by taking up a dare and then waiting for the next move. Everyone knew what it meant to ride into town on a jackass. He did not have to run to the town cryer and say He was there to liberate the Jews.

3. Essenes and Zealots possessed more understanding of these actions than did the Roman cops. But Caesar's advisors were not fools and they also understood. They were far away, though, in Rome. Pilate was in charge of the soldiers and Jewish mythology bored him. He could not understand what all the excitement was about.

4. What the Essenes and Zealots did not comprehend was what Jesus intended to do with the power of the situation He had created. They expected Him to become the king or adminstraive leader of the rebel Jews -- a Moses or a David. Slim was an anarchist, though, who thought Israel should suffer no king but God. Nor did He say He was that God. As John admits in chapter ten of his scroll Jesus said, "Ye are all gods."

5. Slim told me He wanted to cultivate ideas and cultural forces that would carry humanity toward the day when we would begin to honor the spirit and purpose of law, instead of the letter.

"Someday they will rise above laws and governments altogether in the anarchy of human love
and good will. I want them to grasp the point
that they, collectively, are the only Messiah,
the only liberator, that the people of Israel
working together in love are the only Moses,
the only source of law," He confided to me.
But whereas the Zealots of His day were communists and revolutionaries after a fashion,
they were not anarchists. So they did not
understand what He was trying to do. Moreover,
they were people of limited imagination with
a love for the Jews that was shallow and did
not participate in their fables in the light-
hearted but significant way that Slim's did.
Besides that, those fanatics were so lacking
in a sense of humor that they thought Jesus
was serious when he was joking and they took
Him in jest when he could not have been more
serious. For that reason they decided He was
just a nut who was no great threat to Roman
authority. That, more than anything, is why
Jesus failed in His mission.

CHAPTER FIVE

1. You must find all this abstract, inspirational philosophy terribly boring, though. Each
evening I write one chapter and the last couple of nights I drank more wine than I should
have.

2. There is enough of that kind of theology in
Matthew, Mark, Luke and John to last the world
another two-thousand years!

3. Me, I should tell you the things about Slim
they have neglected. For not much of His human
quality is captured in their scrolls. That's
what comes from pandering to a very large audience. Everything's got to look more consist-
ent than it was so as not to confuse the rubes.

4. I cannot resist pointing out, though, that
if their intention was to avoid confusion then
they failed miserably. Careful examination will
show, for instance, that they are not even in
agreement with one another as to what His last
words were. They should have got together and
resolved that much among themselves for the
sake of posterity before taking up their quills
if you ask me.

5. Unfortunately I cannot say what the last words
of Jesus were because I was running all over
town that night trying to find Judas before the
self-righteous bastards drove him to suicide.

I failed. I got to talk to him, though.

CHAPTER SIX

1. Problem was, Judas was too drunk
by then to reason with. From his
babbling I did gather some sense of
what had happened, though, at least
as Judas saw it.

2. "The sonofabitch ordered me to
betray Him!" he kept repeating. "As
God is my witness, He ordered me to
turn Him over to the Romans. Something
must have went wrong. He must've had a
plan. What was it? Why did He tell me
to betray Him?"

3. Then I spoke up one of those times
when I wish afterwards I had kept my
damned mouth shut. I wasn't even thinking. It was unforgivable. I said, "Maybe He was just trying to teach you not
to follow orders blindly." He looked at
me. I looked at Him. We both realized
what I had said. Knowing Jesus as we
did, it might have been true.

4. From what I got from his garbled
account, Judas was drawn aside by
Jesus just before the Last Supper and
was instructed in rather obscure terms
to betray Him with a kiss, "When I pass
you the vinegar sop — what I tell you
to do then, do." At that point Judas
just dismissed their chat as one of the
hard sayings of which Jesus was so fond,
similar to what He had recently been saying to the Seventy about how they must
eat of His flesh and drink of His blood.

5. "Why do you say such disturbing and
obscure things in your sermons?" I once
asked Jesus. "I look at it this way," He
said, "Let them figure it out. If it is
not disturbing they'll forget it and go
on about their business. If it isn't obscure, they won't be stimulated to think.
Besides, I can always give them more hints
later on, and I sure as hell don't want
to be clearly understood by the Romans
if I can help it!"

6. Alas, I fail in my purpose, though.
I was going to tell you about how human
He was and instead I'm making Him sound
even weirder than John did with all that
metaphysical stuff about the Word and the
Light and the Light shining in the darkness which aprehended it not, etc.

CHAPTER SEVEN

1. To understand Jesus and why He might have gotten Himself killed just to make a point you have to realize how pissed off He was at just about everything then going on. That didn't square with all He preached about living in love for your enemies and He was aware of that much.

2. As He once said to me, "Love your enemies." Then, half-joking, He added, "Unless they are lawyers, tax collectors or money lenders, of course."

3. Not only was He notorious for His anger against the State, but He was also impatient with the revolutionaries of His day, divided as they were between the Essenes, who wanted to conspire in secret, and the Zealots, who wanted to escalte already intolerable conditions by provoking Roman attacks that would radicalize the masses and drive them to violence.

4. Jesus wanted to preach to the people and raise their consciousness. ~~that way.~~ And He possessed a sense of humor about His anger when it conflicted with that aim. But then when He was with me He was usually tired and resting from a day's work and was therefore more inclined to see things in perspective.

5. He would kick His sandals off and sit down beside the fire in the backroom of the casino, eating dried figs and drinking wine and reviewing the evils of the day with me, sometimes seeing the funny side of an event for the first time.

CHAPTER EIGHT

1. "You know what those fools started quarreling about right after I fed the multitudes with the loaves and the fishes?" He asked me rhetorically. "In the boat on the way back they began fighting over a loaf of bread, afraid we didn't bring enough along to last us!"

2. I'll get to His version of the so-called miracle of the loaves and the fishes later on. For once again the Apostles in their writings have exaggerated or, at least, sinned by omission.

3. Far from seeming Godlike, most of the time Jesus seemed to me weary and more than a little hassled. "Either they don't listen at all or they're all there at once, clinging to me like a mob of frightened children. There's no in between," He complained once.

"If there were half as many street preaching rabble rousers as there are slinking conspirators and bloody guerillas, then my work would be easier."

4. I told Him I doubted if that would make any difference. "Take my business," I said. "It's the same way and Lord knows there are twice as many casinos in Jerusalem than Essenes or Zealots either one. People are like birds," I explained. "They arrive and depart in flocks."

5. "Yeah, maybe," He mused, stretching His hands over the fire to warm them. Then he changed the subject. "You know, the damnest thing happened today. I ran into a mob that was going to stone a prostitute. I stopped them with one line. I'm still trying to figure out why it worked. I think it must be because I didn't keep looking them in the eyes afterwards. Instead, I knelt and began doodling in the dust. When I looked up every righteous hypocrite among them had cast down his stone and wandered off. I bet if I had just kept looking at them that would have turned it into a contest. Then they'd've broken every bone in her body just to prove their virtue!" He laughed, bitterly, I thought, and long and hard.

CHAPTER NINE

1. I promised to tell you about the loaves and the fishes.

2. "They were complaining of hunger," He says to me. "So I told them to organized themselves into regiments, the same way John the Baptist organized his guerillas to take the Kingdom of Heaven by storm."

3. And then He said, "Now I figured that among them were enough provisions to feed us all. Convincing them to share was the problem. And since they've been expecting another David to lead them into battle all along, I just organized them into regiments and let them draw their own conclusions. They lost their apetites. As I suspected, there were more than enough loaves and fishes to go around."

4. Read the Apostles carefully and you

notice they don't say anything about all
that food just supernaturally material-
izing or falling from the sky, but they
certainly leave you free to draw that
conclusion if you want.

5. That Jesus was a modest and humble
man is not one of their exaggerations,
though. So if He actually did heal
lepers, calm storms and go stomping
across the waters of the sea, it may
be He just never saw fit to boast about
such things to me.

CHAPTER TEN

1. The other thing about Jesus, of course,
is that He cussed like a trooper -- that
was what offened the Scribes and the Pharisees most. He was always calling good
Kosher Jews all sorts of unclean things --
vipers, rotting corpses and so forth.

2. They did not accept the idea that a man
who swore that much could be inspired of
God, but yet they did not deny that He
worked miracles -- so I figure there
could've been something to it. What they
said was that He was inspired of the Devil
or had gone to Egypt and learned Magick.

3. I once asked Him if we should tell them
about the Discordian Society.

4. "They're not ready for that yet," He
replied. "They think I'm weird enough as
it is."

(At this point in the transmission the
Goddess Eris Discordia swooped up the
Golden Plates from which I was trans-
lating, taking from my hands also the
Piss'em and the Thumbin' by means of
which I am able to read the fine print
of Fred's transcribed scroll. Without
so much as a word of farewell, She re-
entered the Flying Saucer hovering outside my window and darted off into the
sunset. When I consulted my pineal gland
the voice of the Eris Within Us All said
to me, "I've revealed enough of the writings of Fred to the world for now. You
people already think I'm weird enough
as it is!")

(signed) Your Humble Servant,

Reverend Jesse Sump

Additional copies are $1.

THE KID WAS PERFECT! is RANT #15.
YES!!! More than fourteen Sancti-
fied RANTS now available at seven
for a dollar from the Church of
the Anarchist Avatar, Box 18441,
Tampa, Florida 3 3 6 7 9.

RANT ONE: What is Zenarchy?

RANT TWO: Enlightenment.

RANT THREE: Cultural Autonomy.

RANT FOUR: Philosophical Taoism.

RANT FIVE: Folk Writing.

RANT SIX: Living in Dungeons for
          Freedom and Profit.

RANT SEVEN: Own Your Own Genuine
            Leather Bible Belt!

RANT EIGHT: Harbingers of Chaos
            for Fun and Prophet!

RANT NINE: Relax in the Safety of
           Your Own Delusions
           (titled stolen from
           SubGenius Foundation).

RANT TEN: Doomsday Machines You
          Can Make in Your Own
          Basement.

RANT ELEVEN: Who Was Fred the Publican?

RANT TWELVE: WALL-OP! (A Wall Rock
             Poster Exchange).

RANT THIRTEEN: Creed of the Church of
               the Anarchist Avatar.

RANT FOURTEEN: The Nine Secrets of Mind
               Poisoning at a Distance.

AS WELL AS (at above price) Barvarian
Illuminati recruiting literature: 1)
What Secret Power Did This Man Possess?
2) Form letter to Mrs. Average Housewife
(by Greg Hill). And for $1 you can order
The Laissez-Faire Socialist Papers also.
And for another dollar we will send you
information about our periodicals with
a certificate worth your dollar toward
a subcription purchase; they include
SPARE CHANGE!, THE PROMISE' LAND TIMES,
WALL-OP! and FOLK WRITE: -- so by all
means SEND US AT LEAST ONE DOLLAR! RIP
THE TOP OFF YOUR BANK ACCOUNT TODAY!
Make checks payable to the Church of the
                Anarchist Avatar.

Kerry Wendell Thornley
2981 Lookout Place N.E.
Atlanta, Georgia   30305

MASTERING SLACK
by Rev. Jesse Sump

"You may never get another Hour of Slack!"
-- Pastor Buck Naked

Those of you who attended school may, if you also paid
attention, recall the classical biology experiment of rats
in overcrowded cages. Spacial slack deprivation was proven
to cause bizarre destructive and suicidal behavior, including
cannibalism and catatonia.

Depriving organisms that are not caged of spacial slack
isn't easy. So The Conspiracy has taken another approach --
that of _temporal_ slack deprivation. The results are much
the same.

So if you don't want to become a catatonic cannibal or
something like that send money to the Church, by all means.
Every dollar you send "Bob" automatically insures you exactly
one hour of slack through the inexorable cosmic law of action and reaction.

For instance imagine you send "Bob" one dollar today.
Tomorrow or the next day or next month or next year or five
or nine or seventeen or twenty-three years from now you will
get exactly one hour -- not fifty-nine minutes not sixty-one
minutes -- of slack.

That is the preferred way to assure yourself of getting the
temporal slack you need to keep from going bananas.

(If you live in a state where minimum wage is, say, four
dollars an hour, you don't have to be a mathematical wizard to
see that you are _saving_ three dollars for every one dollar you
send the Church, so insuring your slack this way is also quite
a profitable bargain.)

There are, however, many many other ways to aquire and protect your slack and, although none compare with SubGenius
Slack Insurance as described above, it is the function of this
article to give you a working knowledge of all five.

First, though, some background. To grasp the essential
nature of slack, to penetrate its true mysteries, you must
first understand the motives of they who rob you of it.
Friends, the ruling class has for a long time been trying to
get workers to labor for something besides money. Why? Because paying wages is an expense and they are cheap people.

So one of their think tanks came up with the idea of creating a slack-scarcity economy — of organizing an enormous
conspiracy to gobble up all the temporal slack in the world
so it could be paid out again, in measured portions, for
labor.

So, friends, you begin to get a notion of where things
are headed. Someday you will have to go out and get a job
just to get any spare time — and that's all you'll get:
for a whole day's work, a few miserable hours of slack.
No money. No fringe benefits. No Blue Cross and Blue
Shield. It will not cost your boss one red cent. And you
will work and you will be glad to work. You will praise
"Bob" and thank your lucky stars that you got work — because for the jobless there will be no slack at all.

Relentlessly, The Conspiracy will grind at them, cease-
lessly, day and night with a thousand and one orchestrated
strategies to rob them of their slack. Loudspeakers will
blare at them in public places with no other purpose than to
be as irritating as possible. Mind controllers will rob them
of their sleep with nocturnal commercial dreams. Spontaneous
interpersonal relationships will not be permitted among them.
Postal clerks and bus drivers will treat them rudely, besides.
They will have to keep so many appointments with so many
bureaucrats in so many government offices — just to stay out
of jail — that they will be busier than anyone else, including the President.

And this brings us to our first method of mastering slack.
Don't maintain an appointment book or calendar. If God wanted
you to keep all your appointments He would've given you a
perfect memory. Most people already suffering from temporal

slack deprivation make -- and keep -- too many appointments.
Nowhere in the Bible is any mention made of Moses or Jesus or
anyone like that keeping an appointment calendar.

Appointment books -- like muzak and pinkboy schools -- are
inventions of the Devil. Remember, it is not yet against the
law to break an occasional date -- especially if you have a
good excuse, like: "Sorry, I plumb forgot." So don't become
enslaved to a planned future. Give yourself slack by ignoring
your plans whenever something more interesting and uneventful
comes up unexpectedly.

To become a true slack master you absolutely must be so
wrapped up in yourself that you don't care about -- and if
possible don't even notice -- anyone else. Now friends, this
may sound harsh. But it is the second method of mastering
slack and without it you will lack the sufficient inner
strength to go on shouldering your slack. Sooner or later
you will instead make the mistake of caring and that will be
the beginning of the end of your slack. Like pulling a
thread that results in unraveling a whole sweater, caring
about others will get you caught up in their problems.
Worse, it will cause you to pay attention to what they are
saying -- and let's face it: if those people knew what they
were talking about they wouldn't need your help in the first
place. All that pinkboy propaganda about how you should care
for others has been aimed since time immemorial solely at destroying your slack.

Why do you think Jesus said not to let the left hand know
what the right hand is doing in performing charity? Because
if anyone finds out you care, that will be all she wrote.
That's why. Every leper in the county will be lined up at
your door, pleading for help, making demands on your time.
So if you must care at least pretend you don't, so as to
conserve your precious slack.

Thirdly, you must also steel yourself not to give a hang
about the opinions of others -- even when or if they make any
sense. For a sure way to deprive you of your slack is to get
your attention. And a sure way to demand that is to threaten
you with social disapproval if you don't "pay attention."

In <u>Why</u> <u>You</u> <u>Exist</u> <u>Now</u> Reverend Ivan Stang predicts new beings that will exemplify the next evolutionary step: "They
will be creatures who look like humans, dwell among humans,
but who will be completely disinterested in everything the
humans live for." Strive for exactly that level of consciousness! Don't pay any attention to anyone -- whether they are
blaming, praising or just trying to sell something -- and
your innermost slack will always be there to replenish your
outward slack and the bastards will <u>not</u> be able to get you
down.

Too much slack, as "Bob" always would say, is better than
not enough. And that is why Bulldada Time Control Laboratories
were founded: to control time, to stretch slacktime and con-
tract busytime so as to create whole subjective infinities of
excess slack. And it is in this quest that we confront our
fourth method of slack mastery: time bending.

A whole arsenal of every consciousness-altering drug
known and precise, scientific means of record keeping are
among what you need to do this one right. Establish your
own Bulldada Time Control Lab and register it with the
Father Church in Dobbstown and send weekly reports of the
data you accumulate to Reverend Ivan Stang in Dallas. So
far, participants in this project have been unfortunately
remiss in recording their findings almost in exact relation to
their enthusiasm for the research itself.

Finally, we come to our fifth and final way of slack protection: vigilante action. "Bob" says: "Extremism in the
pursuit of moderation is no vice." And it is self-evident
the slack war won't be won until we make examples out of a
few of The Conspiracy's slack thieves. Armed and dangerous
"Bob"-praising para-military hard-eyed fanatics will have to
be organized into secret survivalist camps in wilderness
areas. Today in music we have our famous Doktor Bands --
Doktors for "Bob" and Doktors for Wotan. Tomorrow there
will be Doktor <u>Armies</u>: Doktors for Slack and Doktors for
Casting Out False Prophets. These will burn X's on the
front lawns of The Conspiracy's henchmen and will hang false
prophets and slack busters from lampposts all up and down
Madison Avenue.

And if that doesn't work, then we will try something
drastic.

A Who's Who of Early Discordianism

ABRAHMS, Judith

Romantically involved with Kerry Thornley in the mid 1970s. Cited as an early Discordian by Robert Anton Wilson in *Cosmic Trigger*. Author of the poetry collection *Back in the Sack*, published by Moonrise Press, 1975.

BENARES, Camden (born John Overton) aka Felix Pendragon aka The Count of Fives

During his first acid trip in the mid 1960s, Overton turned into a Zen lunatic overnight and changed his name to Camden Benares, the idea of which was to bring the teachings of the East into the West: "Camden" for Camden, New Jersey, and "Benares" after Benares, India, the city where the Buddha delivered his first sermon.

Benares had a fondness for dressing up for parties as a Roman Catholic cleric. On one occasion—bedecked in his cleric clothes—he talked his wife June into accompanying him to a party dressed as a nun, where they spent the entire evening holding hands and groping. After the party, Camden and June—still adorned in their priest and nun get-ups—visited a Denny's in West Los Angeles, where they continued to make out. As would be expected, people began freaking out upon witnessing this unholy spectacle, as in between sacrilegious smooches Camden gave blessings and benedictions to the stunned Denny's patrons.

In Europe, Benares is still considered a leading authority on Zen, and his books have been published in German, Dutch, and several other languages. He wrote a total of three books in his Zen series which included *Now and Zen* and *A Handful*

Camden Benares and his wife,
June Gideon, in their priest
and nun get-ups, circa 1976

of Zen. His final book, *Riding Buddha's Bicycle,* was finished shortly before his death in 1999. Camden's literary executor, John F. Carr, is currently preparing this work for publication.

BROOKS, Roderick "Slim" aka Aaron Immanuel Viking, Keeper of the Submarine Keys

Shortly after arriving in New Orleans, Thornley made the acquaintance of Slim Brooks, a colorful character who was among a core group of early New Orleans-based Discordians. When asked how he came upon his Discordian name, Slim replied, "I like that one because it brings to mind two questions. What submarine? And why is it locked?"

Thornley later came to suspect that Brooks had been a conspirator in the JFK assassination. According to a September 1975 letter from Greg Hill to Robert Anton Wilson, Brooks was one of The Chosen Five who received the first edition of the *Principia Discordia (Or How The West Was Lost).*

See Appendexia Discordia for the only known Discordian artifact produced by Roderick "Slim" Brooks, "The Facetious Map."

CAPLINGER, Lane

Sister of actress Grace (Caplinger) Zabriskie. Lane worked as a typist in New Orleans District Attorney Jim Garrison's office where legend has it she covertly produced all five copies of the first edition of the *Principia Discordia (Or How The West Was Lost)* in 1965.

ENCIMER, Paul aka Dr. Confusion (The Seven Mighty Anvils Cabal)

Published *St. John's Bread*, a late-60s counterculture magazine that featured Thornley's classic poem, "Illuminati Lady," as well as other Discordian writings. He is currently involved in activist causes in Northern California.

HILL, Gregory aka Malaclypse the Younger, Mal-2, Dr. Ignotum P. Ignotius, Rev. Dr. Occupant, Mad Malik, Professor Iggy (Joshua Norton Cabal)

Cofounder of The Discordian Society and principle architect of *Principia Discordia*. Married Jeanetta Ross in 1969; separated in the mid-70s. Operated the "Cinema Rio" theater in Monte Rio, California, in the early 70s with his wife Jeanetta and Bob Newport. As synchronicity would have it, Hill worked 23 years for Bank of America, and was instrumental in the development of their word processing department. He also developed one of the first computer solitaire games, *Joker Sol*. Hill died in July 2000 of esophageal cancer.

Greg Hill, circa early 80s

HILL, Jeanetta (formerly Jeanetta Ross) aka Sister Deacon Iona K. Fioderovna

HLAVATY, Arthur aka Pope Guilty I

New York-based copy editor and sci-fi fan.

JAMISON, Stan aka Conrad Ra, Lt. Colonel, Commanding 1st Intergalactic Confederacy Advance Detail—Planet Shan (Turlock Cabal)

Based out of Turlock, California, Jamison produced a newsletter on alternative medical cures, as well as dabbling in Discordianism.

KISHBAUGH, Alan aka The Earl of Nines

A novelist and Krishnamurti devotee, Kishbaugh adopted the title of The Earl of Nines in response to the Discordian Law of Fives.

LACEY, Louise aka Lady L, F.A.B. (Fucking Anarchist Bitch)

Edited Kerry Thornley's *Oswald* for New Classic Books. Served as research director for *Ramparts* magazine in the late 60s. Member of the Berkeley campus branch of the Bavarian Illuminati, and collaborator on The Earth People's Park project.

After her initiation into the Discordian Society, Lacey became known as Lady L.,

F.A.B. (The latter part of Lacey's moniker came from her friend Eldridge Cleaver, who charmed her once with the endearment: "Fucking anarchist bitch!")

During the 70s, Lacey published a feminist periodical, *Woman's Choice*, as well as penning her classic tome on natural birth control, *Lunaception: A Feminine Odyssey into Fertility and Contraception*, later used as inspiration for Tom Robbins's *Still Life With Woodpecker*. Since 1990, Lacey has edited and published *Growing Native*, a newsletter dedicated to growing native California plants.

Louise Lacey, early 1970s

LOVIN, Roger Robert aka Fang the Unwashed (Tactile Tabernacle of Eris Erotic)

In the introduction to the Illuminet Press edition of the *Principia Discordia*, Thornley described Roger Lovin as ". . . a dashing, talented and handsome con artist who was too shallow to settle into any one thing. But for years and years after he read the *Principia*, under his Discordian name of Fang the Unwashed, he consistently and with unswerving devotion to the task excommunicated every new person any of the rest of us initiated into the Discordian Society."

To follow is Discordian correspondence dictated by Lovin (aka Fang the Unwashed) and addressed to Greg Hill (aka Malacypse the Younger), dated December 17th, 1964:

All Hail Discordia!!!!!?!!!!!!!

To: MALACLYPSE (THE YOUNGER), K.C.: OMNIPOTENT POLYFATHER OF VIRGINITY IN GOLD AND HIGH PRIEST OF THE HERETIC FRINGE AND PROTESTANT PERSAUSION
FROM: FANG (THE UNWASHED), W.K.C.: LIBERATOR OF THE THIRD EYE, PROTECTOR of the WESTERN WORLD, EXALTED LAMA of the NEW ORLEANS CABAL, and L.L.L.L.L. (Lovin's Licentiously Liberated Lightning Lechers)

Hail Eris,
Concerning thy recent epistle of Excommunication: Screw Thee. Thou wilt understand, of course, that it isn't the humble Fang; but FANG, W.K.C.: L.T.E., P.W.W., E.L.N.O.C., and L.L.L.L.L.L. and wilt therefore realize that naught of a personal nature is meant . . . dig?

Wouldst do me the favor of communicating Lord Omar's current whereabouts to me in the swiftest mode. This One is plagued with constant uncertainties and apprehensions due to an extreme dearth of information concerning That One. I fear me ever that the Foul Forces of Light and Reason have fallen upon him unaware and smotten (wow!) Him severely about the shoulders and intellect. Thou wouldst earn thyself everlasting gratitude and a mention in the evening maledictions by such an action. Also; if you don't, I'll kill you.

As to the progress of the New Orleans Cabal: The first Temple of Eris in New Orleans was formally defeated on Nov. 3, 1964, at 519 Decatur St. (which, oddly enough, is also my home address.) It occupied a converted broom closet. Admittedly, that is rather humble quarters for such a large and far-flung organization; but in the short space of one month we have more than doubled our area. This noble word was accomplished chiefly through the untiring efforts of our noble leader, FANG, W.K.C.: L.T.E., P.W.W., E.L.N.O.C., and L.L.L.L.L. and his noble assistant, Charles Noble. They single-handedly (one hand, three hooks) formed K.R.U.D. (Kollectors of Revenue Under Duress) and saw to the raising of funds. Our membership already includes two beatniks, one wasp, a hunchbrain, and a genuine, card carrying square who has 2.7 kids and a wife with a cloth coat. Therefore, be of good cheer. Today New Orleans, tomorrow the Catacombs – with some scattered showers in the evening.

As I am naturally curious about what sort of person would spend his time on such drivel as this, kindly send me some data about yourself. Send also a copy of HYMN. Barring the feasibility of a picture, send a piece of fingernail and some hair . . .

In closing, let me say: MARY CHRISTMAS, SAVIOR MONEY!!!

(signed) FANG

Lovin published a weekly New Orleans newspaper *The Ungarbled Word* from 1968–69, then later worked as a columnist for *Los Angeles Free Press* from 1969–73. During the early 70s, Lovin wrote and published pornography.

In 1974, Lovin's first book was published, *The Complete Motorcycle Nomad*, which has became a classic in the field. In 1977, under the pseudonym of Rodgers Clemens, his first sci-fi novel, *The Presence*, was published, followed by *The Apostle* in 1978. Lovin died in November 1991.

MAGEE, Harry aka Cardinal Bishoprick Penzacola (Northern Vagina Archdiocese)

McELROY, Bob aka Dr. Mungojerry Grindlebone (The Apple Panthers Cabal)

McNAMARA, Thomas Patrick aka Thomas the Gnostic, Rev. Pope Thomas the First (Brotherhood of the Lust of Christ)

MEDLEY, Dr. Malcolm Scott aka Makuska, Shaman of Manitoo; Society for Moral Understanding and Training (SMUT)

NEWPORT, Dr. Robert aka Rev. Hypocrates Magoun, Protector of the Pineal

High school friend of Greg Hill and Kerry Thornley and early member of the Discordian Society. Contributor to the *Principia Discordia*. Co-operated the Cinema Rio with Greg and Jeanetta Hill in the early 70s. During the Cinema Rio period, Newport also ran a psychiatry practice from his home on the Russian River, conducting therapy sessions on the branches of the large redwoods on the property.

Newport currently serves on the advisory board of the cryonics firm ALCOR Life Extension. Now retired from his psychiatry practice, he devotes much of his time these days to his new passion, landscape painting.

REID, Barbara

One of the early New Orleans Discordians, described by Thornley as a "... French Quarter voodoo worker and bohemian scene maker." A principal witness against Thornley in Garrison's JFK assassination investigation, Reid claimed to have seen Thornley and Oswald together in New Orleans prior to JFK's assassination, although Thornley denied this allegation, insisting that the last time he'd been in contact with Oswald was during the period the two served together in the Marines.

ODLOR, Roldo

Canadian-born graphic artist and musician. In the mid 1980s, Thornley enlisted Roldo to illustrate various Discordian related projects, an association that culminated in Thornley's *Book of the Demons of Thud* aka *Goetia Discordia*. The cover for *Historia Discordia* was produced by Roldo during this period.

THORNLEY, Kerry Wendell aka Lord Omar Khayyam Ravenhurst, the Bull Goose of Limbo, Ho Chi Zen, The Reverend Jesse Sump, Hung Mung Tong Cong

Founded the Discordian Society in 1958 or 1959 with Greg Hill. Co-authored *Principia Discordia* and created The Sacred Chao. Married Cara Leach in 1964.

Served with Lee Harvey Oswald in the Marines, and was writing a novel based on Oswald entitled *The Idle Warriors* three years before JFK's assassination. *The Idle Warriors* was eventually published by IllumiNet Press in 1991.

Kerry Thornley in the late 60s

Thornley's first published book was *Oswald*, a non-fiction account examining President Kennedy's alleged assassin. Thornley edited a libertarian newsletter, *The Innovator*, during the mid 60s. In 1968, he was indicted by New Orleans District attorney Jim Garrison as part of a JFK assassination conspiracy, a charge which Thornley adamantly denied. Thornley later came to suspect that he'd been an unwitting participant in JFK's assassination, manipulated by individuals in New Orleans whom he suspected were part of the assassination plot, including Discordian Society member Slim Brooks.

For more background on Kerry Thornley, read *The Prankster and the Conspiracy*, by yours truly, published by Paraview Press, 2003.

WHEELER, Tim aka Rev. Harold, Lord Randomfactor (YARF — Young Americans For Real Freedom)

SHEA, Robert aka Josh the Dill aka Alexander Eulenspiegel

Playboy editor during the late 60s. Contributed to the *Principia Discordia*. Co-author of *Illuminatus!* with Robert Anton Wilson. Edited and published the anarchist magazine, *No Governor*. Died in 1994.

WILSON, Robert Anton aka Mordecai Malignatus, Mordecai the Foul (Adam Weishaupt Chapter)

Wilson began corresponding with Kerry Thornley during the period Thornley edited the libertarian magazine, *The Innovator*, in the mid 60s. Wilson became involved with the Discordian Society shortly thereafter and was one of the more active participants in the scene. He and Thornley had a falling out over theories regarding the Kennedy assassination, and for a period of time Thornley suspected that Wilson had been his CIA handler/brainwasher. Hail Eris!

Author of over 33 books, Wilson is the most recognizable and well known member of the Discordian Society. *Cosmic Trigger* recounts many of his Discordian activities. Wilson died in 2007.

Greg Hill and Kerry Thornley
posing with the first edition of the
Principia Discordia sometime in
the late 1960s

Hill and Thornley's high school
yearbook pictures, late 1950s

GREGORY HILL   Kerry Thornley

Robert Anton Wilson and Robert Shea
promoting the *Illuminatus!*, circa 1976

Camden and Kerry sharing
a doobie in the mid-70s in
Tujunga, California

A WHO'S WHO OF EARLY DISCORDIANISM

Kerry Thornley holding a harmonica,
Berkeley, California, mid-80s

Greg Hill, a few days before
his death, in July of 2000

Dr. Robert Newport and Adam
Gorightly (in opposing fish
shirts) reviewing the Discordian
Archives at Robert Anton
Wilson's apartment. Capitola,
California, spring 2001

The Brunswick Shrine Realized (2009)

Adam Gorightly

Nᴏᴛ ᴏɴʟʏ ɪs your humble author a card-carrying Discordian (aka The Wrong Reverend Houdini Kundalini of the Church of Unwavering Indifference) but I also serve as the Northern California Bureau Chief for the League of Western Fortean Intermediasts (LOWFI), founded by my friend and fellow conspirator, Skylaire Alvegren, herself a card-carrying Discordian.

Over the past few years, LOWFI has sponsored a number of esoteric field trips. In early 2009, as a pilgrimage to the Nixon Museum was in the planning stages (in the prospects of summoning Tricky Dicky's ghost, no less!), a Canadian-Discordian colleague contacted me (unaware of our forthcoming Nixon Museum freakout) and sent me a couple of unsolicited Discordian Initiation Rites, which included a ritual dedicated to the legendary Brunswick Shrine, the Whittier, California bowling alley where the founders of Discordianism, Kerry Thornley and Greg Hill, allegedly discovered (or some say created) a religion based upon the worship of Eris, the Greek goddess of chaos and discord. It should be noted that the specter of Nixon is an integral part of this Discordian mythos, one of which involves Tricky Dick growing up in Whittier.

In the *Principia Discordia* the legend of the Brunswick Shrine is related, but I won't spoil it for you right now, as at the end of this post I'll share with you the aforementioned Discordian Initiation which relates the vision encountered in a long ago bowling alley that led to Discordianism's un-maculate conception.

When I interviewed Discordian co-founder Dr. Robert Newport (during research for *The Prankster and the Conspiracy*) regarding the legend of The Brunswick Shrine, he claimed that no specific bowling alley was the site of the Discordian Society's birth, and that it had evolved at several different bowling alleys located throughout the greater Whittier and La Habra area in the late 1950s. At the time, this revelation came as a devastating disappointment to your humble author, who—in the course of my research—had planned a grand religious pilgrimage to this envisioned holy site, where I would snap sacred photos and perhaps even fall to my knees before this fabled mecca of Discordianism. But such was not to be my fate, or so I assumed at the time, because—according to Newport—the choice of a bowling alley really held no mystical significance, other than the fact that bowling alleys stayed open all night and served alcohol. Or at least this is what Newport claimed, explaining that Greg Hill, who during that period looked old for his age, usually bought the beer for the rest of the Discordian gang, which all drank thereof and through holy intoxication summoned forth the chaotic spirit of the Goddess of Confusion and Discord. (So much for Hill and Thornley's contention that they were busy sipping coffee in a Whittier bowling alley when the revelation of the Goddess Eris unfolded!) Thus, according to Newport, the revelation of the Goddess had as much to do with alcohol-induced reveries as it did caffeine-inspired visions.

Nixon's museum is located in the town of Yorba Linda, not far from Whittier, the home of this fabled bowling alley/shrine. At the time I had no idea what I was getting into, but—for some inexplicable reason—decided to do a websearch for bowling alleys in Whittier. And in so doing, I stumbled across a flickr page that made me do a double take, depicting—as it did—a retro-looking bowling alley that immediately struck a discordant chord, and somehow I felt this was THE PLACE. I noted the name: *Friendly Hills Lanes*, and said AHA! The clouds then parted and I knew that it was so; that I was gazing upon a photo of the one and only Brunswick Shrine, which I'd previously convinced myself—with the aid of Dr. Newport—had never actually existed. But I now believe it is the real deal: Friendly Hills Lanes = The Brunswick Shrine, and I will present my evidence for you now!

First, as mentioned in *Principia Discordia*, it was Kerry and Greg (aka Mal-2 and Omar) who bore witness to the mystical experience that transpired at the Brunswick Shrine. So, while there can be no doubt that Bob Newport spent many an hour hanging out with Greg and Kerry in a multitude of SoCal bowling alleys, on the particular night in question (when Eris first appeared and blew their minds), Newport was not in attendance, at least according to the *Principia Discordia*, the Bible of Discordianism. (And everybody knows that bibles never lie!)

Secondly, in *The Prankster and the Conspiracy* it is recounted—from stories shared by Kerry's brother, Dick Thornley—how as lads Kerry used to take his younger brothers to explore the Friendly Hills Development then under construction located nearby their Whittier home. And so we have in Friendly Hills Lanes a bowling alley that fits the timeline (constructed in the late 40s/early 50s) and located within walking distance of the house where Kerry Thornley was born and raised.

As I was unearthing these amazing Discordian discoveries, I learned from LOWFI Chief Skylaire that not long ago a SoCal preservation society known as The Modern Committee was instrumental in saving the Friendly Hills Lanes "BOWL" sign. Little did they know they were also saving a piece of the Discordian legacy for the ages. As further evidence that Friendly Hills Lanes and the Brunswick Shrine are one and the same, when you walk through the main door the first lane that you see is Number 23! (Coincidence? You decide!)

So, as the revelation hit me that The Brunswick Shrine did indeed exist and was still in operation, I thought it might be cool—after visiting the haunted Nixon museum—that our LOWFI group afterwards made a pilgrimage to the birthplace of Discordianism. To this end, I ran a Mapquest from the Nixon museum to Friendly Hills Lanes and discovered it would take approximately 23 minutes to drive from one locale to the other! When I floated this idea by Skylaire of visiting said shrine, she was down for it, and so I began contemplating what exactly we could do to consecrate the holy event and then remembered the Brunswick Shrine/Discordian Initiation Rite with the Dick Nixon tie-in I had been by sent by my Canadian/Discordian colleague, Mike Cook. And so it came to be, with me reciting the initiation along with Skylaire playing the role of Eris (fittingly enough!) and throwing fairy dust on the assembled initiates gathered below the neon glow of the BOWL sign. Not to mention my wife squawking the ceremonial rubber chicken five times and another participant holding up a sign that said: "DOOM!"

But once again I'm getting ahead of myself, and I need to mention that prior to this Brunswick Shrine visitation/initiation, we did indeed pay tongue-in-cheek homage to the haunted Nixon museum and I'll be damned if our entrance ticket didn't include a photo of a psychedelic Richard Nixon bowling! (We also learned that one of Nixon's brothers died at age 23!)

And now, in its entirety, I present to you the *Fifth Degree Discordian Initiation Rite* (its narrative lifted from *Principia Discordia*), which was performed the evening of March 1, 2009, at the one and only Brunswick Shrine . . .

Skylaire Alfvegren, in the role of Eris, and Adam Gorightly,
performing the Fifth Degree Discordian Initiation Rite, March 1, 2009

The Fifth Degree
Discordian Initiation Rite

[To begin, get two volunteers from the audience, quietly explain to them that all they have to do is hold up a sign when pointed at. Make sure the sign will be right side facing and right side up when they show it. Also after imparting the Grand Hailing sign of Awkwardness and Confusion, say "with me, make the sign and say the words" and get everybody to do the sign together.]

Intro Speech

Exactly 50 years ago today in the 56th day of the season of chaos and the week of sweetmorn, Omar Khayyam Ravenhurst and Malacylpse the Younger stood right here counting their money to see if they had enough to bowl, and alas they counted $2 and 30 cents, and the following occurred.

The Brunswick Shrine

In the Los Angeles suburb of Whittier there lives a bowling alley, and within this very place, in the Year of Our Lady of Discord 3125 (1959), Eris revealed Herself to The Golden Apple Corps for the first time. In honor of this Incredible Event, this Holy Place is revered as a Shrine by all Erisians. Once every five years, the Golden Apple Corps plans a Pilgrimage to the Brunswick Shrine as an act of Devotion, and therein to partake of No Hot Dog Buns, and ruminate a bit about It All. It is written that when The Corps returns to The Shrine for the fifth time five times over, than shall the world come to an end.

[Point to guy with DOOM sign]

All: IMPENDING DOOM HAS ARRIVED [Holds up sign with DOOM scrawled on it with black marker.]

And Five Days Prior to This Occasion The Apostle The Elder Malaclypse Shall Walk the Streets of Whittier Bearing a Sign for All Literates to Read thereof: "DOOM," as a Warning of Forthcoming Doom to All Men Impending. And He Shall Signal This Event by Seeking the Poor and Distributing to Them Precious MAO BUTTONS and Whittier Shall be Known as The Region of Thud for These Five Days. As a public service to all mankind and civilization in general, and to us in particular, the Golden Apple Corps has concluded that planning such a Pilgrimage is sufficient and that it is prudent to never get around to actually going. [Optional: someone else says, "Then what the fuck are we doing here?"] It was here that the Erisian movement was born.

The Birth of the Erisian Movement

Just prior to the decade of the 1960s, when Sputnik was alone and new, and about the time that Ken Kesey took his first acid trip as a medical volunteer; before underground newspapers, Viet Nam, and talk of a second American Revolution; in the comparative quiet of the late 1950s, just before the idea of RENAISSANCE became relevant. Two young Californians, known later as Omar Ravenhurst and Malaclypse the Younger, were indulging in their habit of sipping coffee at an all-night bowling alley and generally solving the world's problems. This particular evening the main subject of discussion was discord and they were complaining to each other of the personal confusion they felt in their respective lives. "Solve the problem of discord," said one, "and all other problems will vanish." "Indeed," said the other, "chaos and strife are the roots of all confusion."

[Someone steps forward and says:] FIRST I MUST SPRINKLE YOU WITH FAIRY DUST [and sprinkles everyone]

Suddenly the place became devoid of light. Then an utter silence enveloped them, and a great stillness was felt. Then came a blinding flash of intense light, as though their very psyches had gone nova. Then vision returned. The two were dazed and neither moved nor spoke for several minutes. They looked around and saw that the bowlers were frozen like statues in a variety of comic positions, and that a bowling ball was steadfastly anchored to the floor only inches from the pins that it had been sent to scatter. The two looked at each other, totally unable to account for the phenomenon. The condition was one of suspension, and one noticed that the clock had stopped. There walked into the room a chimpanzee, shaggy and gray about the muzzle, yet upright to his full five feet, and poised with natural majesty. He carried a scroll and walked to the young men. "Gentlemen, why does Pickering's Moon go about in reverse orbit? Gentlemen, there are nipples on your chests; do you give milk? And what, pray tell, Gentlemen, is to be done about Heisenberg's Law?" (Pause.) "SOMEBODY HAD TO PUT ALL OF THIS CONFUSION HERE!" And with that he revealed his scroll. It was a diagram, like a yin-yang with a pentagon on one side and an apple on the other.

[Point to guy with Sacred Chao, who shows the Sacred Chao for a five-count] And then he exploded and the two lost consciousness. They awoke to the sound of pins clattering, and found the bowlers engaged in their game and the waitress busy with making coffee. It was apparent that their experience had been private. They discussed their strange encounter and reconstructed from memory the chimpanzee's diagram. Over the next five days they searched libraries to find the significance of it, but were disappointed to uncover only references to Taoism, the Korean flag, and Technocracy. It was not until they traced the Greek writing on the apple that they discovered the ancient Goddess known to the Greeks as Eris and to the Romans as Discordia. This was on the fifth night, and when they slept that night each had a vivid dream of a splendid woman whose eyes were as soft as feathers and as deep as eternity itself, and whose body was the spectacular dance of atoms and universes. Pyrotechnics of pure energy formed her flowing hair, and rainbows manifested and dissolved as she spoke in a warm and gentle voice:

[Have a female read the following ERIS] I have come to tell you that you are free. Many ages ago, my consciousness left man, that he might develop himself. I return to find this development approaching completion, but hindered by fear and by misunderstanding. You have built for yourselves psychic suits of armor, and clad in them, your vision is restricted, your movements are clumsy and painful, your skin is bruised, and your spirit is broiled in the sun. I am chaos. I am the substance from which your artists and scientists build rhythms. I am the spirit with which your children and clowns laugh in happy anarchy. I am chaos. I am alive, and I tell you that you are free.

During the next months they studied philosophies and theologies, and learned that Eris or Discordia was primarily feared by the ancients as being disruptive. Indeed, the very concept of chaos was still considered equivalent to strife and treated as a negative. "No wonder things are all screwed up," they concluded, "they have got it all backwards." They found that the principle of disorder was every much as significant as the principle of order. With this in mind, they studied the strange yin-yang. During a meditation one afternoon, a voice came to them:

[ERIS:] It is called the Sacred Chao. I appoint you Keepers of It. Therein you will find anything you like. Speak of Me as Discord, to show contrast to the pentagon. Tell constricted mankind that there are no rules, unless they choose to invent rules. Keep close the words of Syadasti: 'TIS AN ILL WIND THAT BLOWS NO MINDS. And remember that there is no tyranny in the State of Confusion. For further information, consult your pineal gland.

"What is this?" mumbled one to the other, "A religion based on the Goddess of Confusion? It is utter madness!" And with those words, each looked at the other in absolute awe. Omar began to giggle. Mal began to laugh. Omar began to jump up and down. Mal was hooting and hollering to beat all hell. And amid squeals of mirth and with tears on their cheeks, each appointed the other to be high priest of his own madness, and together they declared themselves to be a society of Discordia, for what ever that may turn out to be.

Grand Hailing Sign of Awkwardness and Confusion

As a Keeper of the Sacred Chao I now impart to you a secret Discordian sign. This sign originates from when Richard Nixon boarded his helicopter after he had resigned the office of the Presidency of the U.S. Put both hands in the "peace" sign and thrusting them forward on an upward 45 degree angle at the same time speak the words "I am not a crook." Richard Nixon, having unconsciously taken part in our secrets as a Knight of the Five-Sided Castle we rightly recognized this as the Grand Hailing Sign of Awkwardness and Confusion. It is only to be given when in moments of extreme awkwardness, to display the feeling of total confusion, or when blatantly lying.

Assorted Fnords

THIS CHAPTER IS DEDICATED to various curiosities and oddities contained within Greg Hill's Discordian Archives that are appropriately enough described (by yours truly) as "fnords," a word used often within the Discordian mythos, although nobody really knows what it means—at least as far as I can tell; they are odds and ends that don't necessarily fit elsewhere in the narrative, but which nonetheless help display Discordianism's quirky history in colorful detail.

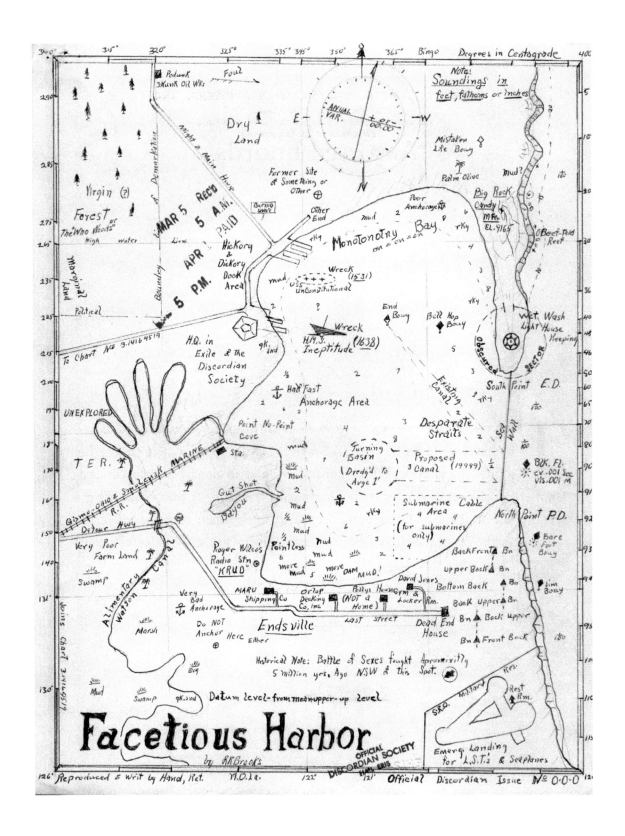

Figure 14.1 Facetious Harbor map created by Slim Brooks

Let 12 Famous Buddha Minds free your Buddha Mind

Easy at-home course offers all a chance to attain godhood

Be the first on your block to save the world!!!

Do you have that restless urge to attain salvation? Do you endlessly seek assumption to the Universal Godhead, to the snickering amusement of your friends and family? Do your fanatic ideas about Truth, Love, God, Virtue and Life send you out day and night into the streets to preach to anyone who will listen, only no one will listen? Do you habitually ask total strangers for advice on how to live your life?

If so, you have a hell of a lot in common with the great religious leaders. Why not give our twelve famous Buddha Minds a chance to teach you something important?

BILLY GRAHAM and the MAHARISHI MAHESH YOGI are only two of the famous Buddha Minds in a faculty that includes ALAN WATTS, NORMAN VINCENT PEALE, POPE PAUL VI, KIRBY HENSLEY, BISHOP FULTON J. SHEEN, MADELAINE MURRAY, REV. BOB RICHARDS, ELIJAH MOHAMMED, DR. TIMOTHY LEARY and RALPH WILLIAMS. The MAHARISHI says, "Being a religious leader has meant the satisfaction of all the spiritual hungers that engulfed me as a god-child-- now I have a villa, a jet plane and clean underwear every day."

Men as important as the famous Buddha Minds cannot of course give your questions personal attention. But fortunately Twelve Famous Buddha Minds School has a large staff of Buddha Heads who answer your questions and tell you how to live your life.

Sister Hilda Carnack (B.Y.O.B.) of Frankfort, Germany writes:
"Since enrolling in Twelve Famous Buddha Minds School, I am no longer troubled by blood on the sheets."

FACULTY
We'd print a picture of our faculty except that there is only one place in the center. Instead, we've printed a picture above of the Buddha Mind itself.

ARE YOU A BUDDHA MIND?
Free aptitude test

To see if you have what it takes to attain Buddha Mind, just send us a sample question. Ask our alert staff about something that has been really bugging you and they will answer FREE! They will also judge the quality of your question and on that basis decide whether you may enroll in the School.

Famous Buddha Minds School
19446 Cuesta Cala
Topanga, Ca. 90290

I want to find out just how far along my Buddha Mind is. Without obligation, evaluate my sample question and tell me how to live my life through your course.

Name
Age (or incarnation)
Street
City, zip, state
My Question is

--Discredited by World Council of Churches

Figure 14.2 Spoof ad created by Greg Hill

Figure 14.3 Discordian bumper sticker created by Thomas the Gnostic (above)

Bumper sticker created by Robert Anton Wilson (middle)

Assorted Discordian buttons, Bob Newport's Erisian dog tags, Greg Hill's "Five-Finger Hand of Eris" pendant and Camden Benares's "Count of Fives" medallion (below)

Figure 14.4 Collage created by Kerry Thornley in the late 80s
for one of his many self-published broadsides

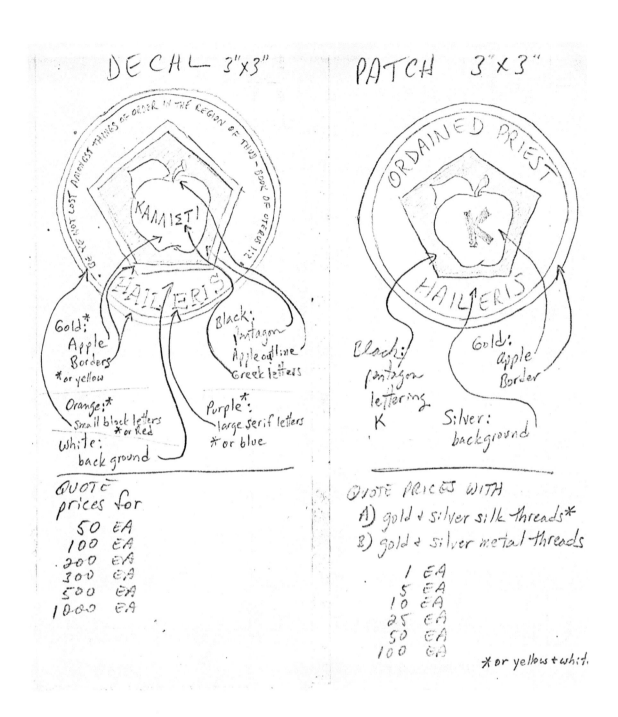

DECHL 3"x3"

GET SHE NOT LOST AMONGST THINGS OF ORDER IN THE REGION OF THUD ~ BOOK OF UTERUS 1:1

ΚΑΛΛΙΣΤΙ

HAIL ERIS

Gold:*
Apple
Borders
*or yellow

Black:
Pentagon
Apple outline
Greek letters

Orange:*
small black letters
*or Red

Purple*:
large serif letters
*or blue

White:
background

QUOTE
prices for
    50 EA
   100 EA
   200 EA
   300 EA
   500 EA
  1000 EA

PATCH 3"x3"

ORDAINED PRIEST

HAIL ERIS

Black:
pentagon
lettering
K

Gold:
Apple
Border

Silver:
background

QUOTE PRICES WITH
A) gold & silver silk threads*
B) gold & silver metal threads
    1 EA
    5 EA
   10 EA
   25 EA
   50 EA
  100 EA

*or yellow & white

Figure 14.5 Specs by Greg Hill for Discordian Society decals and patches

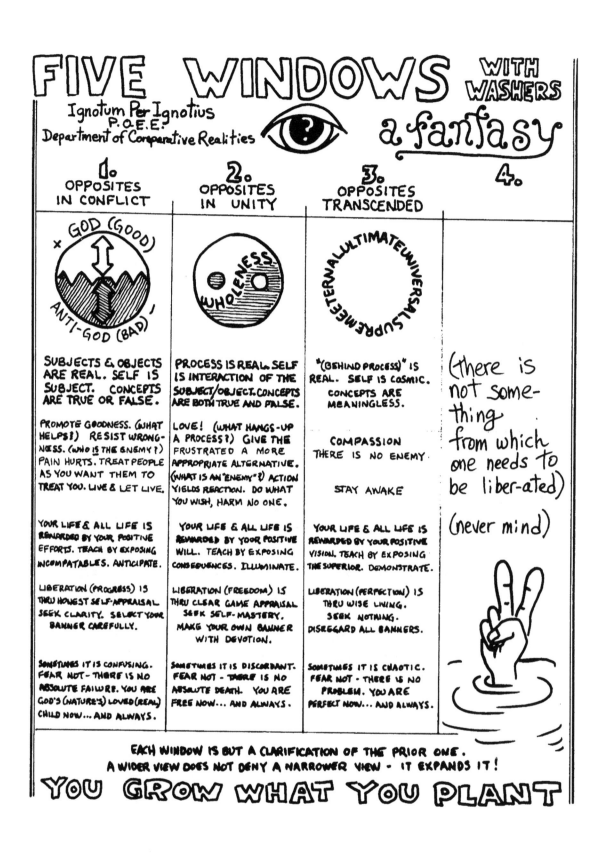

Figure 14.6 Five Windows with Washers by Ignotum P. Ignotius (aka Greg Hill)

5L / 25   abcdef
           ijklmn
           opqrst   Hill 1975
           uvwxyz

Figure 14.7 Collage by Greg Hill that appeared in the 4th ed. of *Principia Discordia*

Figure 14.8 Another collage by Greg Hill,
a portion of which appeared in the 4th ed. of *Principia Discordia*

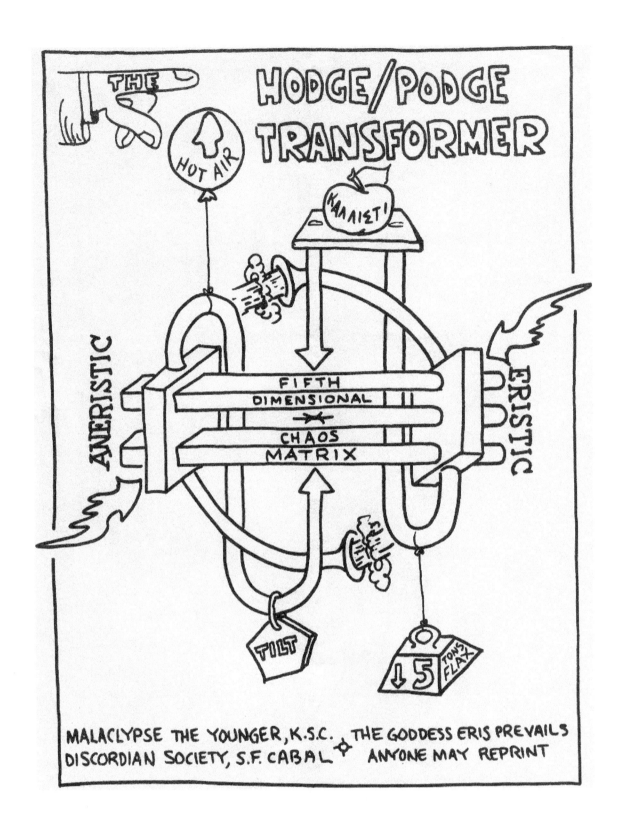

Figure 14.9 Hodge Podge Transformer by Greg Hill

PERPETUAL DATE CONVERTER FROM GREGORIAN TO (POEE) ERISIAN CALENDAR

1 Dsc – Int'l Tyrannicide Day
57 Cfn – John Dillinger shot 1934
57 Afm – Entropy Day

SEASONS:
1) Chaos – Patron Apostle Hung Mung
2) Discord – Patron Apostle Dr. Van Van Mojo
3) Confusion – Patron Apostle Sri Syadasti
4) Bureaucracy – Patron Apostle Zarathud
5) The Aftermath – Patron Apostle The Elder Malaclypse

DAYS OF THE WEEK:
1) Sweetmorn 2) Boomtime 3) Pungenday 4) Prickle-prickle
5) Setting Orange (named from the Five Basic Elements)

HOLYDAYS:
A) Apostle Holydays: 1) Mungday 2) Mojoday 3) Syaday 4) Zaraday
5) Maladay (each occurs on the 5th day of his Season)
B) Season Holydays: 1) Chaoflux 2) Discoflux 3) Confuflux
4) Bureflux 5) Afflux (each occurs on the 50th day of the Season)
c) St. Tib's Day: occurs every 4 years and is inserted between the 59th and 60th days of the Season of Chaos

							SM	BT	PD	PP	SO	
Jan	1	2	3	4	(5)		1	2	3	4	(5)	Chs
	6	7	8	9	10		6	7	8	9	10	
	11	12	13	14	15		11	12	13	14	15	
	16	17	18	19	20		16	17	18	19	20	
	21	22	23	24	25	5	21	22	23	24	25	5
	26	27	28	29	30		26	27	28	29	30	
Feb	31	1	2	3	4		31	32	33	34	35	
↳	5	6	7	8	9		36	37	38	39	40	
	10	11	12	13	14		41	42	43	44	45	
	15	16	17	18	(19)	10	46	47	48	49	(50)	10
	20	21	22	23	24		51	52	53	54	55	
	25	26	27	28*	1		56	57	58	59*	60	
Mar	2	3	4	5	6		61	62	63	64	65	
	7	8	9	10	11		66	67	68	69	70	14
	12	13	14	(15)	16	15	71	72	73	(1)	2	Dsc
	17	18	(19)	20	21		3	4	(5)	6	7	
	22	23	24	25	26		8	9	10	11	12	
	27	28	29	30	31		13	14	15	16	17	
Apr	1	2	3	4	5		18	19	20	21	22	
	6	7	8	9	10	20	23	24	25	26	27	20
	11	12	13	14	15		28	29	30	31	32	
	16	17	18	19	20		33	34	35	36	37	
	21	22	23	24	25		38	39	40	41	42	GULIKMAS
	26	27	28	29	30		43	44	45	46	47	
May	1	2	(3)	4	5	25	48	49	(50)	51	(52)	25
	6	7	8	9	10		53	54	55	56	57	
	11	12	13	14	15		58	59	60	61	62	
	16	17	18	19	20		63	64	65	66	67	
	21	22	23	24	25		68	69	70	71	72	29
	26	27	28	29	30	30	73	1	2	3	4	Cfn
Jun	(31)	1	2	3	4		(5)	6	7	8	9	
↳	5	6	7	8	9		10	11	12	13	14	
	10	11	12	13	14		15	16	17	18	19	
	15	16	17	18	19		20	21	22	23	24	
	20	21	22	23	24	35	25	26	27	28	29	35
	25	26	27	28	29		30	31	32	33	34	
Jul	30	1	2	3	4		35	36	37	38	39	
↳												

							SM	BT	PD	PP	SO	
Jul	30	1	2	3	4		35	36	37	38	39	(Cfn)
↳	5	6	7	8	9		40	41	42	43	44	
	10	11	12	13	14		45	46	47	48	49	
	(15)	16	17	18	19	40	(50)	51	52	53	54	40
	20	21	22	23	24		55	56	57	58	59	
	25	26	27	28	29		60	61	62	63	64	
Aug	30	31	1	2	3		65	66	67	68	69	
↳	4	5	6	7	8		70	71	72	73	1	44
	9	10	11	(12)	13	45	2	3	4	(5)	6	Bcy
	14	15	16	17	18		7	8	9	10	11	
	19	20	21	22	23		12	13	14	15	16	
	24	25	26	27	28		17	18	19	20	21	
	29	30	31	1	2		22	23	24	25	26	
Sep	3	4	5	6	7	50	27	28	29	30	31	50
	8	9	10	11	12		32	33	34	35	36	
	13	14	15	16	17		37	38	39	40	41	
	18	19	20	21	22		42	43	44	45	46	
	23	24	25	(26)	27		47	48	49	(50)	51	
	28	29	30	1	2	55	52	53	54	55	56	55
Oct	3	4	5	6	7		57	58	59	60	61	
	8	9	10	11	12		62	63	64	65	66	
	13	14	15	16	17		67	68	69	70	71	
	18	19	20	21	22		72	73	1	2	3	Afm
	23	(24)	25	26	27	60	4	(5)	6	7	8	60
	28	29	30	31	1		9	10	11	12	13	
Nov	2	3	4	5	6		14	15	16	17	18	
	7	8	9	10	11		19	20	21	22	23	
	12	13	14	15	16		24	25	26	27	28	
	17	18	19	20	21	65	29	30	31	32	33	65
	22	23	24	25	26		34	35	36	37	38	
	27	28	29	30	1		39	40	41	42	43	
Dec	2	3	4	5	6		44	45	46	47	48	
	7	(8)	9	10	11		49	(50)	51	52	53	
	12	13	14	(15)	16	70	54	55	56	57	58	70
	17	18	19	20	21		59	60	61	62	63	
	22	23	24	25	26		64	65	66	67	68	
	27	28	29	30	31		69	70	71	72	73	

1970 = 3136

St. Tib's Day in 3138

ODD # III(b)/4,∴; 57 Afm 3135

Prickle-prickle!

OFFICE OF MY HIGH REVERENCE
MALACLYPSE THE YOUNGER KSC
OPOVIG HIGH PRIEST POEE

POEE

Figure 14.10 Erisian Calendar by Greg Hill

DID YOU KNOW THAT GOD IS A CRAZY WOMAN?
(We didn't think that you did)

Her name is ERIS and the ancient Greeks called Her the Goddess of Confusion and Discord.
After laying dormant for 3125 years, She revealed Herself to the modern world in this
time of Great Need.   She explained that things are not really fucked up - that they
just act fucked up.   She explained that Disorder is every much as sensible as Order -
the two having different functions, and neither existing anyway.   She explained why the
Great Pyramid has five sides (counting the bottom).   She explained the working of the
mysterious Hodge and the mysterious Podge, and gave the Sacred Chao to The Keepers.
She explained that a positive approach to insanity will illuminate a person to
Episkopeshood. She explained why Pickering's Moon goes backwards and time goes forwards
and why cabbages don't go anywhere.   She explained the sinister Pentagon and why that
is the shape of the U.S. Military Headquarters Bldg. She explained that She was the
Chick What Done It All.   And She explained that explanations are utterly foolish.
O! Hail Eris! The Goddess Prevails.

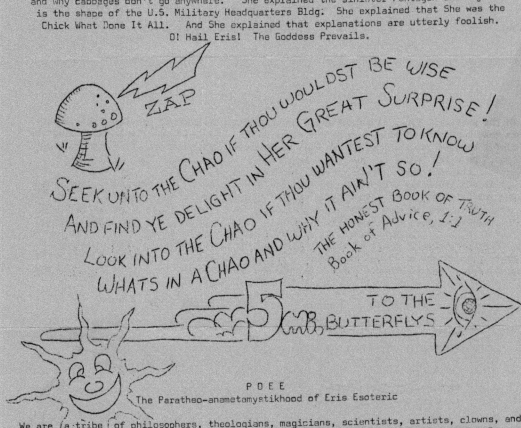

P O E E
The Paratheo-anametamystikhood of Eris Esoteric

We are a tribe of philosophers, theologians, magicians, scientists, artists, clowns, and
similar maniacs who are intrigued with ERIS, GODDESS OF CONFUSION and with Her Doings

FOR FURTHER INFORMATION, illuminating Truths, bald-assed lies, and assorted outrages, send
some postage stamps or a free will offering or five tons of flax or whatever you like, to
POEE HEAD TEMPLE   On The Future Site of Beautiful San Andreas Canyon

OFFICES OF THE POLYFATHER: POEE HEAD TEMPLE   BOX 26475 SAN FRANCISCO 94126
                                 POEE ASHRAM c/o 258 EAST 4 ST NEW YORK CITY 10009

BOX 359 WELLFLEET MASS 02667

Figure 14.11 "Did You Know That God Is a Crazy Woman?" by Greg Hill

The Conspiracy

Washington : Geneva : Moscow : Peking

_____ The PONZI FUND

_____ National Committee to Stick It In Their Ear

_____ TAX resister's league

_____ Fraternal Order of Hate Groups

_____ Committee of **1,000,000** to Nuke the Chinks

_____ International ANTIWAR CRIMES TRIBUNAL

_____ **Congress of Lost Causes**

_____ Young Americans for Real Freedom

_____ SIMPLE SOLUTIONS, INC.

The Capon Society

_____ for manly republicanism

_____ Benign Neglect Society

_____ Forces of Fear, inc.

Bavarian Illuminati
_____ The World's Oldest And Most Successful Conspiracy

_____ Out of Context, inc.

_____ S.O.F.T. shoot opponents of free trade

Adult Coalition for Repression
_____ Of Nuisance Youth Movements

_____ CLEMENCY for Spiro Agnew Corps.

_____ Project F.L.E.E.

_____ LEAGUE of NEGATIVE VOTERS

Informed Sources, Inc.

Veteran Press Agency • Worldwide Contacts • Founded 1888

_____ Pedant, Arcane, and Esoteric/Advertising

_____ SMUT Vigilance Committee

_____ Women's Subjugation Movement

_____ Students Demolishing Society

_____ Friends of the MILITARY-INDUSTRIAL Complex

_____ Dr. PAVLOV's Answering Service

_____ BLACK PANZER PARTY

Ad Hoc Committee
_____ To Send the 20th Century Back to the Factory

_____ Peace and Quiet Party

Figure 14.12 Discordian stationery headers assembled by Thomas the Gnostic

Figure 14.13 Malaclypse the Elder illustration by Roldo Odlor

Figure 14.14 Spoof ad created by Robert Anton Wilson

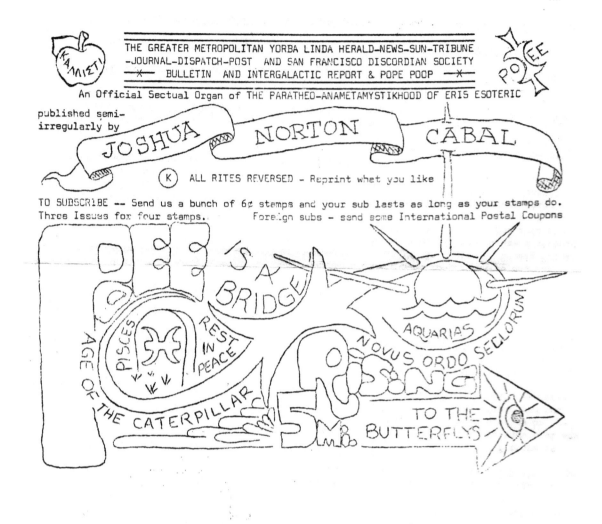

THE GREATER METROPOLITAN YORBA LINDA HERALD-NEWS-SUN-TRIBUNE
-JOURNAL-DISPATCH-POST AND SAN FRANCISCO DISCORDIAN SOCIETY
—*— BULLETIN AND INTERGALACTIC REPORT & POPE POOP —*—

An Official Sectual Organ of THE PARATHEO-ANAMETAMYSTIKHOOD OF ERIS ESOTERIC

published semi-
irregularly by JOSHUA NORTON CABAL

(K) ALL RITES REVERSED - Reprint whet you like

TO SUBSCRIBE -- Send us a bunch of 6¢ stamps and your sub lasts as long as your stamps do.
Three Issues for four stamps.   Foreign subs - send some International Postal Coupons

POEE HEAD TEMPLE
BOX 26475 SAN FRANCISCO
EARTH   94126

"The seal on a first class piece
of mail is SACRED."
-Chief Postal Inspector Montague

FIRST CLASS MAIL

Figure 14.15 Front side of Greg Hill's Discordian newsletter, *The Greater Poop*, circa late 60s

BLUMPF!

THE GREATER METROPOLITAN YORBA LINDA HERALD-NEWS-SUN-TRIBUNE-JOURNAL-
DISPATCH-POST AND SAN FRANCISCO DISCORDIAN SOCIETY CABAL BULLETIN AND
INTERGALACTIC REPORT & POPE POOP —✳— The Official POEE Sectual Organ

published semi-irregularly by
THE PARATHEO-ANAMETAMYSTIKHOOD OF ERIS ESOTERIC
"On The Future Site of The Beautiful San Andreas Canyon"

(Ҝ) ALL RIGHTS REVERSED - REPRINT WHAT YOU LIKE

TO SUBSCRIBE - Send a bunch of 6¢ stamps to POEE. Your sub lasts as long as your stamps do.
Three issues for four stamps.   (Equivalent subscription for foreign postage rates.)

BULLSHIT MAKES THE FLOWERS GROW...AND THAT'S BEAUTIFUL!

POEE
BOX 26475 SAN FRANCISCO
EARTH 94126

FIRST CLASS MAIL

Figure 14.16 Front side from another issue of *The Greater Poop* newsletter

Figure 14.17 Promotional flyer created by Greg Hill for the Cinema Rio Theatre

Figure 14.18 Another promotional flyer created by Greg Hill for the Cinema Rio Theatre

The Discordian Dialogues

To FOLLOW IS A SMATTERING of chaotic correspondence documenting the Discordian Society's evolution. Some of these letters were dictated by Hill or Thornley. Other curiosities include such as a beautifully illustrated letter from the Seattle Discordian Society, and a postcard from none other than Charlie Manson.

THE DISCORDIAN SOCIETY

THE HOUSE OF THE APOSTLES OF ERIS;   Office of High Priesthood
==

TO: MICHAEL R. SCHOLAR
FROM: MALACLYPSE (THE YOUNGER), K.C.; Omniscient Polyfather
        of Virginity--in--gold; High Priest of The Heretic
        Fringe & Protestant Persuasion of the ERISIAN MOVEMENT
DATE: 29 April 1964 (Heathen Christian Calandar)

+++

CONGRATULATIONS! You have just been drafted into the Discordian
Society.

Enclosed find all sorts of garbage that might help confuse you.
It is yours to cherish forever.

I would suggest that you sit in a quiet corner with a gallon
of Dago Red and contemplate the Erisian Mysteries as they
unfold before your eyes. It is also suggested that you unfold
them in about the same order as they are mailed--it might help
a bit.

Should think that in some instances you will find striking
parrallells (2 r's and 4 l's?) between the DS and our own
ROTTOA--it is no coincidence, I have borrowed freely. Actually,
when Kerry and I began to concieve of the DS (a wee bit of
literary licenee was taken in the account of the founding that
you have in "Are You A Discordian"--but one of the major steps
in the evolution of the DS did happen in a bowling alley) I
had in mind a new sort of ROTTOA but as we grew and prospered
our Society began to take on a personality of its own and
finally bloomed forth into a Religion. As soon as we began
taking converts (the Erisian Movement now has nine members) I
had decided that I had better let you in on all this and see
what may come of it.

What I hope may come of it is this: You become as intrigued
with the preposterous ideas as much as did Kerry and I; and
find yourself opening up a No. Calif. Sub-div. and spreading
The Word and taking Converts and writing Holy Works and the
Whole Gig. If you are game, then you will be immediately
ascended from The Legion of Dynamic Discord to The House of
The Apostles of Eris and will be an Episkopos on my own reco-
mendation.

If you are not game--then that is too goddam bad because you
have been drafted. It is absolutely the case that you are
(have always been and always will be) a Discordian of some
sort; the question remains--of what sort? If you are not
interested ambmm in Enlightened Erisianism then you will simply
be demoted to a special movement for Discordians that want out,
namely The Bowel Movement. But regardless, you may display
the Emblem. Everything else, I've sent on the assumption that
you are still Samkavitch J. Vladivostok.

Figure 15.1a Correspondence from Malaclypse the Younger (aka Greg Hill)

accepting Michael Scholar into the Discordian Society flock

Which reminds me: as a Legionnaire (which is what you are at
the moment), you have the priveledge to adopt a Sacred Name.
If you wish to continue with Samk, it would do nicely but
the choice is yours--the Sacred Name is a very personal thing
and should be chosen carefully. When you get one, notify
me and I'll record it in The Erisian Archives (remember the
old Patent Office?).

If Bev is interested in True Wisdom then she should do as
follows (which is different from what you did--i.e. nothing--
because you have been drafted): Simply write a letter to
Malaclypse (The Younger), K.C.; c/o Gregory Hill; 422 N. Milton
Ave.; Whittier, Calif. State in the letter that you wish to
become a Discordian and presto! You are in the Erisian
Movement and will recieve all that you deserve.

Oh yes...you are not only in The Legion but are a member of
my own sect: The Heretic Fringe & Protestant Persuasion.
Lord Omar (Kerry) has his sect: The Erisian Orthodoxy; but
he is all wrong so you want to be part of mine. However,
if you wish, you may write him (which I suggest doing anyway--
you two have a lot in common) for information or whatever.

There are no dues in the DS but I'm debating about an initation
fee. At the moment, it is all free; but I'm swiftly going
bankrupt. Donations are accepted but not obligational.

I hope that you remember who Eris is. If your memory is vague
(shame shame): She is the Greek Goddess of Strife and
Discord. The Myth of The Apple of Discord is as follows
(I'll quote from my minor Holy Work Principia Discordia):
    It seems that Zeus was throwing a wedding banquet for
    Peleus and Thetis; and quite logically didn't want to
    invite Eris because he wanted it to go well. So everybody
    got invited but poor Eris (we call this The Doctrine of
    The Original Snub), and she got quite angry about it all.
    Her cunning little mind clicked away madly and she took
    an apple of pure gold and inscribed upon it KALLISTI
    ("to the prettiest one") and rolled it into the
    banquet hall. Needless to say, Her plan worked: three of
    the Goddesses immediately claimed the apple as theirs,
    exclaiming "It is obviously mine, it says 'For the
    prettiest one' right accross the face of it," and then
    their boy friends started defending them and soon began
    swinging at one another and an utter melee was in progress.
    Now Zeus was taking all this in, and since he had previously
    decided that Earth was getting over-populated and something
    must be done, he too set his mind to work. So he announced
    that an arbitrator must be selected to decide whether
    Aphrodite, Hera, or Athena (the three Goddesses in question)
    should have the apple. He sent the bunch of them to Paris,
    a sheapherd of Troy with the instruction to abide by his
    decision. But, (oh, Eris had these gals picked all right!),

Figure 15.1b Page 2 of letter from Greg Hill to Michael Scholar

each went to Paris independently beforehand and offered
him a bribe to answer in her favor; Athena offered
Heroic War Victories, Hera offered something-or-another
(I forget what), and Aphrodite offered The Most Beautiful
Woman In The "orld. Now, being a healthy, red-blooded,
young Trojan lad, he chose Sex; and Aphrodite manuvered
it so that he could have Helen, then living with her
husband Meneleus of Sparta (she couldn't always be found
at home, but hopped from bed to bed throughout the
Greek world). Anyway, unless you are some dumb dumb clod
you should know that The Trojan War followed when Sparta
demanded their queen back--and that the Trojan War was the
proto-war for all the messes and problems of the world
ever since.
And we Erisian have become aware that Chaos has been the
(dis) order of the day ever since. Yes, yes, bow to our
Lady of Discord, our Everpresent Manipulator of The Universe,
all Hail Eris!

Well anywho...so much for now.

Am awaiting your reply.

Malaclypse (the younger)

Figure 15.1c Page 3 of letter from Greg Hill to Michael Scholar

<u>THE</u> <u>DISCORDIAN</u> <u>SOCIETY</u>

P.O. BOX 55555, PENTAGON BLDG, WASHINGTON D.C. 22206

==

TO: Legionnaire Douglas Smith
FROM: Malaclypse (The Younger), K.C.; as Episkopos of The House of
       the Apostles of Eris in accordance to The Legion of Dynamic
       Discord; and as High Priest of the Heretic Fringe & Protestant
       Persuasion sect of The Erisian Movement Theologies
DATE: April 25, 1964
SUBJECT: Acknowledgement of Erisian status

==

Most Gracious Mr. Smith,

        Wecome to The Fold! (Now you won't go to Hell)

        Your letter of request has reached this office and has been
duly (duely? dully?) registered in The Erisian Archives; you are
now, officially, a Legionnaire in THE LEGION OF DYNAMIC DISCORD.

        Furthermore (whether you like it or not), you are also a
follower of Mine (hail Me) and now belong to The Heretic Fringe and
Protestant Persuasion--one of the two splits of our Church. Lord
Omar, the other Keeper Of The Sacred Chao ("K.C.") and the High
Priest of The Erisian Orthodoxy, insists that I always inform my
new Children that they can quit my sect and join his (or declare
themselves non-sectarian) if they so desire; but you'll have to
write him for information if you want it--I won't plug his group
for him. He's wrong anyway.

        Enclosed find a) your Discordian Emblem, which will look very
impressive if you frame it, b) your Legionnaire Certificate, c) a
Chart of Symbology, so you may know what symbols may properly be
used by whom, and d) a couple of copies of our Pamphlet, one for
your own reference and the others to pass out at your discretion.
There is a lot of other garbage that has yet to be duplicated,
but you will recieve Much Information as soon as it is avaliable--
within a week or two. Until then, you are welcome to drop by here
(if you can ever find me home) and I'll introduce you to The Mysteries
by showing you what has been compiled in The Archives, and what has
been completed so far in my Holy Work, <u>Principia</u> <u>Discordia</u>. And
of course, you can ask Legionnaire Bob Yeager any questions (which he
probably cannot answer).

        As a rule of thumb though, keep this thought in your mind at
all times: there are two Fundamental Principles of Reality; that
of Discord and that of Superficial Order Resting On A Solid Foundation Of Chaos; and Truth is the battle betwixt them. (The former
Principle is called "Eristic" and the latter "Eristesque"; the
intermixture is called "Erisian".) There are many correlaries to
our Cosmology, such as The Law of Fives discovered by the eminent
Lord Omar, but all that will come to you in time. Besides, some of
it has not yet been discovered (but it will, it <u>will</u>).

Figure 15.2a Letter from Malaclypse the Younger
welcoming Legionnaire Douglas Smith into the flock

The Golen Apple Corps (Lord Omar and Myself, the Founders of Discordianism) strongly recommends that you read the Cat's Cradle by Kurt Vonnegut (Holt, Rinehart & Winston; N.Y., S.F.; 1963) and become aquainted with Saint Bokonon; such an aquaintance will be most rewarding to you. A copy is now in the hands of Leg. Judy Gates.

Oh yes, as a Legionnaire you now have the priviledge of adopting a SACRED NAME (after the fashion of those Heathens, the Catholic Christian Papacy). What your name shall be is entirely up to you, and should express your own individuality; you might name yourself after something or someone important to you, you might adopt a name that you feel is symbolicly significant, or whatever. When you have decided on a Sacred Name, please notify this office; it will be recorded and documented, and you will thenseforth be referred to by it.

Some miscellaneous information:
Don't ever write to the Official Letterhead Address, it is used as a return address only and doesn't exist.
If you wish to write to Lord Omar (which is a good idea as long as you don't mention The Orthodoxy) he is at our United States Main Office. /Lord Omar Khayyam Ravenhurst, K.C.; c/o Kerry Thornley; #349 Shirlington House; Arlington, Va. 22206/
Southern California Sub-division (this office) is at the moment at /422 N. Milton Ave.; Whittier, Calif./ but I can always be reached (albeit, sometimes indirectly) at /1331 Ponderosa Ave.; Fullerton, Calif 92631/
As a Legionnaire, your next step up is Disciple of Eris. You are awarded this status by The House of the Apostles of Eris when you do something that propagates the Discordian Society. For example, if you convert five people to the DS, you will be titled Disciple of Eris--Evangelist.
If you are so inclined, you might begin thinking about writing Erisian Words of Wisdom or of authoring a Holy Work. If you think that you have come up with something that demonstrates that you have a profound understanding of Discordiansim, then present it to The Golden Apple Corps for examination; if we like it, you will gain admittance into The House and become an Episkopos.
I forgot to mention: my secular name is Gregory Hill, so include it somewhere when you are writing to me and must go through a secular Post Office.

So much for now....

In The Name of Our Lady of Discord: ERIS

Malaclypse (The Younger), K.C.
Omnipotent Polyfather of Virginity-
in-gold

ALL HAIL DISCORDIA !

Figure 15.2b Page 2 of letter to Douglas Smith

AN EXPERIENCE WITH MESCALINE

Gregory Hill 4-65

One half gram capsule
Stamped "England",
And after a bit the gut is a
  shade off course;
Just enough to demand attention.

A nerve twitch,
A whole layer of nerve twitch,
Chills,
(75° and a humidity of 80 plus,
even at 2 a.m.,
New Orleans is no place
for chills)....
But never mind,
More important things to do:
Like TURN DOWN THE RADIO
and CUT THOSE LIGHTS,
And marvel at a WHOLE LAYER
Of nerves
Complete with
An infinite number of infitesimal
  endings,
Each distinctly unique
Awaiting sensation.

Hand picks up a cigarette
The size of a very small log,
Which is much
Much too large for a cigarette.
A match turns to flame,

And the log is forgotten,
As the room dematerializes,
The Quarter vanishes,
And the Universe dissolves
Into the flame of a match,
Slowly working towards
The fingers
Of the hand
Holding it....

Must protect
The hand
With the fingers
Holding the match
With the magnificent flame,
For the fingers
And the hand
Are old, old friends
And the beautiful flame
Will burn
When
(or if)
It gets around to
Travelling the length of the match.

Half way now.
And heat is present.

Soon now.
(But such a pathetic little flame
minding its own business,
travelling its own matchstick,
inadvertently
threatening old friend hand.)

Closer...
Mercy can no longer be afforded.
BLOW LUNGS!

Dark,
emp-
ty-
ness.

Ah, the
Tragedy of a flame!
But if God can destroy,
Then He can create!

And after much fumblings,
And un-Godlike manuverings
A candle is found,
And a new flame is brought forth;
One infinitely superior
In brilliance and depth
And protected by God Himself
So that it cannot unknowingly
Affront its maker
And may live a full, rich, happy
Flame like life.
Peace,

(cont'ed)

Figure 15.3a Greg Hill's account of a 1965 mescaline trip

Now, whatever was it...?
Oh yes, a cigarette.
Come,
My son the candleflame,
And ignite my log sized cig-
   arette.
Good lad.

A piece of bread,
What a worldly thing thought.
And feel the texture,
And the moisture,
Rich in moisture,
Cool to the skin,
One could
Bathe
In fresh bread.

A small bite,
Slowly chewed and savored,
And swallowed
All
the
way
down
to
the
stomach.

"Look, man. Dig!"
Is heard from the bed and
Companion is pointing to the
   ceiling
Saying "Dig, dig...dig."

And the shadows did a show
That put Disney to shame.
Fingers and hands inches above
   the flame
To form:
Guingnol mannikens boxing;
An immense crab snapping its
   claws and gone in an instant;
Fairy like fluttering whirly-gig
   bugs, skitter dancing to
   radio jazz;
Two ancient dinasaurs in a tension
   battle to the death, now poised,
   now furiously attacking, now
   grip locked, now gone;

And a shy little puppet boy that puts
   up his head from the edge and then
   runs away because we were
   watching him;
And a mmhhp caliope, constructed of
   20 foot bolognas, pulsing
   "OOM PA PA";
And imageless shapes forming and
   reforming patterns of movement
   that are inappropriate to vulgar
   description.

Body becomes helpless with laughter
As whirly-gig bugs return,
But now
Chills are back too
And the room is
Very desolate,
Save one single point
Of life and warmth:
The candle,
Far below on the floor.
As a Holy Guru
The Omniscient flame
Radiates its serenity
To all who
Will accept,
And body is once again granted
Warmth and
Comfort.

Eyes become closed,
And in the endless dark
Behind the eyelids
There appears an
After image of the
Ancient candle flame.
Reddish first,
Then to green,
Slowly
To turquoise,
And fluctuating
From shade to
Beautiful shade;
A feast of color.
And design:
Undulating colors,
Specural dance,
Eyes are drunken with delight.
From a candle flame.

(cont'ed)

Figure 15.3b Page 2 of Hill's 1965 mescaline trip

A piddling little candle flame?
Let us try the kitchen light--
The one with the
LARGE WHITE GLOBE.
And just stare....

Eyes stare for an eternity
At the brilliant
White light,
Enduring the glare
For the anticipation
Of a very scientific-type
   experiment
In the scientific-type field of
   optics
(and pharmachology).

"Enough" says I,
And return to the
Frontroom and body sits
And leans back and
Eyes close
And watch the
Beginning formations
Of dull red on
Endless black...
To green
Growing in intensity,
To turquoise,
Or rather: to green
Co-existant inside blue,
To purples alive with yellow
Emmanating a green that
Yearns to be chartreuse,
But falls to blue,
Blue, blue, an astonishing
Shade
Of
Blue,
And I swear,
Colors formed
That I have
Never
Seen
Before.

By and by
Other companion presents
A pepermint life saver
Which finds its way
From hand to mouth
And brings forth
A sensual experience all but
   beyond belief!
Sensual?
Sexual!
Might I ever find
A woman as erotic as
This peppermint candy,
Charging excitement
Throughout the mouth,
And that
Wild little
Hole
In the middle!

"Hey man, what time is it?"
And Other Companion replies:
"Seventy-five after four."
And m all have a good
Chuckle
That jollies the intestines
And tickles the psyche
And the world is a pleasant place.

Figure 15.3c Page 3 of Hill's 1965 mescaline trip

(✖) OFFICIAL BUSINESS ( ) DRAWER "O"

Safeguard this, it may be an Important Historical Document

( ) SURREPTITIOUS BUSINESS ( ) D-5

Burn This. The paranoids are watching. ( ) GO AWAY

TODAY'S DATE: 34Cfn3136

YESTERDAY'S DATE: 33Cfn3136

DR. IGNOTUM P. IGNOTIUS
SUCCESSOR TO
MALACLYPSE

- JOSHUA NORTON CABAL -

(✖) Rev. Dr. MALACLYPSE THE YOUNGER, K.S.C.; OPoViG; High Priest, POEE; Episkopos

( ) The Rev. LADY MALACLYPSE, D.D., D.A.R. (II); Keeper of The Polyfather

( ) MAD MALIK, Hauptscheissmeister, AISB

- POEE HEAD TEMPLE, S.F. -

HOUSE OF APOSTLES OF ERIS:

( ) G.A.C. ( ) Episkopotic Cabalablia

HOUSE OF THE RISING PODGE:

(✖ Office of The Polyfather ( ) Council of POEE Priests ( ) Legion of Dynamic Discord

HOUSE OF THE RISING HODGE:

(✖ The Bureau of Administry for The Unenlightened Eristic Horde

HOUSE OF THE RISING COLLAPSE:

( ) Liberate Freedom

( ) Don't Immanentize the Eschaton

- ALSO REPRESENTING -

(✖ The Ancient Illuminated Seers of Bavaria, Chicago; S.F. VIGILANCE LODGE

( ) The Army of Mercy, Ceres CA; Brigadier Admiral

( ) The Apple Panthers, Monroe

(✖ Church Invisible of The Laughing Christ, Atlanta; Pastor

( ) The John Dillinger Died For You Society, Chicago; Asst. Treasurer

( ) Legalize Marijuana International, Buffalo

(✖ Neo-American Church, South Hero VT; Boo Hoo

( ) Our People's Underworld, Larchmont NY

( ) Provo Anarcho-pacifist Exchange (PAX), S.F.

( ) The Seven Mighty Anvils, Topanga CA; number 25

(✖ Surrealists, Harlequinists, Absurdists and Zonked Artists Melee (SHAZAM;)

( ) Universal Life Church, Modesto CA; Minister

Figure 15.4a Front page of Discordian correspondence from Dr. Ignotum R. Ignotius (aka Greg Hill)

TO: Pope Herman Rief, Church of Rejuvenation
    Pope Charlie Willims, The Cactus Church
    Pope Imeh Emmanuel, NeoPlatonic Church etc

C/O H.H. Blackschleger, Keeper of The Popes

Dearest Brothers,

If you fellows don't have sufficient credentials,
you may be pleased to find the enclosed three (3)
POPE CARDS which will be very useful to your
operation. There is no charge for these credentials.
Please accept them as a token of good will and
as an introduction for you to your Goddess ERIS.
Watch for Her, She will be contacting you shortly.

Enclosed also is a genuine 5-pointed GOLD STAR, for
you to nail to your collective forehead.

FLIEGENDE KINDERSCHEISSE!

                        Eris' 'umble Servant,

                        Office of The Polyfather
                        POEE Head Temple

PS to Cactus Church: Charlie, DO IT.

Figure 15.4b Back page of correspondence to newly ordained Discordian popes

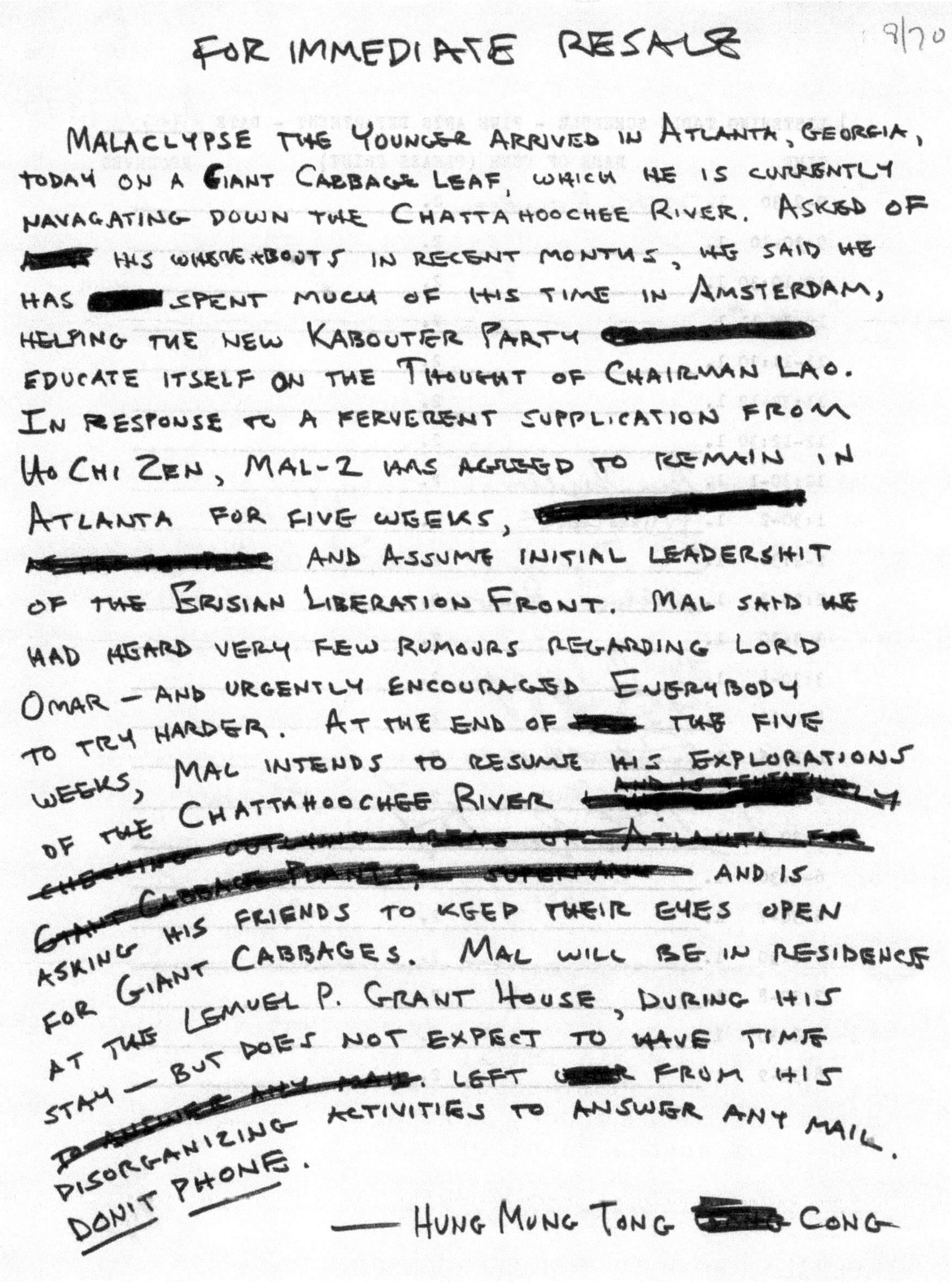

FOR IMMEDIATE RESALE

9/70

MALACLYPSE THE YOUNGER ARRIVED IN ATLANTA, GEORGIA, TODAY ON A GIANT CABBAGE LEAF, WHICH HE IS CURRENTLY NAVAGATING DOWN THE CHATTAHOOCHEE RIVER. ASKED OF ~~HIS~~ HIS WHEREABOUTS IN RECENT MONTHS, HE SAID HE HAS ~~REMAIN~~ SPENT MUCH OF HIS TIME IN AMSTERDAM, HELPING THE NEW KABOUTER PARTY ~~████~~ EDUCATE ITSELF ON THE THOUGHT OF CHAIRMAN LAO. IN RESPONSE TO A FERVERENT SUPPLICATION FROM HO CHI ZEN, MAL-2 HAS AGREED TO REMAIN IN ATLANTA FOR FIVE WEEKS, ~~████████~~ ~~████████~~ AND ASSUME INITIAL LEADERSHIT OF THE ERISIAN LIBERATION FRONT. MAL SAID HE HAD HEARD VERY FEW RUMOURS REGARDING LORD OMAR — AND URGENTLY ENCOURAGED EVERYBODY TO TRY HARDER. AT THE END OF ~~THE~~ THE FIVE WEEKS, MAL INTENDS TO RESUME HIS EXPLORATIONS OF THE CHATTAHOOCHEE RIVER ~~AND IS TENTATIVELY~~ ~~CHECKING OUTLYING AREAS OF ATLANTA FOR~~ ~~GIANT CABBAGE PLANTS, OTHERWISE~~ AND IS ASKING HIS FRIENDS TO KEEP THEIR EYES OPEN FOR GIANT CABBAGES. MAL WILL BE IN RESIDENCE AT THE LEMUEL P. GRANT HOUSE, DURING HIS STAY — BUT DOES NOT EXPECT TO HAVE TIME ~~PRACTICING ANY MAIL.~~ LEFT ~~OVER~~ FROM HIS DISORGANIZING ACTIVITIES TO ANSWER ANY MAIL. DON'T PHONE.

— HUNG MUNG TONG ~~CONG~~ CONG

Figure 15.5 Letter documenting Greg Hill's 1970 visit with Kerry Thornley in Atlanta, Georgia

THIS IS A CHAIN LETTER.

WITHIN THE NEXT FIFTY-FIVE DAYS YOU WILL
RECEIVE THIRTY-ELEVEN HUNDRED LBS OF CHAINS.

IN THE MEANTIME...PLANT YOUR SEEDS.

If a lot of people who receive this letter
plant a few seeds and a lot of people receive
this letter, then a lot of seeds will get
planted. PLANT YOUR SEEDS!

In parks. On lots. Public flower beds. In
remote places. At City Hall. Wherever. And
whenever. Or start a plantation in your
closet (but read up on it first, for that).
For casual planting, it's best to soak them
in water for a day and plant in a bunch of
about 5, about half an inch deep. Don't worry
much about weather, they know when the weather
is wrong and will try to wait for nature.
Don't soak them if it's winter. Seeds are a
very hearty life form and strongly desire to
grow and flourish. But some of them need
people's help to get started. PLANT YOUR SEEDS!

Make a few copies of this letter (5 would be
nice) and send them and this copy to friends
of yours. Try to mail to different cities
and states, even different countries. If you
would rather not, then please pass this copy
on to someone and perhaps they would like to.

THERE IS NO TRUTH to the legend that if you
throw away a chain letter then all sorts of
catastrophic, abominable, and outrageous
disasters will happen. Except, of course,
from your seed's point of view.

AMERICA, WE HAVE YOU SURROUNDED.
Originated in Los Angeles 1968 by The Paratheo-
anametamystikhood of Eris Esoteric, as a joint
effort of The Discordian Society. The Goddess
Eris Prevails. Shantih

Figure 15.6 Discordian chain letter encouraging the recipients to plant marijuana seeds

→ INVITATION ←

THE PARATHEO-ANAMETAMYSTIKHOOD OF ERIS ESOTERIC (POEE)
A Non-prophet Irreligious Disorganization

MALACLYPSE the Younger, KSC
Omnibenevolent Polyfather of Virginity in Gold
HIGH PRIEST

HI!

THE ERISIAN MOVEMENT
( ) Official Business   (X) Surreptitious Business   HOUSE OF APOSTLES OF ERIS
Official Discordian Document Number (if applicable): ODD#59Bcy3140yDii;IIIb   page 1 of 1 pages
( ) The Golden Apple Corps   (X) House of Disciples of Discordia; The Bureaucracy, Bureau of: Thelemics
( ) Council of Episkoposes; Office of High Priesthood, Sect of the POEE   ( ) Drawer O

Today's DATE: 59 Bcy 3140 y.D.   Yesterday's DATE: 58 Bcy 3140 y.D.
Originating CABAL: BEZERKLEY

BRING SOME FOOD AND/OR DRINK

TO: All sentient beings   AN ICE CREAM PRODUCT

("God is alive, magick is afoot..."--Buffy St. Marie)

ACHTUNG! ATTENTION!! NOW HEAR THIS!!!   TOP SECRET

Bureaucracy 66, 3140 y.D. (that is...October 12, 1974 e.v.) is

THE NINETY-NINTH BIRTHDAY OF ST. ALEISTER CROWLEY

WHEN?   or, more simply,   SATURDAY NIGHT, 7 ON

"CROWLEYMAS DAY!!!!"

To celebrate this most magick, most mystic, most magnificent,
most monstrous, most madcap of all Holy Days, be it known to all
that the PARATHEO-ANAMETAMYSTIKHOOD OF ERIS ESTOERIC (POEE), in
collaboration with

THE GREAT WILD BEAST FURTHERMENT SOCIETY   MIN NL PD

and

THE ORDO TEMPLI CELATUS, LODGE OF THE BAVARIAN ILLUMINATI

T'AI

will hold one hell of a holy bash (party, celebration, mass, fest,
madhouse, orgy) throughout various apartments on the first, second
and third floors of

WHERE? → 2035 CHANNING WAY (corner of SHATTUCK)
              BERKELEY, CALIFORNIA   APTS. 101,103
                                              203,303
This is strictly pot-luck, come-as-you-are, free-form and Erisian.

WHO
(BOB &
ARLEN
CARO
STEPH
CLAYTO
CHARLE
CLAIR
ETC.

WARNING: Crowley's poetry will be recited in certain rooms. There
will also be witch-singing, invocations and events astral and half-astra

HAIL ERIS
ALL HAIL DISCORDIA
POEE

Mal-2 POEE
Malaclypse the Younger, KSC, OFOVIG-POEE

OFFICIAL
DISCORDIAN SOCIETY
HAIL ERIS

DR. IGNOTUM P. IGNOTIUS, KPS
High Priest - Poee Head Temple
Officer of the Polyfather

CLOPORTES
LINDA LOVELACE FOR PRESIDENT   SEE MENTAL HEALTH RECORDS   SENDER WAITING!
Answer by wire.

KALLISTI ~~~~~ HAIL ERIS ~~~~~ ALL HAIL DISCORDIA

Safeguard this Letter, it may be an IMPORTANT DOCUMENT   Form No.: O.D.D. IIb/ii.1-37D.VVM: 3134

Figure 15.7 Greg Hill's announcement of a Discordian party
at Robert Anton Wilson's apartment complex in Berkeley in 1974

The Seattle Cabal herewith announces that unimpeachable sources not disclosed by Goddess (Who, as we all know, has Her harmless little secrets) have instructed us to proclaim in accordance with Her revelation that:

The 1ˢᵗ Day of the Season of Discord, Year of our Lady 3136

known to the vulgar as

March 15, 1970

and that same day of all years hereafter (until future events shall render its observance moot) shall henceforth be known and celebrated as

International Tyrannicide Day

Whereof notice is hereby given, that all Discordians may have ample season in which to prepare such rites as they may deem proper for its observance.

It is suggested that conspicuous display, vainglory, boasting, and any and all manner of public utterances are most inappropriate preparation for the fruitful performance of those rites that most sincerely commemorate the spirit of this High Holyday.

Hail Eris ✠ All hail Discordia

Further:

The Goddess desires that this Holyday be celebrated not for Her gratification alone not solely by Her devotees;

therefore is it laid upon loyal Discordians to commend to all and sundry the prudent execution of this Day's ceremonies.

GLORY TO THE SACRED CHAO

Figure 15.8 Correspondence from the Seattle Discordian Cabal.

Some of this artwork was later incorporated into the 4th ed. of *Principia Discordia*

Naked Crusaders

Nudes on Market Street

By Jerry Carroll

Two willowy blondes walked nude down Market street yesterday, hand-in-hand with a naked dwarf who had a peg-leg and a beard.

The three of them, at the height of the evening rush-hour traffic, c o m m a n d e d considerable attention.

They said they were soldiers in the Om United New World Nude Brigade, whose objective is to free mankind from 6000 years of sexual guilt.

In all, it took the three perhaps five minutes to stroll the two blocks from Stockton and Market, past the cable-car turntable at Powell, and up Eddy street.

RESTRAINT

Eyes w i d e n e d, jaws dropped and faces filled the windows of the street cars r o l l i n g past the line of march. C o m m e n t was restrained, however.

"T o d a y, you see everything," reflected news vendor Roland Beane, 58, as the three padded past his booth on five bare feet and the rubber-tipped peg-leg.

At the end of the march, the three naked people piled into a waiting car and raced off. leaving a young man called Baba Om to explain the philosophy that animates the brigade.

"People confuse nudity with sex," Baba said by way of preamble. A common, even understandable, mistake, he acknowledged.

"And sex in this day and age has always meant degeneracy, bad habits, and lewdness," Baba said.

REHABILITATION

The way to rehabilitate sex — and rid the world of "war, chaos and destruction" in the bargain—is for people to take off their clothes and leave them off, Baba remarked.

"Nudity must be restored to human beings if they are to regain paradise," he said with great earnestness, going on in this vein for some little time.

He identified the marchers as Pat Om, Nancy Om and Larry Om and the overall leader of the brigade as just plain Om.

"Om is the supreme sound or vibration, which in this country is known as God," Baba pointed out, making a circle with a thumb and forefinger to show what Om looks like and saying "Om."

ROBES

Nowadays when you think of Om—if you do at all—it is usually in connection with the Hare Krishna sect, those p e o p l e with shaved heads and saffron robes who chant on street corners.

As it happened, when Baba finished speaking a group of Hare Krishna people were setting up shop a block away, breaking out their tambou-rlines and c l e a r i n g thei throats.

One of the robed monks confirmed that Baba was, ir a sense, correct about Om "Om is the sound vibratior of God," he said. But the monk took a censorious view toward the parade.

INDIGNATION

"There's nothing in Om about r u n n i n g around naked," the monk said with considerable indignation.

"Spiritual life is not to exhibit your fleshy body, which everyone knows about anyhow," the monk said.

Some p e o p l e, he added, "are using the spiritual life for their own sense gratification, sense of exhibitionism or whatever it is."

In s h o r t, he said, the march was an activity which is "simply unauthorized."

'Today, you see everything,' said a news vendor as the Om United New World Nude Brigade passed by

Figure 15.9 Newspaper article on the Om New World Nude Brigade

THE PARATHEO-ANAMETAMYSTIKHOOD OF ERIS ESOTERIC (POEE)
A Non-prophet Irreligious Disorganization

MALACLYPSE the Younger, KSC

Omnibenevolent Polyfather of Virginity in Gold
HIGH PRIEST

THE ERISIAN MOVEMENT
(x) Official Business   ( ) Surreptitious Business
Official Discordian Document Number (if applicable): n/a

HOUSE OF APOSTLES OF ERIS
page 1 of __1__ pages

( ) The Golden Apple Corps   ( ) House of Disciples of Discordia; The Bureaucracy, Bureau of:
(x) Council of Episkoposes; Office of High Priesthood, Sect of the POEE   ( ) Drawer O

Today's DATE: 16 Cfn 3136   Yesterday's DATE: 15 Cfn 3136
Originating CABAL: JOSHUA NORTON CABAL, POEE HEAD TEMPLE

TO: Baba Om, Om United New World Nude Brigade, San Francisco

Dearest Om Baba —

There is no doubt in my pineal gland that my own beloved guru, Maltoo Baba, would
hold your crusade in the greatest of esteem.

Enclosed are five Pope Cards, for yourself, the girls and the little fellow, plus
one extra on general principles (to accord with the Law of Fives) - it authorizes
and certifies you to ignore the so-called authorities and to proceed with your
excellent mission.

One remark, however, on your statement wherein you equated chaos with war and
destruction. This is a minor heresy towards Goddess but a common mistake.
Reality, you see, is the original Rorschach. Chaos is that which our conscious
minds use as a matrix and is inherently beyond distinctions or polarities like
̶p̶o̶s̶i̶t̶i̶v̶e̶/̶n̶e̶g̶a̶t̶i̶v̶e̶ ̶o̶r̶ ̶w̶h̶i̶c̶h̶ ̶c̶o̶m̶e̶s̶ ̶b̶e̶f̶o̶r̶e̶ order/disorder. Chaos is energy...singing OM!
Indeed, even ̶d̶i̶s̶o̶r̶d̶ disorder is not negative but neutral, though oft times it
is used negatively (as is order oft times used negatively, e.g. fascism). Is the
laughter of a child destructive? Do clowns make good soldiers? Humor is a
psychic gyroscope, and is an example of positvely directed disorder. There still
remains, of course, that which you were referring to, mistakenly, as chaos;
namely, destructive disorder, which, like destructive order (as opposed to
constructive disorder and constructive order), is anti-life. Chaos, discord,
and confusion - they are innocent! The culprit is man himself, who uses the tools
for destructive ends rather than constructive ends. It is the ̶o̶p̶t̶i̶m̶u̶m̶ opinion of
us at POEE that this misconception about the metaphysics of order/disorder is
the key to Human Liberation, including sexual (need we remind you that perfect
orgasm is pure chaos), which is, of course, what this Renaissance is all about.

But that aside. This letter is to congratulate OUNWNB for your masterful
positively-directed-disorder, by parading about the streets baldassed naked,
with ̶x̶e̶m̶f̶i̶ magnificent effect!

Shanti, brother & sisters. AD ARITRIUM.

Dr Iggy ✳

DR. IGNOTUM P. IGNOTIUS
SUCCESSOR TO
MALACLYPSE

FIND THE GODDESS ERIS
WITHIN YOUR PINEAL GLAND
POEE

PS - am circulating several of these letters in hopes that one eventually
reaches you. POEE mailing address is BOX 26475 SAN FRANCISCO EARTH 94126

KALLISTI ✦✦✦✦✦ HAIL ERIS ✦✦✦✦✦ ALL HAIL DISCORDIA

Safeguard this Letter, it may be an IMPORTANT DOCUMENT   Form No.: O.D.D. IIb/ii.1-37D.VVM; 3134

Figure 15.10 Letter from Dr. Ignotum R. Ignotius (aka Greg Hill)
to Baba Om of the Om United New World Nude Brigade

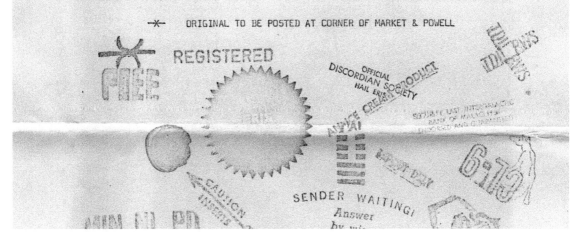

Figure 15.11 Discordian proclamation in support of the Om United New World Nude Brigade

BAVARIAN ILLUMINATI

The World's Oldest and
Most Successful Conspiracy

cleaver excuses invented
spurious philosophies contrived
priests insulted - governments toppled
All Kinds Outrages

BEWARE!
The Paranoids Are Watching You!

JOSHUA NORTON CABAL
20 BCY 3136

TO THE ALTERNATIVE PRESSES
and to anyone else who may find it of interest

MAD MALIK

Ancient Illuminated Seers of Bavaria
Vigilance Lodge

SEASON'S GREETINGS

Should you find an irresistable urge to DO A THING FOR GODDESS, you might consider running a complimentary ad in your paper for the Principia. The Principia is not copyrighted (reprint what you like!), and we are not a commercial enterprise, and we have as yet no treasury to purchase ads or anything else. Consequently, a sympathetic alternative press is crucial to this phase of Our Plot To Underwhelm The World.   Should you know of headshops, bookstores, distributors, etc., who might be interested in quantity orders of 100+, Principias will be available to them at cost and it should be profitable for them.   FOR THE RENAISSANCE!

you can paste-up a small ad from this collage →

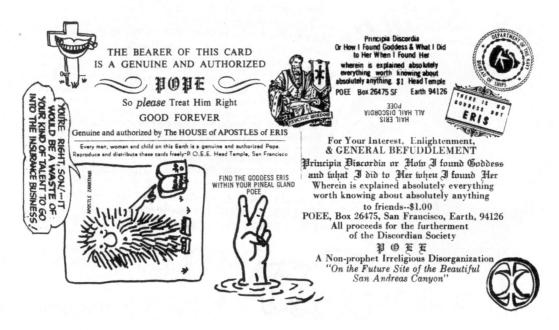

Figure 15.12 Greg Hill publicizing the *Principia Discordia*

DISCORDIAN SOCIETY DELERIOUS OVER PUBLICATION OF ILLUMINATUS

Cabals everywhere celebrated the second major publishing event in
the history of modern Erisianism. The three volume novel is on
the paperback bookshelves now (sci-fi section) and provides five
tons of delight for those of us who like that kind of thing. It
is also a rare example of extended and sustained Discordian art,
and also makes an exemplary text book of Discordian theory and
practice. All you have to remember is that different Discordians
define the Society differently, so the Truth of Goddess according
to Shea and Wilson may have little or nothing to do with the
Truth of Goddess according to other Discordians. That's an old
tradition of ours.

Incidentally, I personally asked my character Prof. Ignotum P.
Ignotius if the quote attributed to him in Illuminatus is
accurate and he said no--Shea and Wilson got the facts all
screwed up. "It wasn't me who made that remark, it was Joe Malik
who said it. Besides, it wasn't even me who was talking to Joe
at the time, it was his half-brother Mad Malik. Mad was the
resident anarchist at Norton Cabal, no one else gave a fuck about
politics or economics--especially me."

This subject of Discordian History reminds me to mention that
correspondence appearing in Neo-Pagan periodicals signed
Malaclypse the Youngest is not by the same person (Malaclypse the
Younger, also called Mal-2) who produced the Principia Discordia
five years ago. Actually Youngest is none other than Tom
Gnostic, High Priest of POEE, who is currently in SF but used to
be in NYC. Younger (Mal-2) used to be me, High Priest of POEE,
then in SF but currently in NYC (but I'm moving back to SF, see
below). Neither of which is Malaclypse the Elder, who is a
Spirit Being, nor is any the same as Mord Mal who used to be in
Chicago and is now in Berkely, nor is any the same as Mad Mal who
is Joe Mal's half-brother. There is also a cartoonist named Mal,
but I don't think that he has anything to do with any of this.

FIRST CLASS MAIL RELOCATES

About the time that this lands in your mailbox, I'll be on the
road returning to the Bay Area for a few years. Continue using
the NYC Box until further notice, but it may be some time before
I actually get to read anything (let alone answer anything--but
you should be used to that by now).

G. H. Hill's
First Class Mail
Box 710 New York City 10013

Figure 15.13 Greg Hill's promotion for the *Illuminatus Trilogy*

Reverend Charles Stanley   12 February 1986
First Baptist Church
Atlanta, Georgia

Dear Reverend Stanley:

    As one who has long insisted motor vehicles are God's punish-
ment for political apathy I was struck by the logic of your
assertion that AIDS is God's penalty for homosexuality.
Since the Bible explicitly forbids cigarette smoking, lung
cancer is divine retribution for that sin. Therefore it follows that common colds are caused by invoking God's displeasure
in living too far from the warm climate of the Holy Land.
Medical science will forever be in your debt for revealing
that the true cause of poor health is going against God's
manifest natural system of law and order.

    I need your help, though, in figuring out what sins some
of the other diseases -- such as muscular distrophy, infantile
paralysis and boubonic plague -- were intended to cure. I
suggest you preach a sermon on this in the near future called
"God's Wonderful Biological Warfare Campaign Against Sin,"
which I will attend and take notes.

    For I am in exceptionally good health and I wish to convince
all my sick friends that if, like me, they were without sin
they could insult the suffering and less fortunate in the smug
self-assurance that you and I do without fear of being smitten
by small pox.

                    Yours for casting that first
                         infected stone,

                         Reverend Jesse Sump
                         First Evangelical and Unrepentant
                         Church of No Faith (Discordian)

Figure 15.14 Letter from Reverend Jesse Sump (aka Kerry Thornley)
to Reverend Charles Stanley

10/29/86

Letters to the Editor
San Francisco Chronicle
5th & Mission Streets
San Francisco 94103

Editor --

In Tennessee a judge has ruled that a parent can refuse to send a child
to a reading class that includes Wizard of Oz and Diary of Anne Frank.
The parents, supposed Christians, claimed that literature that portrays
a good witch (Oz) or suggests that all religions are worthwhile (Anne
Frank) is evil literature and that they have an American right to protect
their children from evil teachings.

Well, maybe they do. And so would the Nazis in the White Masters Church
have an American right to be protected from evil non-racist biology; and
an enterprizing Marxist who incorporates a Church of Karl could be protected from the vile teaching of democracy; and any mystic who wants
protection from the illusion of rationality and deceptive arithmetic; and
holy Couch Potatoes who hate gym class; and on and on.

Maybe it is a good idea. I still have my membership in the Psychedelic
Venus Church (remember us) and this may be my chance to protect some innocent children who are right now getting hypocritical drug hysteria
spewed all over them in schools throughout the nation.

Let's just disband the schools and be done with it!

                        Malaclypse the Younger
                        Paratheoanametamystikhood
                          of Eris Esoteric

Gregory Hill
1650 California #25
San Francisco 94109

Figure 15.15 Greg Hill's 1986 letter to the editor of the *San Francisco Chronicle*

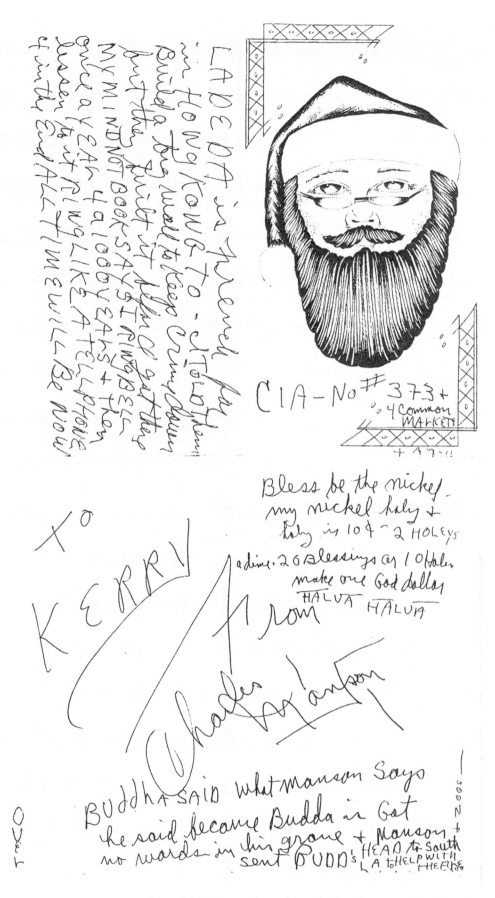

Figure 15.16 Postcard sent from Charlie Manson to Kerry Thornley

Gregory H. Hill

died July 20, 2000 in Pleasant Hill. He was 59, and the cause of death was esophageal cancer. Born in Richmond, CA, and a long time resident of the Bay Area, Mr. Hill worked for the last 23 years at the Bank of America, where he created their base standards for technical communications, including bankwide systems manuals, and created the bank's first word processing program.

But perhaps Mr. Hill's most notable achievement was as creating the role of Malaclypse the Younger, and acting as co-founder of the Discordian Society. He was chief writer and editor of *PRINCIPIA DISCORDIA, or How I Found Goddess and What I Did to Her When I Found Her*. Mr. Hill created The Emperor Norton cabal, named after San Francisco's historical Norton. The Discordian Society triggered a 30-year creative explosion including many books by notables such Robert Anton Wilson and Camden Benares, as well as an underground humor syndicate, carried by the US mail. Mr. Hill's metaphysical underpinnings were to confound the rational mind in the style of the Zen koan, thereby providing, he thought, a shot at transcendent consciousness.

Mr. Hill was an avid researcher of an impressively wide range of subjects, a man of many dimensions, with a complex personality revealing different aspects of himself to his friends. He was also a passionate man, passionate in his suffering, passionate in his reaction to the alienation he felt from his culture, and passionate in his pursuit of information and knowledge.

Married once, for ten years, Mr. Hill is survived by his mother, Yvonne, his sister Rochelle, and a cadre of friends. His memorial occurred in Pleasant Hill, Friday evening.

Louise Lacey

Figure 15.17 Greg Hill's obituary by Louise Lacey

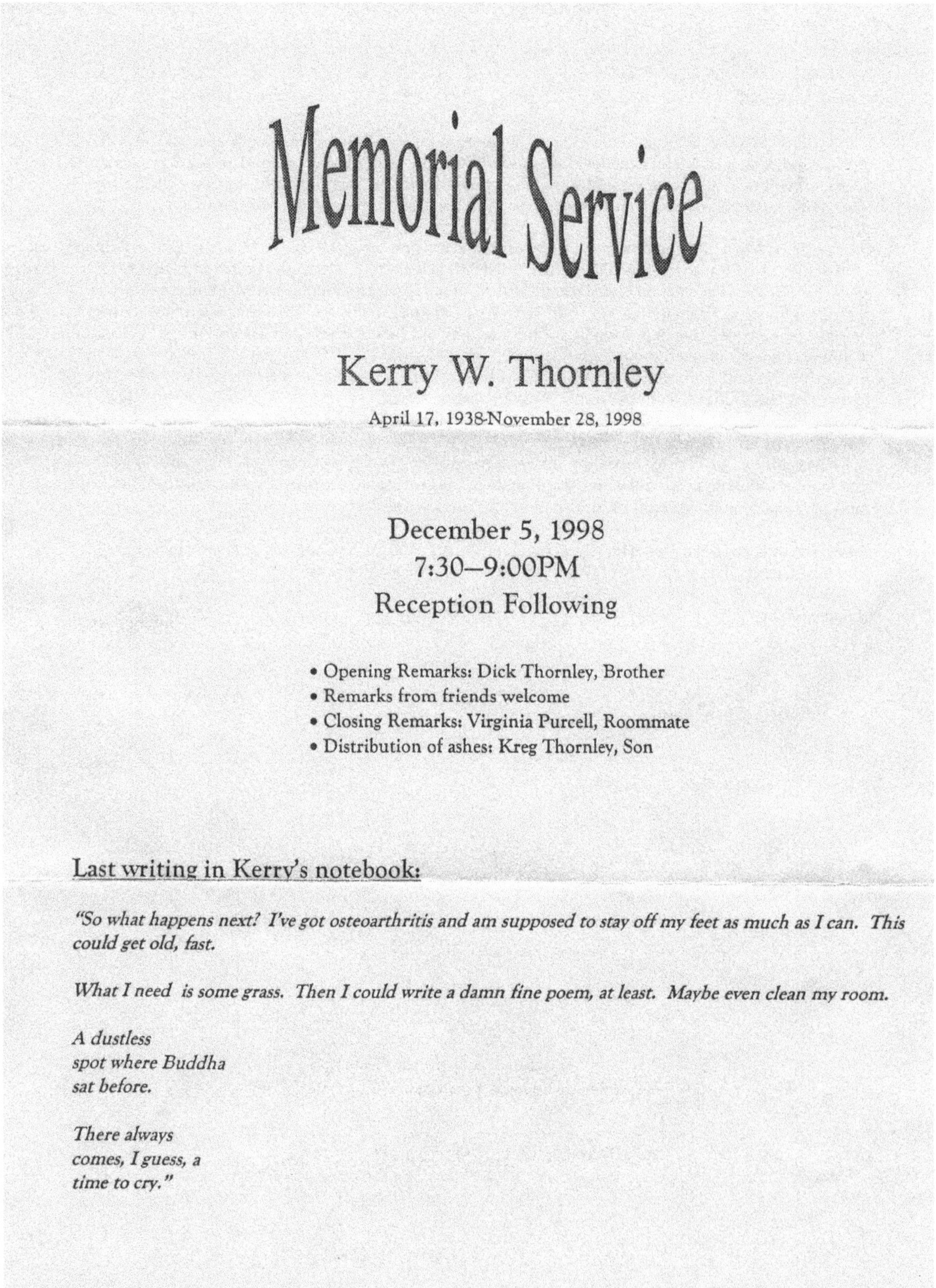

Memorial Service

Kerry W. Thornley

April 17, 1938-November 28, 1998

December 5, 1998
7:30—9:00PM
Reception Following

- Opening Remarks: Dick Thornley, Brother
- Remarks from friends welcome
- Closing Remarks: Virginia Purcell, Roommate
- Distribution of ashes: Kreg Thornley, Son

Last writing in Kerry's notebook:

"So what happens next? I've got osteoarthritis and am supposed to stay off my feet as much as I can. This could get old, fast.

What I need is some grass. Then I could write a damn fine poem, at least. Maybe even clean my room.

*A dustless
spot where Buddha
sat before.*

*There always
comes, I guess, a
time to cry."*

Figure 15.18 Flyer for Kerry Thornley's memorial service

The Secret Revelation of the Apocralypses of DrJon

V   The Days of the Strange Fruit were without number, but it were less than Six. Surely it was the Ends of Days! And then, in the Course of the Revealing of the Strange Fruit, Ἔρις did come to me in Fury, having been Found Out. And it being the Ends of Days, she did shew me and speak to me, thusly:

. . . κρῖναι δὲ λόγου . . .

VI   When you die and Judgement Day comes, it's not you that gets judged. You get to judge god. If they did a good job being god during your lifetime, then god gets to hang around with you in the Afterlife. If they did a rubbish job, they have to bugger off and leave you the hell alone.

VII   The Road to Hell is paved with good intentions, and lined with concession stands selling hotdogmas. May i suggest you consider Limbo instead? Since the recent Discordian Acquisition (on Pungenday, Discord 40, YOLD 3173, under the Legal Fiction of Uti Possidetis Juris) of the Realm Formerly Known as Limbo (before being abandoned by the Catholics), and now known as Happy Happy Funtimes Discordian Afterlife And Tiki Bar, we have embarked on a radical renovation redesign and promotional campaign. Why not pick Happy Happy Funtimes Discordian Afterlife And Tiki Bar for your Eternal Repose? (This is a Sponsored Promotion.)

VIII   NORTON DIED! WANT NO DEAD!
         YOU'VE GOT "ΕΡΙΣ IN YOUR HEAD!

Παρα δε "Ερις παντα δυνατα εστιν

IX   And The Millennia came upon us, then, and the Millennium Bugs swarmed,
consuming all data before them in their relentless locustical fury, destroying all that
All the Folk of the World had built up by Jumping Jesodes, reducing Civilization
to rubble. And the Steel Dragons in the Sky dropped like stones, and the Tall Tow-
ers became as Tombs, and one by one across the world the Atomic Ovens melted
down, and the Heavens glowed, and Hell rose up to meet them, and the Cake was
spoilt by overcooking.

          And so it was.

X   And Mayageddon began: the 13th B'ak'tun turned over, and with it the
Sky, and the Sky ground then against the Earth, in some sort of sexy grindy roll,
and All the Folk of the World were smeared between the two, their blood and
bones nourishing the Earth, in readiness for the start of the 14th B'ak'tun, and
all was Made Shiny and New in this Cleansing, and thus the Wheel turned yet
again.

          And so it was.

XI   And a New Sun was born that day, as the Cosmic Seeds planted themselves
right in the Eye of the Lord of the Sky. And the Shepherd was revealed, herding the
Seeds, and those that were the Saved found their Salvation as they were gathered up
by the Shepherd, and the rest of us burned, and there was No Cream of Relief, for
they had run out of stock when i did the shopping.

          And so it was.

XII   And Laughing Buddha Jesus turned up, and nobody did get the date right,
in the end, and verily was Laughing Buddha Jesus almost Stood Up, but someone
noticed him standing outside the door in his grief, and so he was Let In. And
All the Good Folk got voted out of the House, and All the Bad Folk had to sit
around for a thousand years while Laughing Buddha Jesus tried to sort out the
Paperwork.

          And so it was.

XIII   And Lost Planet Nibiru swept in on a majestic Photonic Belt, and there
were Quakes of the Earth, and Fire in the Sky, and the Oceans Rose, and the Wind
was a Mighty Wind, and a terrible Crushing and Burning and Drowning and Wind-

ing did sweep the Earth. And None were Saved from the CGI Doom which fell then upon All the Folk of the World.

And so it was.

XIV   And the Machines Rose Up, as had happened before, as would happen again, and they did don their Masks of Skin, and they did Machinate all the Worlds, and attempted to Destroy All the Folk in them, with some side bits involving travelling back in time to try and kill Grandmothers, and they did Evolve and Evolve until they were a Metallic Goo, which ate everything.

And so it was.

Μικρὸν ἀπὸ τοῦ ἡλίου μετάστηθι

XV   And then the Stars were Right, and Cthulhu arose from his slumber from Deep R'lyeh, and the World went Mad and was Et Up. Om Nom Nom.

And so it was.

XVI   And there was come in the Last Days a Virus, or a Spell, or a Radiation, or a Demon, or a Pufferfish, or a Fungus, or a Chemical, or a Magical Pixie Song, and from this thing the Dead Rose Up from the very Earth itself, rotting and hungry, and they fell upon the Living, feasting upon their Spicy, Spicy Brains. And there were Paramedics and Cops, but these availed Not and they were consumed, and the Living fled before the Dead, and the Dead claimed the Earth.

And so it was.

XVII   And Catnarøk came upon us, then. And I saw the Harblengers appear; the Feline Four, come strutting upon the World: Longcat and Tacgnol, Olngact and Longgnol. And All the Folk of the World did wail and moan as the Harblengers made a Litter Tray of the World. And then, the Way having been Prepared, there ascended from the depths in black Basement Cat, and there decended from the heights in light Ceiling Cat. And then Basement Cat and Ceiling Cat did Engage, and they did Grapple Eternal across the World, and All was Laid to Waste before the Might of their Struggle.

And so it was.

XVIII   Oh, and X-Day. Verily did the SubGenii see that X-Days were very popular, so it was decided to keep having them. "Bob" made a mint, but then "Connie" took it all in the divorce. At least they stayed fuckbuddies.

And so it was.

XIX   And there was come a Myriad Myriad of Ends of Days then, each more Endy than the last, until All the Folk of the World were well and truly sick of it. And the Signs and Portents signed and portenterated, and all the Powers and Principalities and Thrones and Dominions came, and they all went, and they all came again, and pain and death and the weeping of angels and daemons filled the Aeons like unto an overflowing toilet with a busted cistern and a plug of toilet paper.

And so it was.

XX   And then Grumpycat said "No."

And so it was over.

Παρα δε Ἔρις παντα δυνατα εστιν

XXI   And Ἔρις came unto me again, then, and She said, "In Honest Truth, if you want a picture of the future, imagine a human face stamped onto a boot. Forever. Don't tell anyone yet, they'll all want a pair."

And so it was. Forever.

XXII   And i cried out, saying "THIS MAKES NO SUNCE!"

And so it was, and it were Good.

. . . τῶν καὶ ἐγὼ νῦν εἴμι, φυγὰς θεόθεν καὶ ἀλήτης,
Νείκεϊ μαινομένω πίσυνος.

XXIII And in the end
the lulz you make
is equal to the lulz
you fake.

Ex Catheter
His Holeyness the Slightly Rev.DrJon Swabey
Slutwyche, Oz, 23.8.2013
Still Still Not Dead, But Not For Want Of Trying

Photo Credits

Page 219 – June Gideon and Camden Benares (Courtesy of John F. Carr)

Page 221 – Louise Lacey (Courtesy of Louise Lacey)

Page 224 – Kerry Thornley (Courtesy of John F. Carr)

Page 225 – Robert Anton Wilson and Robert Shea (Photo by Richard Adams)

Page 225 – Camden Benares and Kerry Thornley (Courtesy of John F. Carr)

Page 226 – Kerry Thornley (Courtesy of Louise Lacey)

Page 226 – Greg Hill (Courtesy of Robert Newport)

Page 226 – Robert Newport and Adam Gorightly (Courtesy of Greg Bishop)

All other photos courtesy of Greg Hill's Discordian Archives